# The Ordnance Survey Complete Guide to the BATTLEFIELDS OF BRITAIN

# The Ordnance Survey
# Complete Guide to the
# BATTLEFIELDS
# OF BRITAIN
## David Smurthwaite

Webb & Bower
MICHAEL JOSEPH

First published in Great Britain in 1984 by Webb & Bower (Publishers) Limited,
9 Colleton Crescent, Exeter, Devon EX2 4BY

This paperback edition published 1987 by Webb & Bower (Publishers) Limited
in association with
Michael Joseph Limited, 27 Wright's Lane, London W8 5TZ

Designed by Peter Wrigley

Picture research by Anne-Marie Ehrlich

First impression August 1984
Second impression September 1984

Maps Copyright © 1984.

The maps in this publication are reproduced from
Ordnance Survey maps with the permission of the Controller of
HMSO. Crown copyright reserved.

**British Library Cataloguing in Publication Data**

Smurthwaite, David
 The Ordnance Survey complete guide to the
 battlefields of Britain.
 1. Battles—Great Britain 2. Great Britain
 —Description and travel—1971–
 I. Title
 914.1′04858       DA632

 ISBN 0–86350–157–5

Typeset in Great Britain by Keyspools Limited, Golborne, Lancashire

Printed and bound in Italy by New Interlitho SpA.

914. 1
S66 0

FRONT ENDPAPERS:
'A representation of the Armies of King Charles I and Sir Thomas
Fairfax'. A contemporary engraving.

BACK ENDPAPERS:
'A description of his majestie's army of horse and foot and of his
excellencies Sir Thomas Fairfax . . . at the battle of Naseby, June the
14th 1645'. A contemporary engraving by J. Sturt (1658–1730).

TITLE PAGES:
Attack on a baggage train at Edgehill, watercolour by Richard Beavis
(1824–96).

# CONTENTS

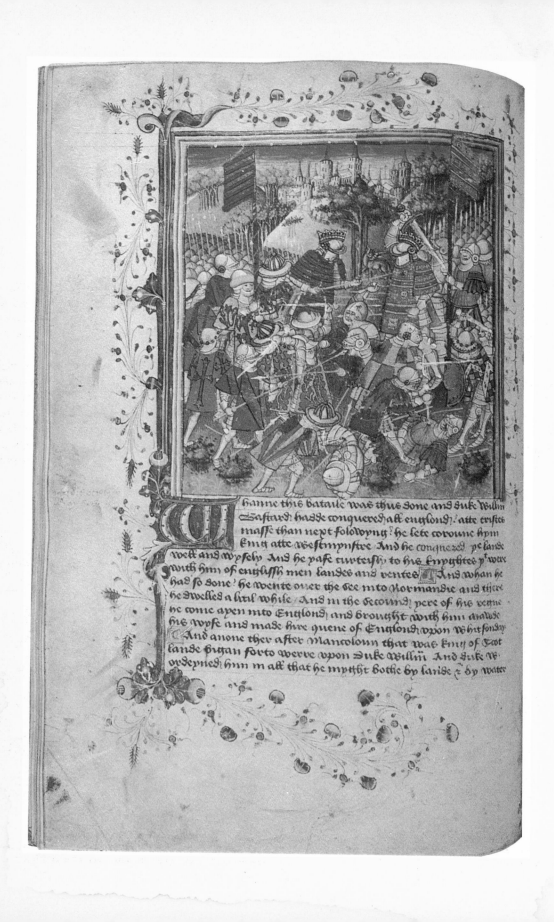

hanne this bataile was thus done and Duke Willm
Bastard hadde conquered all england/ atte tristes
masse than nept folowyng/ he lete corowne hym
kyng atte westmynstre And he conquered pe lande
well and wysely And he paxe curteisly to his knyghtes yt were
with hym of englissh men landes and rentes ❡ And whan he
had so done/ he wente over the see into Normandie and there
he dwelles a litil while And in the secound yere of his regne
he come ayen into England and brought with hym alisse
his wyfe and made hire quene of england vpon whitsonday
❡ And anone ther after Mancoloun that was kyng of Scot
lande bygan forto werre vpon Duke Willm And duke W
ordeyned hym in all that he myght bothe by lande & by water

# INTRODUCTION

Anyone who embarks upon even the briefest exploration of our countryside is likely to stumble upon at least one example of the often-forgotten and dilapidated assortment of crosses, obelisks and cairns which stand as memorials to battles fought on British soil. Many of the most important dates in Britain's history are linked with such battles, but singularly little is done to explain the significance of the spot on which they were fought. In North America the visitor arriving at a battlefield will more often than not find the full resources of a visitor centre placed at his disposal to explain why the battle was fought, who took part in it, how the fighting developed and what the outcome was. In Britain, by contrast, the battlefields are allowed to slumber on, and the only occasion on which they receive public attention is when someone threatens to drive a motorway across one of them.

There are, of course, many reasons for this neglect. The last battle to be fought on British soil took place over two hundred years ago. Many sites have suffered the encroachment of urban expansion and they are now host to factories, housing estates, roads, railways, farms and even, appropriately, military camps. It might also be argued that as Britain is already so richly endowed

LEFT:
A medieval view of the battle of Hastings, 1066. From a fifteenth-century manuscript.

ABOVE:
A view of Glen Feshie in the Highlands of Scotland, a mountainous region which provided a natural barrier against enemy forces.

with easily visible and understandable historic sites, the effort of marking routes and erecting display boards on battlefields is superfluous. Yet the pioneering work of several local authorities and of bodies such as the National Trust for Scotland has shown what can be achieved in battlefield interpretation (at Hastings, Bosworth Field, Bannockburn and Culloden, for example), and has also demonstrated the ready and enthusiastic response of both British and overseas visitors. There can be few better ways of spending an afternoon than by walking the ground upon which the fate of a monarch was decided, the success of an invasion confirmed, or the nature of government altered. The details of strategy, tactics and deployment, which can remain complex on paper, often fall easily into place when the ground upon which a battle was fought is seen.

The geographical position and the landscape of Britain have played a major part in moulding its history, and they have exercised a fundamental influence upon the strategy and tactics of the warfare conducted on British soil. The most immediate geographical influence is the fact that Britain is an island. As a result, once the Roman, Anglo-Saxon, Danish and Norman invasions had run their course warfare in Britain was largely a parochial affair, fought out between the English, Scots, Welsh and Irish. Armed intervention by a foreign power was always a problematical undertaking which could lead to a naval battle in the Channel, an opposed landing, and the severance of the lines of communication of any force that did get ashore. Appeals for foreign help were nevertheless made by the warring parties and although on occasion they were answered, the efficacy of such support was always in doubt. Firstly, the aid that a foreign power could provide was often too little, too late, and the employment of foreign troops in an English campaign usually served only to ensure that the opposition closed ranks in the face of such unwarranted interference.

The mountains and rivers of Britain channelled armies into certain parts of the country which became well-trodden ground. Until General Wade built his network of roads through them in the eighteenth century, the Highlands of Scotland were a region beyond the capacity of any army to control, and similarly the Welsh forests and mountain ranges provided the ideal base for the waging of guerrilla warfare. The Pennine Range dominated the invasion route between Scotland and England, forcing armies to choose between a march through western or eastern

England. For many commanders it was a decision which provoked a good deal of heart-searching and which determined the subsequent pattern of a campaign. A river-crossing was a formidable undertaking for most armies, particularly if it was opposed, and the rivers Thames, Severn, Trent and Forth were important strategic factors in many campaigns. A rapid march for a crossing over one of these rivers could often lead to a sudden battle. It is no accident that the majority of decisive battles in our history took place on open ground or that Edward Dummer could describe Sedgemoor on the night before he took part in the fight against Monmouth as 'a place copious and commodious for fighting'.

The field of Flodden, looking towards the English position and the memorial on Piper's Hill.

For many British battles the historian can provide a clear identification of the site on which they were fought and offer firm suggestions as to the deployment and tactics of the opposing forces. For others he can locate the general area in which the battle took place, but the exact site and nature of the fighting must, for lack of evidence, remain conjectural. To the visitor in search of an understanding of the manner in which ground influenced a battle both these categories of site can be rewarding. The former provides the clarity and vigour of a personal confrontation with the physical evidence of history, and the latter allows the visitor to form his own judgement of the military and geographical validity of the site. A proportion of British battles,

however, remain elusive, and the visitor must assess for himself the merits of alternative sites.

Although a number of battlefields have escaped the intrusion of later centuries to an extent that the commanders of the armies which fought there would still be able to identify the ground without hesitation, this is by no means always the case. Having armed himself with the historical background, maps, binoculars, and sturdy footwear, the visitor must remember to include one indispensable commodity for the study of battlefields – his imagination.

9

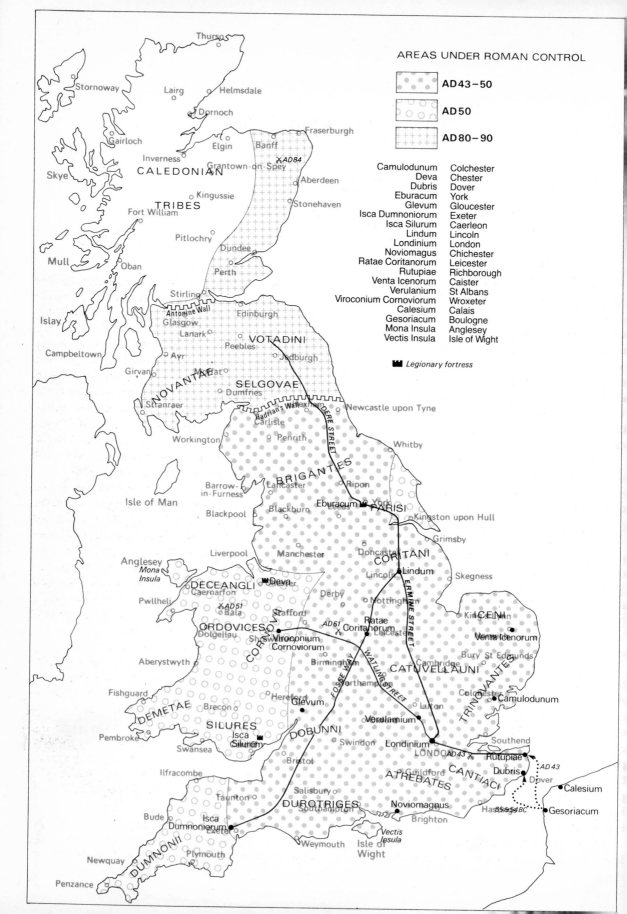

AREAS UNDER ROMAN CONTROL

AD 43–50

AD 50

AD 80–90

| | |
|---|---|
| Camulodunum | Colchester |
| Deva | Chester |
| Dubris | Dover |
| Eburacum | York |
| Glevum | Gloucester |
| Isca Dumnoniorum | Exeter |
| Isca Silurum | Caerleon |
| Lindum | Lincoln |
| Londinium | London |
| Noviomagus | Chichester |
| Ratae Coritanorum | Leicester |
| Rutupiae | Richborough |
| Venta Icenorum | Caister |
| Verulanium | St Albans |
| Viroconium Cornoviorum | Wroxeter |
| Calesium | Calais |
| Gesoriacum | Boulogne |
| Mona Insula | Anglesey |
| Vectis Insula | Isle of Wight |

*Legionary fortress*

# THE ROMANS
# IN BRITAIN
## 55 BC—AD 409

he Roman Army was the first professional military orce to fight in Britain. Although its campaign began in arnest in AD 43, Roman legions under the command of ulius Caesar had established temporary bridgeheads in outh-east Britain in both 55 BC and 54 BC. The first ncursion lasted for three weeks and involved only two egions. The second expedition a year later was a more erious venture, employing 5 legions supported by ?000 cavalry. On this occasion the Romans stayed for hree months and the legions penetrated to the Thames Valley.

To the legions who ventured across the strip of ocean between Gaul and Britain it was a voyage beyond the known world. According to their reason and logic Britain ought not to exist, since both Greek and Roman geographers had shown that the contemporary world was surrounded by an empty ocean. For Britain to rise as a land mass in that ocean meant that it was part of another world and to a superstitious soldiery that was quite enough to raise doubts about the wisdom of the enterprise. In AD 40 the invasion army assembled by the Emperor Gaius refused to sail and three years later the egions of Aulus Plautius embarked only after a near mutiny.

In Books IV and V of *The Conquest of Gaul* (*De Bello Gallico*) Caesar recorded his campaigns in Britain. Although he misunderstood much of what he saw of the island and its people, he provided the earliest eye-witness account of life and warfare in Britain. Caesar could speak with authority only of the south-east, and particularly Kent, since this was the region of which he had first-hand experience. The area was inhabited predominantly by the Belgae, a group of settlers who had arrived from Gaul in a series of migrations beginning about 150 BC.

The Britain which the Romans encountered was an Iron-Age country in which the pattern of change in economic, social and political life was accelerating. The speed of cultural development varied greatly across the country, and in the remote uplands of Scotland, northern England and Wales it was hardly discernable; but in the south-east a dynamic and successful society was emerging in the lands dominated by the Belgae. The vigorous Belgic culture overlapped its own boundaries to the east, north and west, bringing innovation to the neighbouring Iceni in East Anglia, the Coritani in the east Midlands, the Dobunni in Somerset and Gloucestershire, and the Durotriges in Dorset. It was to be the very success of the Belgae as warriors, farmers and traders which focused Rome's attention on Britain.

The Roman conquest of Gaul had been accomplished only after bitter fighting against the Belgae in the north and the Veneti in Armorica (Brittany). These tribes had close links with Britain; the Belgae with the south-east and the Veneti through trade with the south-west. Caesar claimed that both had received moral and material support from Britain. He could thus add military necessity to the arguments of wealth, power and prestige which he advanced to justify an extension of Roman influence across the Channel.

Rome dealt with hostile powers either directly by invasion and conquest or, where expedient, by diplomacy and treaty. For diplomacy to be successful it needed information about the country in quest'' Caesar opened diplomatic contact with the south-eastern Britain by sending an env king of the Atrebates, although it appe to provide the desired military info therefore, the invasion of 55 reconnaissance in force, justifie what kind of power lay to the w second invasion in 54 BC faile enclave for Rome but it did ac main Belgic tribes, the surrenc

CUNOBELINUS    COMMIUS    TINCOMMIUS    EPATICCUS

Settlers from Belgic Gaul introduced the practice of striking coins to Britain, and the first examples were based on the gold stater issued by Philip of Macedon in 348 BC.

payment of tribute. Although the island's inhabitants were to keep their freedom for nearly a century the choice of friendship or enmity towards Rome was henceforth a political consideration which could not be ignored.

After the Roman withdrawal, Belgic migration continued, principally through the movement of the Atrebates, the tribe of Caesar's erstwhile ally Commius. Tribal capitals became more prominent and local power centred increasingly on the re-occupation of hillforts and the establishment of *oppida* or defended settlements. The power struggle in south-eastern Britain was between the Catuvellauni in Hertfordshire and the Trinovantes in Essex. By AD 10 the Trinovantes had lost their capital Camulodunum (Colchester) and their independence to the Catuvellaunian ruler Cunobelinus (Cymbelline). In a reign which spanned nearly forty years Cunobelinus contrived to extend his power over most of south-eastern Britain without provoking direct Roman intervention. He even encroached upon the territory of the Atrebates whom Rome had supported as a counter-balance to the growing power of the Catuvellauni. It seems possible therefore that Cunobelinus was able, if not by alliance, then at least by the force of his personality and diplomacy, to persuade Rome that this accretion of power was a purely British affair.

With the death of Cunobelinus around AD 40 the position deteriorated alarmingly. His pro-Roman son Adminius had already fled the country and power was assumed by his remaining sons Caratacus and Togodumnus. They were determined to enlarge the empire they had inherited and both nurtured a hatred of Rome. ˙st Adminius and then Verica, the defeated king of the ˙s. arrived in Rome to seek help. The arguments ˙n now seemed overwhelming. Verica ˙flight was an insult to Roman d further the destruction of s of Rome, the Druids; and all, an openly hostile power ˙e north-western frontier of ˙e, too, that the emperor ˙share of military glory, saw relatively inexpensive way ˙h. That Rome possessed the

military means to achieve these aims had been demonstrated by her legions across the length and breadth of Europe and the East.

A Roman legion of 6000 men formed a self-contained fighting force, a small army in its own right. Besides over 5000 infantry organized as nine cohorts each of 480 men and one cohort of 800 men, it contained its own supporting troops such as armourers, despatch riders, carpenters, engineers and medical staff. The cohort was the main tactical unit of the legion and with the exception of the larger 1st cohort, which had 5 double centuries, each was composed of 6 centuries of 80 men. The legion was a shock force of heavy infantry trained for close-quarter fighting. Each legionary was equipped and armed accordingly. To protect the upper body he wore a segmented strip-and-plate armour (*lorica segmentata*) which was sufficiently flexible to allow for movement while fighting or working. A bronze helmet reinforced with an iron skull-plate protected the face, head and neck. The curved shield of wood edged with bronze or iron was large enough to cover most of the body, and when linked closely with the shields of other legionaries it was an impressive mobile barricade.

The legionary's weapons were the *pilum* and the *gladius*. The *pilum* was a javelin with a four-foot wooden shaft topped by three feet of iron with a hardened point. In addition to being a deadly missile, the *pilum* was also a disabling weapon. When it lodged in an enemy's shield the weight of the shaft bent the iron, anchoring it firmly in the shield. The chances of surviving combat with an advancing legionary while your shield arm trailed seven feet of javelin cannot have been high.

Besides two *pila* the legionary carried a *gladius*, a double-edged sword with a blade twenty-four inches long and two inches wide, designed as a short-range thrusting weapon.

As well as a fighting soldier the legionary was also a military pioneer capable of building camps, forts and roads. On campaign the legions constructed a marching camp when they halted for the night and although these were temporary structures they could cover an area in excess of 100 acres. They were encircled by a shallow ditch and an upcast mound topped by a palisade of

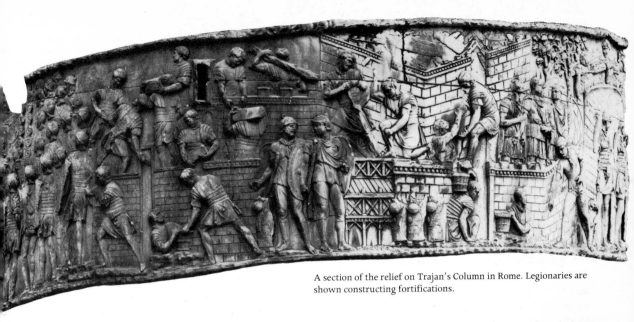

A section of the relief on Trajan's Column in Rome. Legionaries are shown constructing fortifications.

Legionaries foraging. A relief from Trajan's Column.

A bronze helmet from the special parade armour worn by the cavalry of the *auxilia*. Made towards the end of the first or early in the second century AD the helmet has a vizor-mask and a crown embossed with fighting scenes. Discovered at Ribchester in Lancashire, this helmet is now in the British Museum.

seven-foot wooden stakes, two of which formed part of every legionary's equipment. Permanent forts were constructed when more lengthy occupation was planned and these were sited in strategically important positions dominating mountain passes, river crossings or trackways. Where possible, the forts were sited within a day's march of one another along a linking road system. Their defences were more substantial than those of the marching camps, with a higher and thicker rampart, gates and towers, and a more formidable ditch. Stone replaced wood as the main building material at the beginning of the second century. All fortresses were built to the same basic plan, although they varied in size according to the type of unit stationed there. A fortress garrisoned by auxiliaries would occupy approximately five acres, that for a legion fifty to sixty acres.

The legion was thus a sophisticated military unit whose prime function was to allow highly trained and disciplined infantry to enter battle in the most advantageous tactical formations and with the most appropriate weapons. It was a formula which had enabled Rome to conquer Italy, Sicily, Carthage, Greece and Gaul.

The *auxilia*, as its name implies, was an important adjunct to the legions. Recruited from the tribes and nations allied to Rome it was initially little more than a collection of barbarian levies raised for the duration of a campaign. Gradually, however, it became an essential and permanent support to the legions both in the field and in garrison, for while the citizens of Rome were adept at fighting as shock troops they were less skilful as cavalry or light infantry. Rome quickly saw the tactical advantage to be gained from the use of slingers from the Balearic Isles, archers from Syria and cavalry from North Africa.

The *auxilia* formed three types of unit: cavalry, infantry and mixed formations of both cavalry and infantry, the *cohors equitata*. This dual formation was particularly common in Britain and as with the other types of auxiliary unit its strength was normally 500 men and exceptionally 1000. Although raised as expendable troops designed to take the first shock of enemy contact, the *auxilia* assumed an increasingly important tactical role. Throughout the Empire Roman commanders came to depend on the *auxilia* in battle, and in Britain it bore the brunt of both conquest and defence as the legions settled into the routine of garrison life, fortress construction and road building. At the battle of Mons Graupius, Agricola was able to achieve victory using only his auxiliary force of cavalry, British levies, and Batavian and Tungrian infantry from the lower Rhine. As the *auxilia* assumed a more important tactical role, a new force, the *numeri*, was recruited from the tribes on the periphery of the Empire to serve as light troops. In AD 175, 5500 Sarmatian cavalry raised as *numeri* in eastern Europe arrived in Britain to reinforce the garrison.

As Britain was an overseas province, a seaborne arm was necessary for the initial conquest and subsequent defence. Accordingly a special fleet, the *Classis Britannica*, was formed, but the Roman navy was not an independent fighting force and it operated under the firm control of the army. The fleet's principal duty was the transportation of men and supplies and although it operated out of several harbours in Britain its main base was at Boulogne in Gaul. The *Classis Britannica* did take part in offensive operations, notably during Vespasian's campaign in the south-west, during the conquest of Wales by Frontinus and during the campaigns undertaken by Agricola and Severus in the north.

In both 55 BC and AD 43 the native forces defending Britain could hardly have stood in bleaker contrast to the military power that was moving against them. The army which the tribal kings could field against the Romans consisted of ill-armed levies stiffened by a warrior aristocracy. Tribal warfare must have accustomed many to the sight and sound of battle but that same struggle prevented the evolution of a trained and disciplined fighting force. Such warfare was often resolved through individual combat between warriors and it provided little schooling in how to defeat the professional army of Rome. Moreover, since the use of manpower in tribal wars was governed by the needs of agriculture it was not possible for a British army to remain in the field indefinitely.

Because they lacked the discipline and cohesion of a standing army the Britons, once launched into battle, were incapable of manoeuvring in response to the tactics of their opponent. Predictably, therefore, they lost the major battles in which they challenged the legions to open combat. They fared little better behind fixed defences and few of the hill-forts and *oppida* the Romans encountered caused anything more than minor delay to their progress.

This is not to say that the Britons were an easy prey. The legions had often to fight hard for their victories. The Battle of Medway in AD 43, for example, lasted two days, and on many occasions the tribal levies showed a remarkable moral and physical resilience in defeat. The problem for the British was that their traditional form of warfare was obsolete in the face of the most successful army the world had seen. Typical of this obsolescence was the chariot, a weapon which had not been employed on the Continent for decades. Initially, its very unfamiliarity disconcerted the Romans and Caesar described British tactics in some detail:

In chariot fighting the Britons begin by driving all over the field hurling javelins, and generally the terror inspired by the horses and the noise of the wheels are sufficient to throw their opponents' ranks into disorder. Then, after making their way between the squadrons of their own cavalry, they jump down from the chariots and engage on foot. In the meantime their charioteers retire a short distance from the battle and place the chariots in such a position that their masters, if hard pressed by numbers, have an easy means of retreat to their own lines. Thus they combine the mobility of cavalry with the staying power of infantry . . .

The weapon of the British warrior emphasized his individuality in battle, since the long Celtic sword could only be used effectively when there was sufficient space for an extended swing. The warriors therefore fought in open order and this placed them at a tactical disadvantage when attacking the close order formation of the legion. It is little wonder that the ancient Briton, protected only by a small shield, painted his body with blue woad to gain the defence of ritual symbolism and to strike terror into his foe.

By the end of the first century the essential pattern of Roman conquest in Britain had been set, and thereafter the central, south-eastern and south-western areas of the province enjoyed 200 years of comparative tranquility. The north and to a great extent the west remained militarized zones, constantly garrisoned and patrolled. Normally the garrison of Britain was a strong one, somewhere in the region of 50,000 men, but at times of crisis within the Empire its strength would be depleted by the transfer of troops to deal with whatever emergency had arisen. The inevitable result was a resurgence of conflict on the now under-garrisoned frontier. For a time the raiders, whether they were Scots, Picts or Saxons, could wreak considerable havoc, attacking forts and looting settlements. Once the wider emergency had been settled to Rome's satisfaction retribution followed, often in the form of an imperial task force which restored order by burning tribal strongholds, destroying livestock and crops, and building yet more forts. It was when Rome could no longer deliver such retribution that imperial rule in Britain began to falter. On at least three occasions imperial authority was usurped by local commanders who effectively withdrew Britain from the central empire. In AD 259 Postumus initiated a political break which lasted fifteen years, in 286 Carausius established an independent administration which lasted for ten years and in 383 Magnus Maximus used a victorious campaign in Britain as a platform on which to launch a separate western empire. On each occasion central authority was eventually restored by Rome but as the tempo of crisis within the empire quickened during the later years of the fourth century it became more and more difficult to deliver effective military force where it was needed. Diocletian's reorganization of the army into units for garrison duty and units which formed a highly mobile field army to be used as a strategic reserve went some way to providing a solution. In 402, however, the majority of the field army in Britain was withdrawn for the defence of Italy, and by 409 the province had expelled the remaining Roman officials and set about organising its own defence. After a military occupation which had lasted 366 years Britain had again to face the threat of a new invasion.

# INVASION 55 and 54 BC

Julius Caesar landed on the south-east coast of Britain with the VIIth and Xth Legions in the last week of August 55 BC. The risks he took in mounting such an enterprise were considerable. The campaigning season was already well advanced and his attempts to gain intelligence of Britain through interrogating merchants and dispatching a scouting vessel had yielded little of value. Yet Caesar pressed ahead with his preparations, assembling transports for the legions and auxiliaries at Boulogne and for the cavalry at Ambleteuse. The object of such warlike activity was perfectly evident to the tribes in southern Britain and several of them had sent peace envoys.

Caesar sailed on the night of 25/26 August, anchoring off Dover the following morning to await the arrival of the cavalry transports. The latter, which had been delayed in embarkation, fought a losing battle against wind and tide and were forced to return to Gaul. The cliffs above Dover were lined with British warriors eagerly awaiting battle and a landing there was clearly impossible. Caesar's force sailed northwards to the open beaches between Walmer and Deal, where it found that the British cavalry and chariots had kept pace with it: the beaches were already strongly held. The legions were not equipped for an opposed amphibious landing, lacking both suitable assault boats and the necessary supporting weapons. The heavily laden troops could gain the shore only by jumping into the sea and wading up a shelving beach under close-range fire. The legionaries hesitated and only began to disembark after the famous gesture by the standard-bearer of the Xth Legion who, jumping into the sea alone, placed the Eagle of the Legion in danger of capture. To avert such dishonour, the legionaries followed and a wild mêlée developed at the water's edge as they reached the Britons. Supported by warships on the flanks and by a floating reserve of troops packed into ships' boats, the legionaries were gradually able to deploy on dry land. With a concerted charge they swept the Britons from the beach. Denied cavalry, Caesar was not able to turn the retreat into a rout but for the moment a bridgehead had been established.

As news of the British defeat spread, tribal chieftains appeared at the Roman camp offering submission and bringing hostages, but before Caesar could exploit this good fortune disaster struck. A combination of high tide, full moon and a violent storm shattered the Roman fleet. Of the seventy to eighty ships Caesar had brought with him twelve were completely destroyed and not one escaped damage. The expeditionary force, with barely 10,000 men, was stranded on a hostile shore. The British were not slow to realize their opportunity and the tribes were again summoned to battle. British tribesmen surprised and roughly handled a foraging party of the VIIth Legion, and a major, though unsuccessful, attack was made on the Roman camp. It was clearly time for Caesar to return to Gaul.

A statue of Julius Caesar in the Museum of the Palazzo dei Conservatori, Piazza Senatorio, Rome.

By a combination of good fortune and military skill the expeditionary force had survived an ill-starred venture. The failure to discover a secure natural harbour on the British coast had nearly resulted in complete disaster, while the non-arrival of the cavalry denied the legions decisive gains from their victories. Caesar had also made several errors of judgement, the most serious being his failure to safeguard his seaborne communications from the risk posed by the weather and the sea. After the storm he was effectively besieged on the coast of Kent and his return to Gaul was little more than an emergency evacuation. Yet the reconnaissance had not been a total failure. Caesar had seen Britain for himself, the legions had demonstrated their superiority in battle, and the need for both cavalry and a good anchorage had been underlined.

With an opponent of the calibre of Julius Caesar Britain could not expect to escape so easily a second time and the invasion of 54 BC was altogether more formidable. It was launched with 5 legions, 2000 cavalry and 800 vessels, and it made an unopposed landing near Sandwich in the first week of July. The British, overawed by the sight of so vast a fleet, had retired inland to a defensive position behind a river. This was probably the River Stour near Canterbury, and the legions had to fight their way across in the face of British charioteers and cavalry. The British retreated again, this time regrouping within the *oppidum* at Bigbury. Caesar described the British position as a 'well-fortified post of great natural strength, previously prepared, no doubt, for some war among themselves, since all the entrances were blocked by felled trees laid close together'. Protected by a shield wall and using earth ramps built against the perimeter of the fort, the VIIth Legion breached the defences and drove the Britons out of the *oppidum*. But before the advance could be resumed news arrived that the fleet had suffered severe storm damage with forty ships sunk. Caesar gave orders for all the ships to be beached, the walls of the camp extended to enclose them, and repairs carried out at all costs. This gave the British a breathing space and during the next ten days they assembled a new army under the command of a single leader, Cassivellaunus, who was probably king of the Catuvellauni.

When Caesar resumed his march inland the Britons harried the flanks of the legions and drew the Roman cavalry into skirmishes. As the legions halted to construct their marching camp a British force attacked from the cover of the surrounding forest and broke through the Roman lines. The legionaries were impressed by the speed, mobility and open order fighting of the tribesmen, and it was clear that any units detached from the main Roman column would be in constant danger from surprise attacks. The next foraging party consisted of three legions and all the cavalry, a force of nearly 20,000 men, and they were prepared for battle. When the attack came, the legions were able to fight their way out of encirclement, counter-attack and launch a cavalry charge which routed the Britons with heavy losses. This reverse broke the alliance of British tribes and Cassivellaunus withdrew his remaining forces north of the Thames. The pursuing legions successfully forced a defended river crossing close to London and began to lay waste the territory of the Catuvellauni. Realizing that he could not hope to defeat the legions in pitched battle, Cassivellaunus disbanded his infantry, retaining only 4000 charioteers as a mobile guerrilla force. Making good use of the heavily wooded countryside north of the Thames Cassivellaunus harried the legions searching for his stronghold.

The Romans had made little progress when a diplomatic breakthrough brought Caesar the intelligence he was seeking. The Trinovantes of Essex, old enemies of the Catuvellauni, appealed for help against Cassivellaunus. Other tribes, equally fearful of the growing power of the Catuvellauni, offered submission to Rome and revealed the location of Cassivellaunus's stronghold. This fortress, hidden by forest and marsh, protected by rampart and trench, and crammed with men and cattle, has been identified by archaeologists as the massive earthwork at Wheathampstead in Hertfordshire. Despite its natural strength it fell quickly to a legionary attack delivered simultaneously from two directions. Caesar had captured his enemy's base. However the remains of the confederacy forged by Cassivellaunus could still strike back and four Kentish tribes were even now able to mount a surprise attack on the Roman naval camp.

Both Caesar and Cassivellaunus were ready for peace. The British leader, whose generalship had shown a disconcertingly high level of strategic skill, leadership and pertinacity, accepted the far from harsh Roman terms. Although he now dominated the south-east of Britain, Caesar had already decided to withdraw for the winter to Gaul. He probably planned to return the following summer but events elsewhere prevented him from ever again seeing the island which, for a brief span, he had brought to the forefront of Rome's attention.

# THE MEDWAY AD 43

A *Richborough*  B *The Medway*

By proving that the legions could campaign success-fully across the Channel, Julius Caesar had taken the first step in transforming Britain into a Roman pro-vince. It was to be nearly 100 years before a Roman army sailed for Britain again but in 34, 28 and 27 BC expeditions were planned, only to be abandoned owing to the pressure of events elsewhere.

Four legions provided the fighting strength of the expedition which sailed in AD 43. In the early summer the IInd Augusta from Strasbourg, the IXth Hispana from Pannonia, the XIVth Gemina from Mainz and the XXth from Neuss began to assemble at Boulogne, along with 20,000 auxiliary troops, both infantry and cavalry. Command was given to Aulus Plautius, gover-nor of Pannonia, and amongst his legionary comman-ders were some of the army's best officers, including the future emperor Vespasian.

The delay caused by the troops' refusal to embark meant that a Roman expeditionary force again arrived in Britain late in the campaigning season. This time, however, the majority of the 40,000 legionaries and *auxilia* came ashore in a natural harbour at Rutupiae (Richborough) on the coast of Kent. It has been suggested that part of the force landed on the Sussex coast close to Chichester but it seems improbable that the expedition's strength would have been divided so early in the invasion, even though this second landing might have expected help from friendly tribes.

The landing at Richborough was unopposed since the Britons, misled by the non-appearance of the Romans, had disbanded their army. It now proved difficult to find the tribes who had melted away into the forests and marshes, leaving the legion's scouts search-ing vainly for a foe. At least two skirmishes occurred with independent forces led respectively by Togodum-nus and Caratacus. These rulers of the Belgae may well have been testing Roman strength while the tribal levies reassembled behind the River Medway in Kent. Camped on the northern bank the Britons waited for the pursuing legions, reassured, no doubt, by the belief that so defensible a river line must halt the Roman advance. Here they underestimated the Romans, for the first crossing, carried out by auxiliaries who swam the river with their weapons, took the defence by surprise. Before the British charioteers could mass to destroy this bridgehead a shower of javelins directed at their horses threw their ranks into confusion.

While the Britons were preoccupied with stemming the advance of the auxiliaries, a second landing, this time by the fully armed legionaries of the IInd Augusta was made on the opposite flank. Again the defence was taken by surprise and a second bridgehead was secured. Boats and possibly a pontoon bridge would have been used to reinforce the IInd Augusta and as night fell Roman strength on the enemy bank was growing rapidly. The Britons knew that the legionary bridgehead was the most dangerous threat and on the second day they turned all their strength against it. Although they were now attacking more than one legion, the Britons penetrated deeply into the Roman position and the bridgehead commander Gnaeus Hosidius Geta narrowly escaped capture. For the Britons the critical point in the battle and indeed in the whole campaign had been reached, but as reinforce-ments continued to cross the river the initiative passed to the legions who were at last able to break out for a decisive advance. Realizing their defensive line was breached, the British disengaged and withdrew.

The Medway was the decisive action of the invasion campaign and a classic bridgehead battle. A tribal army defending a water barrier had been thrown off balance by a diversionary attack and further confused by a surprise landing on the opposite flank. A tenacious defence of the landing ground enabled fresh troops to be fed into the bridgehead until sufficient strength had been assembled for a breakout. The legions had put to flight a tribal army of 60,000–80,000 men and it is possible that one of the kings of the Belgae, Togodum-nus, was mortally wounded during the fighting.

The British retreated across the River Thames into Essex, correctly reasoning that the Romans' next objective would be Camulodunum (Colchester) the Belgic capital. With further skirmishing the Romans established themselves north of the river where they paused to await the arrival of the emperor Claudius. He remained in Britain for sixteen days, long enough for a triumphant entry, with elephants, into Camulodunum and to accept the submission of the increasing number of British tribes seeking surrender terms. Caratacus, his kinsmen in disarray, his capital in enemy hands and his cause bereft of allies, retreated with those who would follow to the mountains of Wales, there to continue a guerrilla war against the invader.

*The site of the battle for the Medway crossing has never been positively identified although a number of locations*

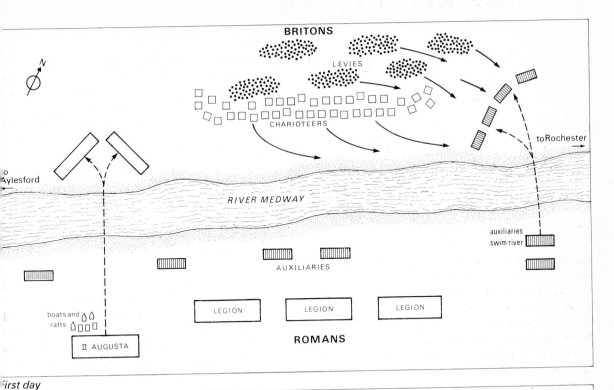

*First day*

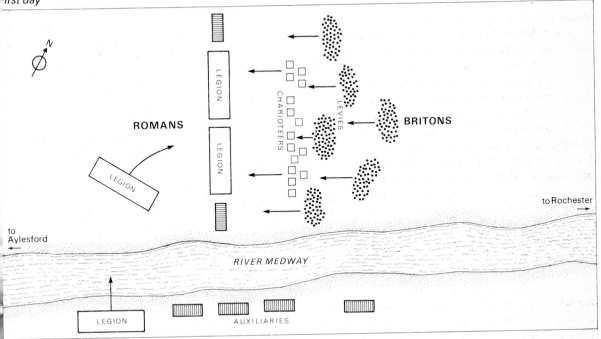

*Second day*

have been suggested. It seems certain that the battle took place at a point between Rochester and Aylesford. Although the river is much narrower towards Aylesford its banks are surrounded by marshes which would undoubtedly have impeded both Britons and Romans alike. The sand and shingle banks where the river widens near Rochester would have been a more practical crossing point for an army and its impedimenta. The most convincing site for the battle would seem to be close to the present Medway Bridge which carries the M2 motorway over the river.

While Claudius was savouring the defeat of the tribes in the south-east, Vespasian and the IInd Augusta had begun an advance into the south-west. It was most probably a combined land and sea expedition and it involved hard fighting. Vespasian's biographer, Suetonius Tranquillus, mentions the capture of the Isle of Wight, the reduction of at least twenty *oppida*, thirty battles, and the subjugation of two warlike tribes — certainly the Durotriges of Dorset and Somerset, and possibly the Dumnonii of Devon and Cornwall. Vespasian's progress was marked by a series of violent if brief struggles for the possession of hillforts such as Maiden Castle, Hod Hill, Spettisbury Rings, and Ham Hill. It is probable that Vespasian reached Exeter and his campaign may have extended as far west as Cornwall.

There is no literary evidence for the activities of the remaining legions in Britain but the archaeological record suggests that the XXth remained at Colchester to establish a firm base and act as a strategic reserve; that the IXth Hispana advanced northwards to the area around Peterborough, eventually to reach Lincoln; and that the XIVth Gemina moved north-westward through the Midlands to Shropshire. It seems likely that strategically important areas were controlled by sizeable detachments from particular legions and from the *auxilia*. These detachments were based in a network of camps and forts which formed a buffer zone between the settled territory of the Claudian conquest and the turbulent regions to the north and west. The Roman road known as the Fosse Way, running from Topsham in Devon through Leicester to Lincoln, provided an effective line of communication through a broad frontier zone stretching from the River Severn to the River Humber.

Thus in AD 47 Aulus Plautius passed a considerable military and administrative achievement to his successor as governor of Britain, Publius Ostorius Scapula.

Maiden Castle, an Iron-Age hill fort in Dorset. Hill forts such as Maiden, Hod Hill and Spettisbury Rings formed the power base of independent chieftains of the Durotriges and there is evidence that Maiden was the scene of a ferocious and successful assault by the II Augusta under Vespasian. In addition to the defence in depth provided by its banks and ditches the fort's gateways could only be approached by an oblique route commanded by the banks.

substantial part of the island had been occupied as a province of Rome and for the moment at least the occupation appeared reasonably secure. A continuing problem, however, was that the tribes outside the conquest refused to accept the frontier and no sooner had Ostorius Scapula arrived than he was faced by a crisis in the west. It was precipitated by a potent combination of Druidism, Caratacus, and the tribe of the Silures.

The Druids exercised considerable authority from their base at Mona (Anglesey) and their hatred of Rome was implacable. It seems probable that they helped Caratacus to become a supra-tribal leader in Wales, and they may also have furthered his attempts to enlist the support of the Brigantes in Yorkshire and the Iceni in East Anglia. As Ostorius Scapula began his tenure as governor the Silures launched an attack across the Severn, deep into his new province. Scapula responded rapidly, marching with a force of *auxilia* to disperse the insurgents and drive them back to their mountain strongholds. Despite the speed and ease of his victory Scapula realized that he would need to deal permanently with Caratacus and that to do so the present frontier would have to be pushed westwards. To reduce the risk of rebellion during his absence in Wales, Scapula decreed that any tribes of doubtful loyalty must be disarmed. The inevitable result was rebellion and before he could move westwards he had to crush a revolt among the Iceni, an act which left a legacy of hatred towards Rome.

Scapula began the search for Caratacus early in AD 48 but it was to be a cautious campaign involving thorough preparation in the deployment of the legions and the construction of forts and supply bases. The Silures, and in the north the Deceangli, waged an effective guerrilla war and penetration of their territory proved difficult and costly. During the summer of AD 50 Caratacus eluded probing attacks from both north and south but only at the cost of devastated tribal lands. Moving north-west to the territory of the Ordovices, he resolved to give battle the following year.

Caratacus may have believed that only a decisive victory would spread his cause throughout Britain and to achieve that victory he needed the help of a strong defensive position to break the advance of the legions. The Roman historian Tacitus described the chosen battlefield as one 'where numerous factors – notably approaches and escape-routes – helped him and impeded us. On one side there were steep hills. Wherever the gradient was gentler, stones were piled into a kind of rampart. And at his front there was a river without easy crossings.'

A tribal army, possibly as strong as 10,000 men, was positioned on the hills and behind the ramparts. Its levies and warriors came from most of the tribes of Wales, from the Belgae and perhaps from the Brigantes of Yorkshire. The Roman force would almost certainly have outnumbered them, probably by between 2000 and 5000 men. Both sides realized the importance of the forthcoming battle and Caratacus and his chieftains moved amongst the tribes encouraging them to fight as their ancestors had against Caesar.

Dismayed by the apparent strength of the British position and by the ferocious shouts and war cries of the tribesmen Scapula apparently decided to retreat. The legions' eagerness for battle changed his mind and after reconnoitring the British position he led his troops forward. The river was forded with little difficulty although casualties were suffered on the lower slopes as a storm of missiles rained down from above. Locking their shields above their heads in the *testudo* (tortoise) formation, the legionaries swarmed over the ramparts driving the Britons before them to the summit. Here the superior weapons and tactics of the legions took heavy toll of the lightly equipped tribesmen and their resistance collapsed. The terrain would have precluded the use of either Roman cavalry or British chariots and there was no general pursuit. Although his wife, daughter and brother were captured, Caratacus evaded the legions and made his way to the territory of the Brigantes from where no doubt he hoped to renew the war. Brigantia, however, was still a client kingdom of Rome and its ruler Queen Cartimandua owed her authority to Roman support. There was little room for manoeuvre and Caratacus was dispatched as a captive to Italy.

---

*There has been considerable speculation about the site of the battlefield on which Caratacus challenged the legions. All that can be said with any certainty is that the site is in northern or central Wales amongst a group of hills topped by a plateau, with a sizeable river at their base. Only the Rivers Dee and Severn appear to fit these requirements and it is on the Severn that two possible sites are to be found. Traditionally Cefn Carnedd, rising to a height of 908 feet (276 metres) to the west of the Severn between Caersws and Llanidloes, has been the most convincing site. Another at Dolforwyn Castle three miles to the east of Newtown also has arguments in its favour.*

# BOUDICCA AD 61

Although they adopted much of the style and substance of Roman life many of the tribes who surrendered at the conquest still looked to the day when their freedom would be restored. At the very least they expected Rome, in return for their allegiance, to preserve their territory and respect the dignity of their tribal rulers. In their dealings with the Iceni of Norfolk and the Trinovantes of Essex the Roman administration was to fall disastrously short of these expectations.

When Prasutagus, king of the Iceni, died (probably in AD 59) the terms of his will made the emperor Nero co-heir with the king's two daughters. To assess the extent of the estate due to the emperor, an inventory of Prasutagus's possessions and land should have been taken. Instead the local Roman administrators began to plunder the whole territory of the Iceni. When the royal family resisted, the king's widow, Boudicca, was flogged and his daughters raped. The Trinovantes, still resentful of the confiscation of their lands for settlement by retired veterans of the legions, joined the Iceni in rebellion. In 61 the tribesmen led by Boudicca descended upon the *colonia* at Camulodunum (Colchester), massacring the veterans and their families. A detachment of the IXth Legion hurrying to their aid was ambushed and destroyed. The Roman governor Gaius Suetonius Paulinus, who had been campaigning in Wales, returned to London with all speed but without the majority of his troops. As the Britons swept towards London Suetonius retreated northwards to meet his approaching legions and the city was left to its fate.

Following Suetonius the tribes paused to destroy Verulamium (St Albans) and the governor rejoined his main body of troops, comprising the XIVth Legion, part of the XXth, and auxiliaries summoned from local garrisons. It was fortunate for Suetonius that with only 10,000 men he was able to give battle on ground of his own choosing.

The Roman battle line, with the legions flanked by auxiliaries in the centre and cavalry on the wings, was drawn up in a defile with a forest to the rear and an open plain to the front. Boudicca's host, estimates of whose strength have ranged as high as 230,000, paused to form a loose battle-array and then charged up the slope towards the enemy position. The Romans halted the charge with a storm of javelins and then counter-attacked in a wedge formation. The British were driven back and trapped against the wagons bearing their women and children. The legionaries slaughtered the draught-oxen creating a killing ground on which they proceeded to massacre warriors, tribesmen and non-combatants. Tacitus put the final toll at 80,000 Britons and 400 Romans. Boudicca escaped, later to commit suicide, while Suetonius, reinforced by legionaries and auxiliaries from the Rhine, laid waste the territory of the rebellious tribes.

*Boudicca's defeat occurred somewhere in the Midlands and a site at Mancetter, to the south-east of Atherstone, has been suggested.*

Marcus Favonius Facilis, a centurian of the XXth Legion. From his tombstone at Colchester.

# MONS GRAUPIUS AD 84

In the fourteen years from 71 to 84 three men succeeded to the governorship of Britain: Petillius Cerialis (71–4), Julius Frontinus (74–8) and Julius Agricola (78–84). Under their command the legions pacified first northern England, then Wales, and finally began an attempt to conquer the Highlands of Scotland. In the north Cerialis advanced the Roman frontier into the territory of the Brigantes. Under Frontinus the scene of military activity moved to Wales and his defeat of the Silures and Ordovices was later consolidated by Agricola in a swift campaign which ended in the capture of Anglesey. Agricola then turned to the north where he planned to build upon the defeat of the Brigantes by the expansion of Roman control to the west of the Pennines and into Caledonia.

Between 79 and 81 Agricola pushed forwards with legionary columns from Chester in the west and York in the east. He reached the line of the Forth–Clyde isthmus and then pushed on to the Tay estuary, establishing forts to consolidate the ground won. In the summer of 83 Agricola planned to bring the Caledonian tribes to battle, even though his own command had been reduced by the transfer of both legionaries and auxiliaries to the defence of the Rhine frontier. Using the *Classis Britannica* to harry coastal settlements, Agricola advanced with his legions in an attempt to encircle the Highland massif, building forts to block the exits provided by the glens. A serious reverse befell the IXth Legion when a Caledonian force broke into the legion's camp during a night attack. The situation was only restored by the arrival of Agricola with reinforcements. The campaigning season ended without a decisive engagement and the Romans had to wait until the following year for the battle they sought.

Determined to restore the security of their Highland refuge, the Caledonian tribes assembled their greatest strength and confidently awaited Agricola's approach at Mons Graupius. A tribal army of 30,000 men under its leader Calgacus confronted a Roman force of roughly equal strength. Agricola kept the IXth and XXth legions in reserve, forming his main battle line from 8000 auxiliary infantry and 5000 auxiliary cavalry. Since the Caledonians occupied the high ground and their position was screened by a line of chariots, Agricola launched his cavalry against the charioteers while his infantry engaged in an exchange of missiles with the enemy. When the charioteers began to give ground, Agricola advanced with his Batavian and Tungrian infantry to bring the tribesmen to hand-to-hand conflict. As the auxiliaries drove into the enemy line the mass of tribesmen to the rear began to move forward down the slope, overlapping the Roman flank. Agricola halted this threat with a charge by auxiliary cavalry which broke through the opposing line and wheeled round to take the enemy infantry in the rear. As more and more cavalry broke into their ranks, the tribesmen turned and fled, leaving 10,000 dead on the battlefield. According to Tacitus the Roman loss was 360 auxiliaries. It was a remarkable outcome, particularly as it had been achieved solely by auxiliaries, but it was not the victory for which Agricola had hoped. Nearly seventy per cent of the Caledonian army had escaped leaving the tribes with sufficient strength to threaten the northern border of the province.

---

*The site of Mons Graupius has still not been conclusively identified but the location of a large Roman camp near Inverurie to the north-west of Aberdeen suggests that the mountain known today as Bennachie 1733 feet (528 metres), could indeed be Mons Graupius.*

The tombstone at Colchester of Longinus Sdapezematycius, a *duplicarius* (non-commissioned officer) of the 1st *ala* of Thracians.

# THE DEFENCE OF A PROVINCE AD 105–409

A *Antonine Wall*  B *Hadrians Wall*

By the end of the first century AD the period of Roman expansion in Britain was over. As troops were withdrawn for service elsewhere in the empire consolidation became the predominant concern. The transfer of the IInd Adiutrix from Chester to the Danube had meant the abandonment of the territory won by Agricola beyond the Forth–Clyde line, and within twenty years this was followed by a further withdrawal to the Tyne–Solway line.

To deter raids from the north the forts along an existing military road, the 'Stanegate', were refurbished and additional posts built. Serious fighting occurred in Britain between 118 and 122 and following a visit by the emperor Hadrian the decision was taken to strengthen the defences of the north by the construc-

tion of a permanent wall beyond the Stanegate. Despite the tremendous effort of construction involved in Hadrian's Wall the new emperor Antoninus Pius decided shortly after his accession in 138 to abandon it and reoccupy Lowland Scotland. There he built a new wall 100 miles to the north spanning the Forth–Clyde isthmus. The Antonine Wall was 37 miles (59 kilometres) long and constructed of turf and it was abandoned temporarily in the 150s, probably again in the 160s and then finally at the beginning of the third century. Thereafter, Hadrian's Wall remained the principal fortified line until its abandonment in 409.

Detail from the Bridgeness Slab excavated in West Lothian in 1868. Stone slabs such as this commemorate the construction of a particular length of the Antonine Wall and are known today as 'distance slabs'. The Bridgeness Slab records the completion of $4\frac{2}{3}$ Roman miles (7.4 km) of the wall by men of the IInd Augusta. In this detail a Roman soldier is seen riding down barbarians.

The nine forts of the Saxon Shore as shown in the *Notitia Dignitatum*, a list originally drawn up about AD 400 as a guide to the deployment of troops throughout the Roman World, including Britain. The section devoted to the command of the Count of the Saxon Shore lists nine coastal forts on the following sites: Bradwell, Dover, Lympne, Brancaster, Burgh Castle, Reculver, Richborough, Pevensey, Portchester.

In the west and east the province came under attack by seaborne raiders. From Ireland, which the Romans had never attempted to conquer, raids were launched against the west coast of Britain, and coastal forts such as Cardiff and Lancaster were enlarged or constructed in an attempt to deal with this threat. By the end of the second century Saxons were already raiding the southeast coast and the erection of forts at Brancaster and Reculver in the early third century was the beginning of a major coastal defence system. The series of fortifications from the Wash to Southampton Water which became known as the Saxon Shore, denied the raiders entry to the river estuaries which could carry

## HADRIAN'S WALL

ABOVE:
A bronze head of the Emperor Hadrian retrieved from the River Thames at London Bridge. The portrait shows Hadrian, who ruled from AD 117–138, with a full beard.

RIGHT:
Hadrian's Wall, Northumberland, near Housesteads Fort.

Serious unrest occurred in Britain between 118–22 and following a visit by the Emperor Hadrian the decision was taken to strengthen the defences of the north by the construction of a linear barrier along the Tyne–Solway gap. The completed wall ran for 80 Roman miles (120 kms) from Wallsend in the east to Bowness on Solway in the west. Although originally conceived as an outpost line in advance of a supporting garrison 15 forts were added during construction to reinforce the milecastles and to allow the main garrison to be moved to the wall itself. This increased the strength of the garrison from 2000 men to approximately 10,000. Legionaries from the IInd Augusta, XXth Valeria Victrix and VIIth Victrix were employed on building the wall, together with auxiliaries and men from the *Classis Britannica*. On its completion it required a garrison numbering in the region of 20,000 men. The front of the wall was protected by a ditch, in places over 30 feet (9 metres) wide and 12 feet (3.6 metres) deep and the wall itself was 8–9 feet (2.4–2.7 metres) wide and in parts 15–20 feet (4.5–6 metres) high. To prevent civilian access to this military zone a ditch 20 feet wide, 10 feet (3 metres) deep and flanked 30 feet on either side by 20 foot mounds was dug to the south along the entire length of the wall.

them inland. The forts served as a base from which garrisons could contest Saxon landings, and ships of the *Classis Britannica* could attempt to meet the enemy at sea. In 367 Roman Britain suffered a major attack by barbarian forces from the Highlands, Ireland and Gaul. Of the two principal commanders of Britain's defences, the Duke of Britain and the Count of the Saxon Shore, the former was captured and the latter killed. By 370 Count Theodosius had restored order. He rebuilt the damaged portions of Hadrian's Wall, withdrew the outlying garrisons and relied on treaty relationships with neighbouring tribes to provide a buffer zone to the north of the province.

Barbarian raids continued but despite rebellions by the Roman commanders of Britain and the withdrawal of troops from the garrison no large scale campaigns were needed against the Picts, Scots and Saxons until those launched by Stilicho in 396 to 398. Until the final Roman withdrawal, a major responsibility for defence appears to have rested with a mobile field army of infantry and cavalry commanded by the Count of the Britains (*Comes Britanniarum*).

# EARLY ENGLAND
## 410–1060

The 650 years stretching from the withdrawal of the Roman garrison at the beginning of the fifth century to the conquest by William, Duke of Normandy, in the eleventh century are of supreme importance to English history. From this period of invasion and settlement by Anglo-Saxons, Scandinavians and Normans, emerged an England in which the pattern of racial, cultural and linguistic development was established. The early centuries of this achievement, from roughly 410 to 600, are traditionally known as the Dark Ages. While as a judgement of British society this epithet requires qualification, it does hold a substantial element of truth when applied to the sources available to the historian. Written evidence in the form of manuscripts such as the *Anglo-Saxon Chronicle*, the *De Exidio et Conquestu Britanniae* of the monk Gildas, Bede's *Ecclesiastical History of the English Nation* and the tenth-century compilation known as 'Nennius' *History of the Britons*, allow the outline of events to be reconstructed, but the interpretation placed on them by these sources may be at best ambiguous, and at worst totally misleading. Fortunately additional evidence in the form of charters and laws, the archaeological record and the study of English place names, can be used to qualify and expand the narrative. The major themes which emerge are the transition of England from a grouping of small kingdoms into a single monarchy, the assimilation of two migrant peoples, the Anglo-Saxons and the Vikings, and the conversion of the English to Christianity. The outcome of battle was fundamental to the development of the first two, and war, on occasion, was the precursor to the advance of Christianity.

The Roman legions came to Britain as professional soldiers under orders to conquer an island whose possession might further the interests of Rome. The English (Angles, Saxons and Jutes) came as a people hungry for land and loot. Finding that Britain could satisfy their desires, settlement and eventually folk-migration followed. This English invasion was resisted by the native Britons, but gradually they were pushed westwards and the political focus of England centred on the struggles of the kingdoms of the Heptarchy: Wessex, Mercia, Northumbria, East Anglia, Essex, Sussex and Kent.

We will never know the full extent of the fighting between Briton and Anglo-Saxon but sources such as the *Anglo-Saxon Chronicle* do throw some light on the nature of warfare at the time. The desire to annexe and settle enemy territory was one of the prime reasons for war, but there were other motives. Battles could result from feuding between rival claimants to a throne, from the harbouring of dynastic exiles, from the attacks of marauding war-bands, and from raids aimed at seizing desirable loot such as cattle. Warfare took a number of forms, including attempts to repel seaborne landings and to capture defended strongpoints involving Roman fortifications or pre-Roman hill-forts and, most common of all, actions at river crossings.

River lines formed a natural defensive position and battles often centred on fords or other crossing points. Of the twelve battles fought by Arthur, seven were connected with rivers. It has been suggested that actions fought at river crossings would have given mounted Britons a natural superiority over the English infantry, but in fact the advantage of deploying mounted troops probably lay in the speed and mobility they offered in reaching the battlefield. Arthur's horsemen were not the heavy cavalry suggested by the legends of the Knights of the Round Table and they would have been unable to deliver effective shock action. They did not ride down opposing infantry with horse and lance but used the horse as a mobile platform from which to throw their spears before attacking with the sword. The emphasis of warfare still lay firmly with individual feats of arms rather than with the unity of action required in a disciplined cavalry charge.

It is difficult to estimate the numerical strength of the British and Anglo-Saxon armies. On occasion, the *Chronicle* numbers battle deaths in thousands, but if armies that could sustain such high casualty figures did exist it is difficult to accept that such numbers represented warriors alone. These totals must have included a high proportion of followers and possibly civilians arbitrarily struck down in the pursuit. The Laws of Ine (688–94) declared that 'we call up to seven men "thieves"; from seven to thirty-five a "band"; above that is an army'. Numerically weak forces obviously possessed military credibility; indeed, in 786 Cyneheard had almost captured Wessex with a force of eighty-five men. The initial Anglo-Saxon invading forces numbered between two to five ship's companies, or 100 to 250 men, and the strength of the army which attempted to crush Northumbria in *c.*600 is recorded in the poem *Y Gododdin* as 300 men. The *Gododdin* raises another interesting aspect of Dark Age warfare, namely the remarkable mobility and endurance of armies and war bands. Though the Gododdin mounted their expedition from Edinburgh they were defeated in battle at Catterick in Yorkshire, nearly 150 miles (240 kilometres) to the south. Before reaching the battlefield at Chester in *c.*615 Æthelfrith's army had to march the 210 miles (336 kilometres) from his capital of Bamburgh. The logistics of such deep penetration of enemy territory argue that both defending and attacking forces would be numbered in hundreds rather than thousands.

The cadre of an army was the king's bodyguard or war band, formed of warriors serving in return for weapons, food and a share of the spoils. It was very much an institution of a heroic age in which skill at arms and prowess in battle were both a duty and a pastime. In return for their lord's protection and beneficence, the war band remained loyal to the death and the climax of many battles came with the last stand of the warriors of the household around their slain or dying king. Their weapons were the sword, the spear, occasionally the axe, and the shield. The sword was less common than the spear and its use appears to have been confined to the nobility. The *spatha*, the Anglo-Saxon sword of the pagan period, had a doubled-edged, parallel-sided blade and was usually between 75 and 80 centimetres in length. A single-edged long-knife, the *scramasax*, which could range in length from 3 inches to 2 foot 6 inches (7.5–75 centimetres), might also be slung at the

## THE SUTTON HOO TREASURE

ABOVE:
Sword, scabbard and baldric mounts.

RIGHT:
The Sutton Hoo helmet, reconstructed in 1971, which can be seen the British Museum.

The Sutton Hoo treasure and ship-burial is the richest discovery ever made in a pagan grave in Britain. It was excavated in 1939 in the mound of a barrow cemetery overlooking the River Deben in Suffolk. The treasure was resting in a burial chamber situated in the middle of a ship, of which only heavily rusted nails and lines of staining in the sand remained. It has nevertheless been possible to reconstruct the design of the ship which was nearly 90 feet (27 metres) long, 14 feet (4 metres) at its greatest beam and capable of propulsion by sail or by thirty-eight oarsmen. The date of the burial has been estimated from coin finds as between 625 and 660 but archaeologists are still uncertain as to whether it ever included a body. The treasure has been linked with a number of kings and it has been suggested that it represents grave-goods for the East Anglian King Raedwald who died in the 620s or Aethelhere who was killed at Winwaed in Yorkshire in 655. The treasure is of a predominantly military character and includes equipment such as the masked helmet which although the work of Nordic craftsmen, is in the style of the parade-armour of a high ranking late-Roman officer.

hip with the sword. The spear was used for both hunting and war and it represented, together with a circular wood-and-leather shield, the main weaponry of the average warrior. Body armour in the form of mail and helmet was rare and was probably worn only by the highest ranks of the British and Anglo-Saxon armies. With weapons such as these, most battles resolved themselves into grim hand-to-hand mêlées in which frightful wounds were inflicted and received. The shield wall gave some protection during the initial exchange of spear and arrow, but it was not the rigid formation of interlocking shields that its name suggests. Such a precise and formal arrangement was alien to the Anglo-Saxon military art and its application would have severely restricted the fighting room of the warrior.

In the ninth and tenth centuries the Vikings of Denmark, southern Sweden, and Norway spread terror throughout western Europe, but of all their attacks, those against Britain were the most savage and the most constant. This was partly for reasons of geography – the waters of the North Sea were scant protection against a race capable of sailing to the New World, and partly a reflection of the divisions, not simply into Pict, Scot, Briton or Saxon, but also between kingdom and sub-kingdom, which existed in Britain at the end of the eighth century. England was rich, both in wealth and good land, and the Viking raiders of the late eighth century had changed by the middle of the ninth into men intent upon conquest and settlement. The campaigns waged by the great Viking armies of 865 to 880 resulted in the conquest of most of East Anglia, Northumbria and eastern Mercia. London came under Viking control and their attacks bit deeply into Wessex. That the Viking advance was held and in some areas pushed back was due primarily to the military and administrative talents of Alfred, King of Wessex (871–99).

In the year Alfred succeeded to the throne the 'Great Army' of the Danes which had been campaigning successfully in England since 865 had been reinforced by the arrival of a 'Great summer Army'. For the next seven years, until Alfred's victory over the Vikings at Edington in 878, Wessex fought desperately for its survival. The mobility of the Viking armies, which could move quickly by sea or on horseback, made them a difficult enemy for Alfred to counter. Their men were professional warriors, well armed with axes, swords and spears and possessing a remarkable talent for living off the land. As a result they were frequently able to

The Gokstad ship. The Viking warship made of oak and measuring 76 feet 5 inches (23.3 metres) in length which was used for a royal

retain the strategic initiative throughout a campaign, successfully avoiding Alfred's attempts to intercept their penetrations into Wessex. To redress the balance Alfred used the fourteen years of comparative peace after Edington to embark upon a series of military and administrative reforms designed to keep the Vikings at bay.

The time required to summon the West-Saxon fyrd (that part of the army formed from men owing personal or territorial military service) left the defence of Wessex vulnerable to sudden raids. Alfred therefore organized the fyrd so that half of its manpower remained on active service while the other half stayed on the land to ensure the success of the harvest. The two halves exchanged roles at regular intervals and Alfred was provided with the services of what amounted to a standing army. Alfred's thegns also rotated military service with the supervision of their estates, serving the King for one month out of three. If a thegn neglected his military duties he could be fined 120 shillings and a ceorl (a freeman) 30 shillings. To provide for the defence of specific areas Alfred initiated a system of fortified localities known as burghs. Thirty-one burghs are listed by name in a document known as the *Burghal Hidage*, which dates from the reign of Edward the Elder (899–924). The burghs were spread throughout southern England in order, at least in theory, that no area was more than a day's march (roughly 20 miles/32 kilometres) away from a fortress. They acted as assembly points for the local fyrd and provided a base for garrisons. Each burgh was kept in repair and garrisoned when necessary by men drawn from the surrounding villages on the basis of one soldier from every hide of arable land. Although Alfred also began a programme of shipbuilding it was primarily through the reorganized West Saxon army and the burghs that he evolved a military system capable of fighting the Danes to a standstill.

burial. Excavated from a layer of blue clay in 1880 it is now displayed in the Viking Ship Museum at Bygeoy near Oslo.

# MOUNT BADON (Mons Badonicus) c.490–9
# DYRHAM (Deorham) 577

## MOUNT BADON

With the removal of Rome's military support around 410 the centralized administration of occupied Britain disintegrated, although the form and values of Roman life were not instantly overthrown. It was still hoped that Britain would become a Roman province again and an appeal for military aid was made to a Roman army campaigning in Gaul as late as 446. Two military policies appear to have been put forward to deal with the barbarian threat after the break with Rome. Each policy was supported by rival adherents whose partisanship developed into mutual hostility and war. The rival leaders may have been Vortigern and Ambrosius Aurelianus; it appears that the former, whom Gildas describes as a *superbus tyrannus*, was the principal military leader in the early fifth century. The name Vortigern can be translated as 'high king' although the exact status of this figure remains uncertain. It is widely accepted that he was responsible for bringing Saxon mercenaries to Britain as a defence against attack by Picts and Scots. It is possible the real significance of this stratagem was as a defence against a Roman landing from Gaul in support of Ambrosius. Thus Vortigern's decision to base Saxons in East Anglia and to surrender Kent as an area for further Saxon settlement can be explained by the need to create a buffer zone against an attack from across the Channel.

Vortigern's employment of barbarian allies was by no means original and it is probable that Germanic settlers co-operated in the defence of forts and towns even before the Romans withdrew. Whatever the precedents, Vortigern's policy was a catastrophe for the Britons. The mercenaries comprised Angles, Saxons and Jutes and it seems certain that their role as allies started earlier and developed more gradually than is suggested by Bede's account of a single mass descent led by Hengist and Horsa around 450. At first all went well and the Saxons accepted land and money in return for their military service, but as reinforcements arrived from Germany and their strength increased they were encouraged to rebel by the apparent weakness of their hosts. Consolidating their hold on the east, they launched savage raids to the west and north. Hengist and Horsa fought Vortigern at a site called Ægelsthrep where Horsa was killed, and then Hengist and his son Æse won a decisive victory against the Britons at Creacanford, another site which cannot easily be identified.

Vortigern disappears from the historical record b 460 and thereafter British resistance to attacks centre on the leadership of two men bearing Roman names Ambrosius Aurelianius and Arthur. The fortunes of war swung between the Britons and the Anglo-Saxon but the Britons seem to have begun and ended a series of campaigns lasting nearly forty years with significant victories. The first was achieved under Ambrosiu Aurelianus, but the concluding victory at Mount Bado was probably gained by a force under Arthur's command. The *Historia Brittonum* lists twelve battle fought and won by Arthur of which only one, Cat Coi Celidon, the battle of the Caledonian Forest in souther Scotland, can be attributed to a particular site with an degree of confidence. Mount Badon, the last of th twelve, was probably fought between 490 and 499 on site in southern England.

Arthur was not a king but rather the military leade of the forces of a number of small British kingdoms, and the entry for 'Year 72' in the *British Easter Annals* link Arthur specifically with the battle: 'Battle of Badon i which Arthur carried the cross of our lord Jesus Christ three days and three nights on his shoulders and the Britons were victorious.' The detail of the entry should not, of course, be interpreted literally. 'Three days and three nights' merely implies a lengthy battle and Arthu would have borne the cross as a symbol, perhaps in the form of an amulet. Gildas supports the contention that the battle was a series of attacks and repulses, for he describes it as the siege of Mons Badonicus – *obsessio Montis Badonici*. The clear implication is that either the Britons or the Anglo-Saxons occupied a hill-top from which they were prepared to resist the attacks of the enemy.

This does not necessarily imply that one of the combattants occupied an existing hill-fort; it may simply have been that the Anglo-Saxons occupied an elevated position in order to reduce the effectiveness of Arthur's cavalry. The Britons still managed to launch decisive attacks and a statement in the *Historia Brittonum* describes a single charge in which Arthur and his followers slew 960 of the enemy. It is difficult to accept the historical accuracy of such a precise figure but the victory gained by the Britons was undoubtedly comprehensive. While it is probably overstating the results of the battle to suggest that the Saxon threat was eradicated for half a century, Gildas does describe the far-reaching consequences of Badon, stressing the resulting peace and the cessation of foreign wars. The Britons had at least gained a breathing space in which to prepare to meet the renewal of Saxon pressure.

*Attempts to identify the site of the battle have centred upon the search for a suitable hill-fort. It has been suggested that the British name for the site was* Din Badon, *meaning 'Badon Fort', and that the defeated Saxons translated this into* Baddanburg *or 'Badda's Fort', thereby implying a link with one of the five modern Badburys between Dorset and Lincolnshire. Favoured sites have included Badbury by Liddington Castle in Wiltshire and Badbury Rings in Dorset. There are however a number of objections to a hill-fort site, and Welsh tradition identifies Badon with Caer Vadon, or Bath. It is possible that the battle was fought on one of the hills surrounding the town.*

## DYRHAM

The entry for the year 577 in the *Anglo-Saxon Chronicle* records that 'Cuthwine and Ceawlin fought against the Britons and killed three kings, Conmail, Condidan and Farinmail, at the place which is called Dyrham; and they captured three of their cities, Gloucester, Cirencester and Bath'. That this decisive battle took place near the modern village of Dyrham, seven miles north of Bath, is beyond doubt, and a precise location has been proposed. Approximately one mile to the north of Dyrham there is a hill-fort identified on the Ordnance Survey map, *'Southern Britain in the Iron Age'*, as 'Dyrham Camp'. Many historians have accepted this as the immediate site of the battle. However the name 'Dyrham Camp' is of late-nineteenth-century origin; in the eighteenth century the site of the fort was known as Barhill and in the seventeenth as Burrill. It would thus seem rash to accept uncritically that the fighting occurred at the hill-fort, although this remains a possibility.

The battle of Dyrham resulted from the aggressive westward advance of the descendants of the Saxon dynasty established on the Hampshire coast by Cerdic early in the sixth century. The Saxon drive towards the Severn Estuary threatened to isolate the British settlements in the south-west from those in Wales. In the path of this advance stood the British towns of Bath, Cirencester and Gloucester, which, although still populated, no longer possessed the political and economic importance they enjoyed under Rome. A Saxon presence astride the commanding 600 foot (180 metres) escarpment at Hinton to the north of Dyrham was a

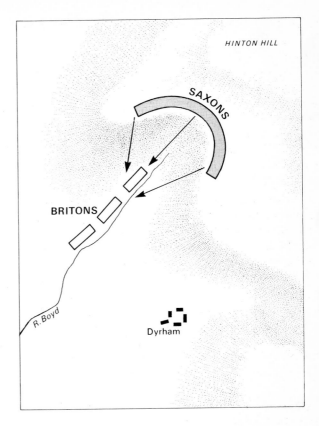

challenge which the Britons could not ignore, and the forces of the three towns combined under their kings, Conmail, Condidan and Farinmail, for a concerted attack upon the army of Cuthwine and Ceawlin.

The battle may have taken the form of an attack by either side upon the fort on Hinton Hill but it could equally, and perhaps more probably, have been fought on the banks of the tributary of the River Boyd which flows below the south-west face of the escarpment. The battle went decisively in favour of the Saxons, for all three British kings perished, suggesting that the Britons ended the battle surrounded and unable to escape. A Saxon attack launched at dawn from the escarpment, with the advantage and impetus of a downhill charge, may have swept through the British position before they could form to receive it. Defeat would have followed very quickly.

*Hinton Hill lies between the* B4465 *and the* A46 *approximately 7 miles (11 kilometres) north of Bath.*

# THE BATTLES OF NORTHUMBRIA 603–85

A 603 *Degsastan*   B 615 *Battle of Chester*   C 616 *Battle of the Idle*   D 632 *Haethfelth*   E 633 *Heavenfield*
F 641 *Maserfelth*   G 655 *River Winwaed*   H 678 *Battle of Trent*   I 685 *Nechtanesmere*

By the close of the sixth century Britain was still a nation fragmented into a number of small kingdoms. Pre-eminent amongst these were the seven kingdoms of the Heptarchy; Kent, Sussex, Wessex, Essex, East Anglia, Mercia and Northumbria. At the beginning of the seventh century Northumbria was divided into the two separate Anglian kingdoms of Bernicia and Deira, the former centred upon Bamburgh, the latter upon the Yorkshire Wolds. The transformation of these isolated English settlements into the most powerful kingdom in northern Britain was begun by Æthelfrith, the last pagan king of Bernicia, who reigned *c.*593 to 616.

The expansion of Bernicia was achieved through Æthelfrith's considerable military skill, and his first opponents were the Scots of Dalriada (Argyll). Under their king, Aedan Mac Gabran, the Scots pushed southwards into Bernicia but were defeated by Æthelfrith at Degsastan in 603. Aedan's army was all but wiped out and this decisive victory secured Northumbria from attack from the north.

Æthelfrith next turned south-west, moving against the Britons of Powys in north Wales. Whether he advanced southwards from Carlisle or westwards through the kingdom of Elmet it must have been a difficult march, but such was his speed that the Britons were taken by surprise and forced to give battle before their full strength had been mustered. Only the followers of Selyf Map Cynan of Powys, supported by men from the most easterly province of Gwynedd under Cadwal Crisban of Rhos, took the field against Æthelfrith at the battle of Chester in *c.*615. Nearly 1200 monks from Bangor-on-Dee also appeared on the battlefield but whether merely to offer prayer in support of the Britons or to fight alongside them is not entirely clear. Whatever the monks' purpose, Æthelfrith's troops were not troubled by any possible distinction between warriors and non-combatants and they slaughtered the monks as a preliminary to the main battle. The Britons were completely defeated and Selyf and Cadwal were killed. It is difficult to say whether Æthelfrith launched the campaign as a raid or as a deliberate attempt to drive a wedge between the Britons in Wales and those in Strathclyde, but if the latter was the case it is strange that the battle was not followed by Northumbrian settlement in the west.

The absence of any lasting result from the battle of Chester may perhaps be explained by the death of Æthelfrith only one year later at the hands of Raedwald

of East Anglia. King Raedwald had attacked in support of Edwin, heir to the throne of Deira, who had been exiled by Æthelfrith, and the latter's defeat at the battle of the River Idle in 616 gave Edwin the kingdom of Deira and Bernicia. Edwin became the first Christian king of Northumbria and his great military strength enabled him to conquer the British kingdom of Elmet and to lead an army to victory as far south as Wessex.

Edwin's invasion of Gwynedd and his conquest of the Isle of Man and of Anglesey led to a counter invasion of Northumbria. In 632 the allied forces of Penda of Mercia and King Cadwallon of Gwynedd defeated the Northumbrian army on the plain called 'Haethfelth' and slew Edwin. The Britons attempted to cement their victory through the devastation of Northumbria but although the kingdom was again split into the territories of Deira and Bernicia, Cadwallon was himself defeated in 633 at Heavenfield by Oswald of Bernicia. This victory reunited Northumbria and destroyed hopes of a British revival led by Gwynedd.

Under Oswald, Northumbria rose to pre-eminence in England but a clash with the growing power of Mercia could not long be postponed and on 5 August 641 Penda defeated and killed Oswald at Maserfelth. Penda assumed Oswald's mantle as the most powerful ruler in England and Northumbria again reverted to separate kingdoms, Oswine ruling Deira and Oswiu Bernicia. The Mercian king was still determined to destroy the residual power of Bernicia and in 654 Penda mobilized a formidable coalition, including King Æthelhere of the East Angles, and the British Prince Cadafael of Gwynedd. Faced by this massive array of strength Oswiu sued for peace, even offering a lavish bribe of treasure which Penda refused. Although outnumbered and on the verge of defeat, Oswiu vanquished the Mercian army at the River Winwaed in 655, killing Penda and most of his royal allies. Mercia and southern England acknowledged Oswiu as their overlord and it was only with his death in 670 that Mercian power began to reassert itself under the leadership of Penda's son Wulfhere. In 674 Wulfhere invaded Northumbria with an army drawn from all of southern England but he was repulsed by Oswiu's son Ecgfrith. In 678 Ecgfrith was defeated in turn by Wulfhere's brother Æthelred at the battle of Trent, in what proved to be the last clash between the armies of Mercia and Northumbria for a generation. It was also the final attempt by Northumbria to secure control of southern England and henceforth the kingdom's concern would rest primarily with the north.

In 685 Ecgfrith led an army northwards against the Picts. He did so despite the protests of his advisers, for his expedition was considered by contemporaries as unnecessary aggression. The Picts, led by their king Brude Mac Beli, retreated before Ecgfrith's advance, drawing him into the difficult country of the Sidlaw Hills. On 20 May the Picts turned upon their pursuers and defeated them in battle near a loch called Nechtanesmere, by Dunnichen, south-east of Forfar. The battle was probably a running fight or mêlée with the Northumbrians, disorganized by the speed of their pursuit, finally trapped against the shore of the loch between Dunnichen and Letham. Evidence suggests that a fortified settlement existed on the south side of Dunnichen Hill and its presence would further have restricted the Northumbrian deployment and presumably have provided a source of reinforcement for the Picts. Ecgfrith's bodyguard made a last stand around their lord, but both he and most of his army were slain. With Ecgfrith's defeat, English ascendancy in northern Britain was replaced by an independent kingdom of the Picts. To the south the immediate future lay with Mercia, whose rise foreshadowed the decline and eventual collapse of Northumbria.

---

*Dark Age battle sites remain notoriously elusive despite the attempts of generations of historians, archaeologists and antiquarians to place them in specific locations. Thus the argument that the site of Degsastan is Dawston in Liddesdale must be received with caution and the identification of Maserfelth with Oswestry in Shropshire and of the River Winwaed with the area of Leeds in Yorkshire are possible but by no means certain conclusions. The site of the battle of Haethfelth is traditionally linked with Hatfield Chase on the southern border of Northumbria and the Idle was fought near the spot at which the Roman road from Lincoln to Doncaster crosses the river. The battle of Heavenfield took place at Denisesburna to the south of Hexham while the Battle known as Dunnichen Moss or Nechtanesmere was fought on the banks of a loch which has since disappeared. Its location has been pinpointed to an area between Dunnichen and Letham which lie south of the A932 between Forfar and Arbroath.*

---

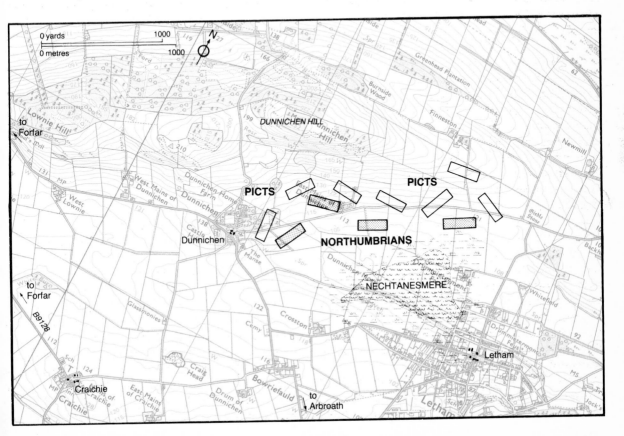

## ELLANDUN

Between the seventh and ninth centuries the centre of power in England passed from Northumbria to Mercia and then to Wessex. Offa, the son of Thingfrith, took the throne of Mercia amidst the civil war which followed the assassination of King Æthelbald in 757. Distracted by internal conflict, Mercia temporarily forfeited its supremacy in the south and Offa's re-establishment of that dominance brought him into conflict with Sussex, Kent, Wessex and Wales. A crippling blow was struck against Wessex in 779 at the battle of Bensington in Oxfordshire, and it was not until Egbert, exiled by Offa, returned to take the throne of Wessex in 809 that the southern challenge to Mercia was rekindled. We know little of Egbert's reign during the next twenty years but it is safe to assume that he was preparing for the period of intense military activity which he unleashed in 825.

Egbert first turned westwards advancing to Galford

BELOW:
Offa killing the son of Riganus from a twelfth century source (*The Lives of Offa*), which while being completely anachronistic for Offa is a useful representation of the warfare of its own period.

where his defeat of a British army brought east Cornwall within his control. Beornwulf, king of Mercia, had mobilized his forces but he did not take advantage of Egbert's absence to attack the heartland of Wessex. Egbert, justifiably alarmed at the presence of this Mercian host on his northern border, returned eastwards and the armies of Wessex and Mercia confronted each other at Ellandun. Although heavily outnumbered, Egbert chose to attack and after a protracted struggle his army gained the field and a decisive victory. Mercian losses were heavy for, in the words of the *Chronicle*: 'Egbert had the victory and a great slaughter was made there.' Beornwulf, who succeeded in escaping from the battlefield, fled eastwards only to be killed by the East Angles. The ascendancy of Mercia was at an end and henceforth the Anglo-Saxon destiny would be controlled by Wessex.

Egbert dispatched his army with his son Æthelwulf to Kent where they defeated Baldred and secured the submission not only of Kent but also of Essex, Surrey and Sussex. Four years later in 829 Egbert invaded and conquered Mercia, taking the title 'King of the Mercians' for a year before the kingdom regained its independence. Egbert's campaigns of 825 and 829

marked an important stage in the growing political unity of the English: he brought the resources and strength of the south, from Kent to Cornwall, under centralized authority at the time when the very existence of England was to be challenged by the warriors of Scandinavia.

*The location of the battlefield of Ellandun was at first thought to be Amesbury in Wiltshire, but the claims of Wroughton, to the south of Swindon, now take precedence.*

## THE VIKINGS

For the *Anglo Saxon Chronicle* the year 793 was one of awesome significance: 'In this year dire portents appeared over Northumbria and sorely frightened the people. They consisted of immense whirlwinds and flashes of lightning, and fiery dragons were seen flying in the air. A great famine immediately followed those signs, and a little after that in the same year, on 8 June, the ravages of heathen men miserably destroyed God's church on Lindisfarne, with plunder and slaughter' (Manuscript D).

The Viking attack on Lindisfarne was not the first Norse raid on Britain but to contemporaries it was the most dramatic example yet of a force that was to become a deadly threat to the English kingdoms. For at least another generation, however, that threat was to remain unfulfilled, and although isolated raids took place England did not become a major focus of Viking attention until 835. Thereafter the extent and frequency of Norse raids increased although their object was still plunder rather than settlement. The raids were widespread and included attacks on Northumbria, Lindsey, Mercia and East Anglia, with the heaviest raids falling on the south and east of England. The Vikings were not always successful and several of their expeditions were attacked by strong English forces. A joint Norse–British army was defeated by Egbert in 838 at Hingston Down and in 851 his son Æthelwulf wiped out a Viking force transported by 350 ships at the battle of Aclea, somewhere south of the Thames.

The Vikings had wintered in England in 850 and 854 but their expeditions had always ended in a return to Scandinavia. In 865, however, a new and more dangerous situation arose with the arrival in East Anglia of a massive Viking army prepared to remain in England for many years. Led by the sons of Ragnar Lothbrok ('Leather-breeches'), including Healfden, Ubba and Ivar the Boneless, the Vikings spent their first year in

Helmet and head of a Viking warrior from Sigtuna, Sweden.

England subduing East Anglia and equipping themselves with horses so that they could undertake the conquest of Northumbria as a mounted force. In November 866 they captured York and in March 867 defeated a Northumbrian army which had succeeded in storming the Roman walls of the city. Two Northumbrian kings perished in the attack and the Danes installed an Englishman named Egbert as their puppet ruler. The army next turned against Mercia but was content to come to terms when confronted by a joint Mercian and West Saxon force. For the next thirty years the dominant struggle in England would be between the Danes and Wessex, the strongest of the surviving Saxon kingdoms.

# ASHDOWN 8 January 871

In 870 the Vikings turned their attention to Wessex, marching from Thetford to Reading where in late December they established a fortified camp between the rivers Thames and Kennet. A foraging party pushed out to the west was scattered at Englefield by a force under Æthelwulf, the Ealdorman of Berkshire. Four days later the main Saxon army joined Æthelwulf and together they drove the Danish outposts into Reading and attacked the enemy camp. Their attack failed, Æthelwulf was killed, and the Saxons retreated to the north-west where their king Æthelred and his brother Alfred attempted to rally their men. The twenty-two-year-old Alfred held the rank of *secundarius*, or heir to the throne, and his authority in the Saxon army was already considerable.

The Saxons were still within 15 miles (24 kilometres) of Reading and on 7 January 871 the Vikings marched out of camp to attack them. It seems probable that Æthelred and Alfred had received local reinforcements, if not those they so eagerly awaited from Mercia, and they had also used the short breathing-space since the attack on Reading to revitalize their army. Viking and Saxon spent the night of 7–8 January camped just 1000 yards (900 metres) apart astride the Ridgeway on the Berkshire Downs to the north-west of Reading. The entry in the *Anglo-Saxon Chronicle* recording the subsequent battle is brief and we are fortunate to have a fuller account in Bishop Asser's *Life of King Alfred* written only some twenty years after Ashdown. Although Asser was not present at the battle his friendship with Alfred, established in 885, must have meant that he heard an account of the battle from the King himself. Asser certainly visited the site of the battle and though his account of the action must be regarded as partisan he provides valuable detail of the terrain and deployment of the armies.

Despite their recent defeat, Saxon morale was high and they were determined to fight. At dawn on 8 January 871 the Danes formed their battle-line, dividing their force into two, one division commanded by the Kings Bagsecg and Halfdan and the other by the Danish earls. The Saxons conformed to this disposition, forming their army in two columns with the column commanded by Æthelred opposite that of the Danish Kings and the column led by Alfred opposite the earls. A pause now ensued and Æthelred decided to utilize the time in prayers for victory. When warning arrived that the Danes were preparing to attack Æthelred refused to move before he had finished hearing Mass, declaring 'that he would not forsake divine service for that of men' (Asser 37).

Alfred had to act quickly to avert a major crisis. The Danes had deployed on a ridge higher than that of the Saxon position and if he allowed them to charge down upon the Wessex forces, only half of whom would be ready to receive the attack, defeat would be certain. Alfred decided that the only chance of victory lay in taking the initiative and attacking the Danes with his own column. Led by Alfred 'acting courageously, like a wild boar' (Asser 39), the Saxons gave a tremendous shout and charged into the advancing Danes. The battle-lines met at a point marked by 'a rather small and solitary thorn-tree' (Asser 39) and a furious mêlée began in which Æthelred's troops also joined. The King may still have been at his devotions and it is possible that his late arrival accompanied by his retainers, who would be

The rolling downland of Berkshire where the battle of Ashdown was fought.

a useful and fresh reinforcement, tipped the balance of fighting in favour of the Saxons.

As their casualties mounted, the Danes began to give ground until they suddenly broke and fled from the field in what became a complete and bloody rout: 'one of the two Viking kings [Bagsecg] and five earls were cut down in that place, and many thousands on the Viking side were slain there too – or rather, over the whole broad expanse of Ashdown, scattered everywhere, far and wide' (Asser 39). Æthelred called off the pursuit as night fell but the remnants of the Danish army did not regroup until they were safely within the earthworks at Reading.

Although the Saxon victory was complete it provided little strategic advantage since two weeks later Æthelred and Alfred were defeated by a Danish army at Basing to the south of Reading. A further defeat followed at a site called Meretun and in April 871 Æthelred died, perhaps as a result of wounds received in battle. Alfred succeeded to the throne and although

he continued the fight success evaded his armies. At Reading the Danes, now substantially reinforced, scattered the Saxon troops opposing them, and Alfred himself was worsted by two Danish armies at Wilton. After a year of heavy fighting the Danish threat was as strong as ever and Alfred was forced to buy peace.

*The site of the battle was long held to be near White Horse Hill above Uffington, but this theory is now discredited. Although we can still not pinpoint the location of the battle precisely the most likely area is that around Lowbury Hill north-west of Streatley along the Ridgeway. The Downs can be reached from Reading by following the A329 northwards and turning onto the B4009 to Aldworth at Streatley. From Aldworth a lane signposted to the Downs leads a further $2\frac{1}{2}$ miles (4 kilometres) until it meets the Ridgeway. This junction is probably the centre of the battlefield.*

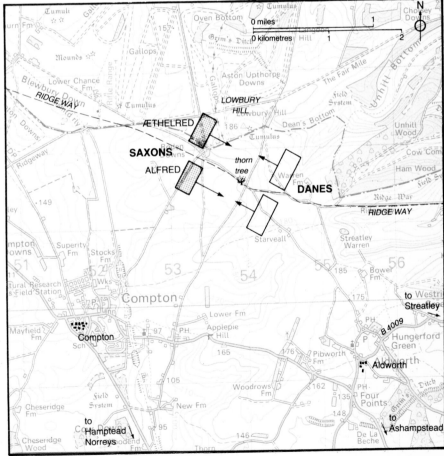

# ETHANDUN (Edington) May 878

In accordance with their peace terms with Alfred, the Vikings left Wessex and wintered in London where they also came to terms with the Mercians. In 872 they moved to Northumbria to suppress a rebellion against their puppet ruler Egbert before returning to the east midlands to establish their winter quarters at Torksey. In 873 they advanced into the centre of Mercia, defeating King Burgred in the following year. Since the arrival of their 'Great Army' in 865 the Danes had campaigned as a single unit and this concentration of force had been a vital factor in their success. The survivors of the original army were now in their ninth year of warfare and they decided to settle and support themselves in Northumbria. In so doing they established the northern Danelaw, centred on the Viking kingdom of York. The army that had landed in 871 was relatively fresh and its leaders, Guthrum, Oscytel and Anund, were determined to destroy Wessex.

and keep the initiative during the campaign of 875–7, partly because expected reinforcements were lost in a storm off Swanage and partly because they had been surprised by the speed with which Alfred had countered their moves.

With the departure of the Vikings, Alfred believed that he had secured a firm truce. He disbanded his weary army and went into winter quarters. In January 878 the Danes launched a surprise attack and Alfred, spending Christmas at Chippenham and unable to offer effective resistance, was forced into hiding with a small band of followers. Wessex was overrun, its people obliged to choose between flight overseas or submission to the Danes, and its King reduced to the life of a fugitive in the woods and fens of Somerset.

Alfred began the fight to secure his kingdom and the survival of the English by launching guerrilla raids from a fort built in the marshes at Athelney. The Saxons won an early and unexpected success with the defeat at Countisbury Hill in Devon of a Viking army of 1200 men from a fleet of 23 ships. Over 800 of the Vikings were killed by a force commanded by the Ealdorman Odda, and Guthrum's hopes of a concerted attack upon

Alfred the Great in a late thirteenth century manuscript.

Alfred's stronghold were dashed. Guthrum now lacked the necessary manpower to confine Alfred to the marshes of Somerset and the King was able to raise troops from Somerset, Wiltshire and Hampshire.

In the second week of May 878 Alfred marched his new army to Iley Oak near Warminster en route for the Viking camp at Chippenham. Alfred found the Vikings at Edington about 15 miles (24 kilometres) south of Chippenham and in Asser's words, 'fighting fiercely with a compact shield-wall against the entire Viking army, he persevered resolutely for a long time; at length he gained the victory through God's will'. The Saxons pursued the Danes to Chippenham and blockaded the enemy camp. After two weeks of siege the Vikings sued for peace, offering Alfred hostages but requiring none in return. Their King, Guthrum, and his leading

The Vikings advanced into Wessex late in 875 and after a year of fighting, which appears to have ended as a draw, a peace on equal terms was ratified with treasure, hostages and sacred oaths. Although the Vikings had agreed to leave Wessex, they evaded a shadowing force and marched from Wareham to Exeter where they wintered in 876–7. Confronted by Alfred, they made a new peace and left Wessex for Mercia in August 877. The Vikings had found it difficult to gain

followers accepted Christianity and at the close of 878 the Viking army left Wessex and returned east to settle. Thus East Anglia was added to the Viking settlements in Northumbria and Mercia to form what became known as the Danelaw.

Ethandun was a remarkable battle in many ways, not least because it completely reversed the fortunes of Alfred and Wessex. In a few short weeks Alfred was restored from a fugitive to the most powerful English ruler and Wessex from foreign domination to freedom. The victory also saved England from total Danish conquest. Although the Saxons would be called upon to fight at Rochester in 884, and at London in 886, Wessex enjoyed relative peace until the arrival from Flanders of two Viking armies in 892. The defensive measure taken by Alfred in the 880s now bore fruit and the Danes, faced with a war of attrition rather than with raid and counter-raid, and challenged at sea by Alfred's fleet, despaired of ever making real progress against Wessex. By 896 they were ready to give up the attempt and to settle in the Danelaw or return to France.

The Westbury White Horse cut in the eighteenth century on the site of an earlier representation.

*It is generally accepted that the site of the battle of Ethandun is to be found in the area of Edington in Wiltshire. Exactly where is more problematical. Two possible sites are the hill fort of Bratton Castle, whose slopes bear the Westbury white horse, and by Edington Hill. The B3098 running from Westbury to Edington connects both sites. Bratton Castle is signposted and Edington Hill lies approximately 900 yards (800 metres) south of the village.*

# BRUNANBURH 937

*choice of 3 locations*   A *Axminster,*   B *Between Derby and Rotherham,*   C *Bromborough*

Although Alfred the Great had prevented the Danes from conquering Wessex, the kingdom's interests were still threatened while the Danelaw existed. For the West Saxon dynasty to be fully secure the land occupied by the Danes had to be brought under English lordship. The reign of Alfred's son Edward the Elder saw the expansion of Saxon rule over the territory south of the Humber. The reign of Edward the Elder's son Athelstan saw that rule extended northwards to encompass Northumbria and provide substance to the title 'King of England'.

The death of Sihtric, King of York, in 927 provided Athelstan with an excuse to invade Northumbria and drive out the Scandinavian monarchy. Following this campaign the Welsh princes and Constantine of Scotland acknowledged Athelstan's suzerainty. The settlement appears to have been challenged in 934, for Athelstan mounted a combined land and sea operation which penetrated Scotland as far as Caithness without meeting serious opposition. Athelstan's success alarmed the British, Scots and Scandinavian rulers of the North and Ireland and an armed coalition was formed by Olaf Guthfrithson in 937. With Constantine of the Scots, Olaf invaded England, sailing up the Humber with a fleet of 615 ships to rendezvous with further troops from the north-west. Forming a very large army, (estimates have ranged from the widely exaggerated figure of 60,000 to the more reasonable estimate of 20,000), the coalition forces proceeded to ravage the north of England.

It took Athelstan some time to raise an army large enough to cope with this threat but towards the end of 937 he met the invaders in battle at Brunanburh. His joint Mercian and West Saxon army attacked at dawn in two divisions, Mercians against Scandinavians, Saxons against Scots. After a ferocious mêlée the invaders broke, and in the words of the *Chronicle*, 'The whole day long the West Saxons with mounted companies kept in pursuit of the hostile peoples, grievously they cut down the fugitives from behind with their whetted swords'. Casualties were heavy and included five kings, seven earls and a son of the Scottish king. In England the victory was seen as a national triumph and it was a further step along the path of national unity.

---

*Although countless historians have attempted the task, no satisfactory location of the battle had yet been found. There has been strong support for a site in Scotland (Burnswork) but it seems inconceivable that the battle was fought north of the border, particularly if we accept that Olaf landed on the Humber. The sites suggested in England have included Axminster, a location between Derby and Rotherham, and Bromborough on the Mersey.*

---

Athelstan from the *Chronicle of Abingdon.*

# MALDON 991

The entry for 991 in the *Anglo-Saxon Chronicle* (Manuscript A) provides a bare outline of the events surrounding the battle of Maldon: 'In this year Olaf came with 93 ships to Folkestone, and ravaged round about it, and then from there went to Sandwich, and so from there to Ipswich, and overran it all, and so to Maldon. And Ealdorman Brihtnoth came against him there with his army and fought against him; and they killed the ealdorman there and had control of the field.'

This major Scandinavian attack followed a series of probing raids begun in 980 against centres of prosperity and population, which yielded rich spoils in the form of Saxon treasure and slaves. Although the number of ships and raiders involved had been relatively few their attacks had been wide-ranging. Cheshire, Devon, Cornwall and Dorset had been particularly hard hit and Southampton, London and the monastery at Padstow had been sacked. These successful ventures must have encouraged the massive expedition of 991 in which the Norwegian Olaf Tryggvasson and the Danes Guthmund and Jostein led a fleet of 93 ships against the south-east of England. As stated by the *Chronicle*, the battle at Maldon came after successful raids in Kent, Essex and Suffolk, and it seems probable that by this stage of the expedition the Viking fleet would be reduced in number by the dispersal of ships on a number of ventures, or by the return of vessels filled with loot to Scandinavia. The *Chronicle* suggests that Brihtnoth fought specifically against the followers of Olaf, and the Viking army engaged at Maldon may thus have been substantially less than the total available from a fleet of 93 ships.

Ealdorman Brihtnoth was a military leader of some experience. He had held office since at least 956 and had evidently dealt with Viking raids before, including the defeat of an earlier one at Maldon in 988. We would know little of what took place during Brihtnoth's second and fatal encounter at Maldon, were it not for the survival of two contemporary historical sources, the *Life of St Oswald*, and *The Battle of Maldon*, an incomplete epic poem dealing with the engagement. The latter is one of the finest battle poems of any period in British history and although the beginning and ending of the poem are missing it supplies an evocative account of the battle itself and of Brihtnoth's leadership.

The Vikings had established themselves on an island separated from the Essex mainland by a tidal river. The river could be crossed by a causeway, but only at low tide, and although Brihtnoth deployed his army on the opposing shore the Vikings were unable to engage the Saxons because it was still high water. As the armies waited for the water level to fall the Vikings attempted to negotiate peace terms, a messenger shouting their offer across the water: 'Bold seamen have sent me to you, and bade me say, that it is for you to send treasure quickly in return for peace, and it will be better for you all that you buy off an attack with tribute rather than that men so fierce as we should give you battle.' The Maldon poem also presents Brihtnoth's defiant answer: 'Not so easily shall you win tribute; peace must be made with point and edge, with grim battle-play, before we give tribute.'

Brihtnoth's army consisted of his hearth-troop of warriors and the local militia and he had taken great care to supervise their initial deployment, suspecting that the loyalty and steadfastness of some of his force might not be all that he could wish: 'he rode and gave counsel and taught his warriors how they should stand and keep their ground, bade them hold their shields aright, firm with their hands and fear not at all. When he had meetly arrayed his host, he alighted among the people where it pleased him best, where he knew his bodyguard to be most loyal.' As the tide began to recede the Danes prepared to cross to the mainland but Brihtnoth ordered three warriors, Wulfestan, Ælfhere and Maccus to hold the western end of the causeway. Brihtnoth was presumably seeking to inflict casualties on the Vikings with minimum loss to his own force and also to demonstrate to his levies that the enemy was not invincible. The defence offered by the three warriors was so successful that the Danes abandoned their attempts to force a passage. Instead they asked that they be allowed to cross the causeway unhindered and Brihtnoth agreed. Although the poem criticizes the Ealdorman for this decision it is difficult to see that he had any alternative. Having at last run the raiders to earth it made little sense to refuse battle, for the Vikings would then simply return to their ships and sail away to menace another part of the coast.

The Saxons fell back to allow the advancing Danes room to deploy and Brihtnoth ordered his men to 'form the war-hedge with their shields, and hold their ranks stoutly against the foe'. Well aware of the military deficiencies of his levies Brihtnoth had no plans for executing any elaborate manoeuvre and he based his

The causeway at Maldon which the Vikings crossed to meet Brihtnoth in battle.

tactics on the ability of his men to absorb a frontal assault by the Danes. The battle opened with a discharge of spears and arrows followed by the savage, initial shock as the armies met: 'They let the spears, hard as files, fly from their hands, well-ground javelins. Bows were busy, point pierced shield, fierce was the rush of battle, warriors fell on either hand, men lay dead.' The Saxon line stood firm and the Vikings must have fallen back to regroup. At this point a Danish warrior 'strong in battle' advanced towards Brihtnoth who, perhaps interpreting this movement as a specific challenge, stepped forward to meet him. It seems rash for a commander to hazard himself in this way but there may have been compelling reasons for accepting the challenge. Both armies were watching to see how the Saxon leader responded and Brihtnoth may have considered that the maintenance of his army's morale required that he accept. His hearth-troop would in any case be close at hand should the Danes attempt any subterfuge.

From the first moments the combat went against Brihtnoth. He was twice wounded by spear thrusts, though not seriously enough to prevent him killing two of his attackers, and a Dane succeeded in disabling his sword arm. Sinking to the ground, Brihtnoth continued to urge his men forward but the Danes closed in and cut him down along with two warriors, Ælfnoth and Wulfmaer, who had rushed to their earl's defence. With Brihtnoth's death a large part of the Saxon army fled and only a small band of his retainers continued the fight, determined to die alongside their lord. The warrior Ælfwine rallied the survivors of the hearth-troop: 'Remember the words that we uttered many a time over the mead, when on the bench, heroes in hall, we made our boast about hard strife. Now it may be proved which of us is bold! ... Thegns shall have no cause to reproach me among my people that I was ready to forsake this action, and seek my home, now that my lord lies low ...' Their victory at Maldon inspired the Vikings to attempt the permanent occupation of England, and the Saxons, disheartened by their defeat, made the first of those payments of tribute that were to be known as the Danegeld.

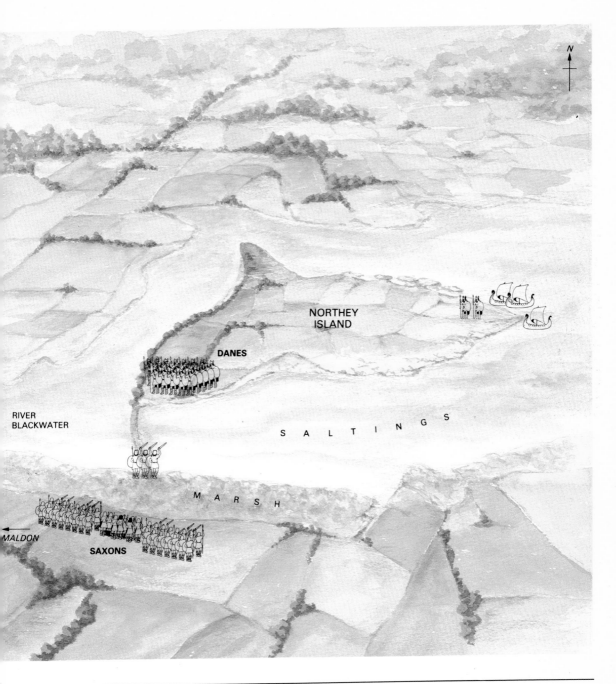

N

NORTHEY
ISLAND

DANES

RIVER
BLACKWATER

S A L T I N G S

M A R S H

MALDON

SAXONS

About 1¾ miles (3 kilometres) down-river from Maldon lies the island of Northey and it was here that the Viking force assembled. The causeway which allowed the Danes to cross the River Blackwater in 991 is still there although it has been widened to allow cars to cross. The battlesite can be reached by car by following the B1018 to the lane leading to South House Farm (the lane is not a right of way for vehicles) and then by continuing on foot across agricultural land to the river. Alternatively a path starting at the marina in Maldon provides an easy walk along the riverbank to Northey. Today the island is a National Trust Bird Sanctuary.

# ASSANDUN (Ashingdon) 18 October 1016

Olaf Tryggvasson, the victor of Maldon, returned to England in 994 allied with Sweyn Forkbeard, King of Denmark. Their expedition comprised 94 ships and its objective was London. Its citizens, however, defended their homes so effectively that the astonished Vikings were forced to abandon the attack and revert to their customary practice of ravaging the south and east coasts. To halt these destructive forays a Danegeld of £16,000 was paid for which the English received an additional benefit. In the winter of 994–5 Olaf Trygg-vason, with King Æthelred of Wessex as his sponsor, was baptised a Christian and promised never to return to England in hostility. Unfortunately no such promise was given by Sweyn Forkbeard or his son Cnut the Great. The raiding which began in 997 was followed by almost twenty years of warfare, relieved only by fragile truces secured through payment of Danegeld or by the resistance offered by London, by Ulfcetel, Ealdorman of East Anglia, and after Æthelred's death in April 1016 by his son Edmund Ironside.

Although London chose Edmund as Æthelred's successor many of the noblemen of Wessex swore fealty to Cnut and Edmund's first campaign was directed at restoring the kingdom's allegience to the old dynasty. After laying siege to London, Cnut followed Edmund westwards and indecisive battles were fought at Pensel-

wood in Dorset and Sherston in Wiltshire. Turning to the offensive, Edmund relieved London, parried a raid into Mercia, and drove Cnut into Sheppey. With this change in Danish fortunes, some of Cnut's English supporters, including Ealdorman Eadric of Mercia, changed their allegiance to Edmund.

Embarking on another raid, Cnut sailed from Sheppey and anchored in the River Crouch near Burnham in Essex. Edmund moved to prevent the Danes, now loaded down with booty, from returning to their ships and in the words of the *Chronicle* he 'pursued them and overtook them in Essex at the hill which is called Ashingdon, and they stoutly joined battle there' (Manuscript C). Edmund had mustered a large army with contingents from Wessex, East Anglia and Mercia and although his ill-trained levies could not match the Danes man-for-man, his superiority in numbers offered the chance of a decisive victory. As Edmund's army made camp on Ashingdon Hill on the evening of 17 October 1016 the enemy was in full view just over 1½ miles (2½ kilometres) away.

Cnut now had little choice but to fight. To avoid battle and escape by land he must abandon both the spoils of his latest raid and his fleet. With an undefeated enemy so close at hand it would be foolhardy to attempt an embarkation when his army would be hard put to

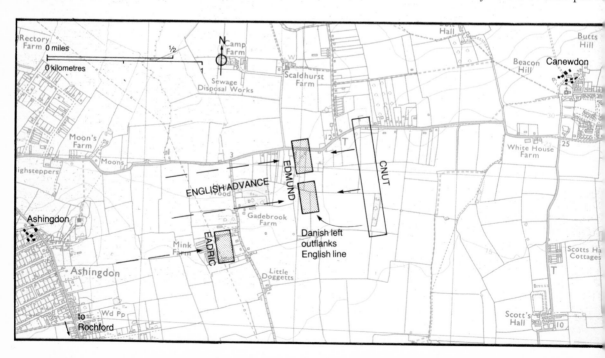

efend itself. Cnut therefore assembled his force on the ill at Canewdon which stood between Edmund and the anish fleet. A low ridge connected the hills from which the two armies faced each other, but at the anish end of the ridge a slight rise about 1000 yards )00 metres) in front of Canewdon offered Cnut the pportunity to advance without losing the advantage of igher ground. Edmund may have deployed his army in hree divisions, with the Wessex contingent under his own command, the Mercians under Eadric, and the East Angles under Ulfcetel. Eadric, now in favour once again, was probably stationed on the right flank, with Edmund in the centre and Ulfcetel on the left.

Edmund began the battle by charging down the hill at Ashingdon towards the Danes. The English left, probably because of the nature of the ground, advanced far more quickly than the right and a rapidly increasing gap opened between the respective flanks. As Edmund

The battlesite at Ashingdon.

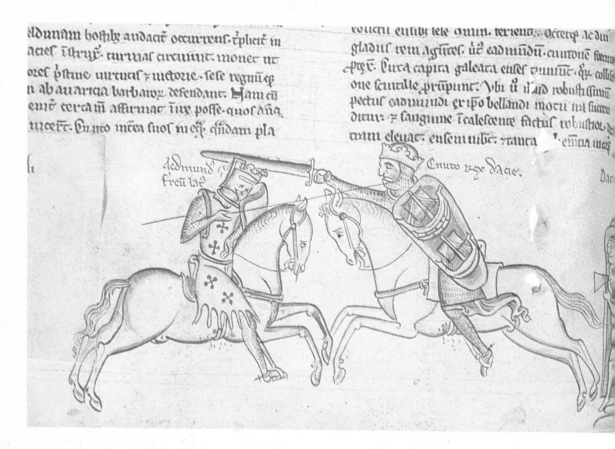

aldunam boftlg audaue occurrent. ipliat in
aaes iftrup. turuas arcuunt. mouet ne
ozes þftine uirtuas ꝛ uictoue. fefe regniu ꝙ
n ab auariaa barbauoꝛ defendant. Ham cu
eure cercam affirmac iure poffe. quoſ dña
uceft. Hu neo inea fuoſ meſſ ꝙndam pla

couceli euiluꝯ tele omin. terteuaꝯ. acceꝛꝯ ac dui
gladiuf rem agitates. uꝛ eadmudu. cuutone fecm
epgt. Hura capita galeata euſeſ omiſiue. ꝙꝛ colluſ
one feintille prupunt. Vbi u iſud robuftiſmu
pectuf eadmundi gripo bellandi moeu na fucceu
dieur: ꝛ fanguune tealeſcence fieiuf tobuftioꝛ
mim eleuat. enfemuibuꝯ: ꝛ tauca ꞏemua iueſſ

*Aedmund
freu las*

*Cnuto ꞏꝛex dace.*

*Dac*

ABOVE:
A duel at Deerhurst between Edmund Ironside and Cnut the Great
depicted in the manuscript *Historia Major* by Matthew Paris
c. 1200–1259.

OPPOSITE:
Ethelred from the *Chronicle of Abingdon*.

and Ulfcetel clashed with the Danish line at least a third
of the English strength remained uncommitted for
Eadric had halted his division well to the rear. The
Danish left, finding no troops to their front, turned
inwards to envelop the unprotected English flank.
Eadric and his contingent retreated from the field and
Edmund was left to fight on for as long as possible.
Although outflanked and outnumbered, the English
continued the unequal struggle until late in the afternoon and Edmund was eventually able to escape with
the survivors of his army. Ulfcetel, a large proportion of
the English nobility, and the majority of Edmund's
troops were killed.

Edmund retreated to Deerhurst on the Severn where
shortly after the battle he and Cnut met to agree the
partition of England. Edmund would rule in Wessex
and Cnut in the north. In November, however, Edmund
died and Cnut was made King of England in 1017. For
the next twenty-five years England was to be part of a
Scandinavian empire.

*Ashingdon lies approximately 5 miles (8 kilometres) to the
north of Southend-on-Sea and it can best be approached
along the B1013 which connects Rayleigh and Southend.
Uncertainty as to where the action took place means that a
visit to the battlesite is not particularly rewarding, but
Ashingdon Church and the surrounding views are worth
the detour.*

# THE MIDDLE AGES
## 1066–1450

The impact of the Norman Conquest on Anglo-Saxon England has been the subject of conflicting argument. For long it was held that the Normans were the bestowers of an entirely new form of life and government which rescued Anglo-Saxon society from exhaustion and decadence. Revisionists countered by arguing that a vibrant Anglo-Saxon heritage not only survived the conquest but eventually absorbed the invader, and that the achievements of the Norman settlement were due in no uncertain measure to strong Anglo-Saxon foundations. It is in fact a measure of the strength and durability of both Anglo-Saxon and Norman society that a new monarchy and new instrument of government could be imposed by an alien race while at the same time preserving the continuity of English life. That the Norman invasion of England was essentially different from those carried out by the Anglo-Saxons and the Vikings is beyond doubt. The Normans established themselves through sudden conquest rather than through a period of prolonged invasion and settlement. William had to fight hard to retain his new kingdom but by the time of his death in 1087 the English had been subdued under Norman rule. Perhaps it is because of the dramatic developments which flowed from the defeat inflicted on Harold at Hastings that the slender nature of the military superiority which brought victory on that October day tends to be overlooked.

The Norman victory at Hastings is often seen as the inevitable outcome of the superiority of cavalry, supported by archers, over dismounted infantry. As a result the comparison that tends to be drawn between Norman and English military capabilities centres upon the successful use of mounted force as opposed to an obsolete reliance on infantry. The mounted knight emerges as the dominating tactical feature of the battle, despite the fact that it took almost eight hours for the Normans to overcome the English defence. Harold's force was composed of hoursecarls and those members of the fyrd who had been able to answer their king's summons. The housecarls were professional men-at-arms, a permanent royal bodyguard founded by Cnut, and they were ranked by contemporaries as an elite amongst the soldiers of Europe. They were a mobile force since they usually rode to the site of the battle before dismounting to fight on foot. Although they were essentially infantry, the housecarls were well-equipped to challenge the armed dominance of the mounted knight. Their most distinctive weapon was the long-handled war axe which was quite capable of bringing down both a horse and his rider with one blow. The axe-men would be supported by other housecarls equipped with javelins and swords and all were offorded the protection of a tunic of mail ('hauberk') which reached to the knees, a conical helmet with nasal bar and a round or kite-shaped shield.

Beyond 50 yards (46 metres) the fire of archers using the Danish short bow was virtually ineffective against these defences and provided the housecarls could maintain a solid formation they were a potent deterrent to cavalry. The mounted Bretons fled when faced by housecarls at Hastings and only weight of numbers appears to have overcome the surviving housecarls as darkness fell. That the horsemen could compete at all with these heavy infantry was due to the stirrup, which had been introduced in Europe during the eighth century. This provided cavalry with a firm seat from which they could strike downwards with sword or lance. Despite the emphasis on cavalry as the professional elite of their army, the Normans were well aware of the efficacy of infantry tactics and when necessary their knights dismounted and fought on foot, as at the Battle of the Standard. To the Normans it was never axiomatic that heavy cavalry should always fight

King Cnut and Queen Emma present an altar cross to the New Minster at Winchester. From the eleventh-century *Liber Vitae*.

concept of the war-band, the lordship of Norman society had developed beyond that point to a feudal relationship based upon homage, fealty and the holding of a fief, usually in the form of land. The tenant of the land was the military vassal of the lord who granted the fief. By 1087 the whole of England, with the exception of the land held by the king and the church, had been granted to lords as fiefs and in return they rendered military and knightly service to the monarch. The church did not escape the obligation to support the king and William received knight-service from the religious houses and bishoprics of at least the south of England. In turn, the lords holding fiefs from the king proceeded with subinfeudation by granting fiefs to the knights and vassals upon their own estates. The number of knights to be provided by the tenant in return for his fief was set by the granter; it has been calculated that William obtained the potential service of some 5000 knights through his enfeoffments. Through feudal service he was able to field an elite striking force of heavy cavalry with which to maintain his hold upon England and Normandy.

The knights who served William were armed in many respects as their English opponents, wearing mail hauberks and conical helmets, and carrying kite-shaped shields, lances, swords and maces. Beneath the hauberk it was customary to wear a gambeson (a tunic padded with wool) to give added protection should a spear or arrow penetrate the hauberk. Mail consisting of interlinked iron rings remained the most usual form of body protection during the thirteenth and fourteenth centuries, and swords (with an increased blade length), maces and lances continued to be the main weapons of mounted knights. A range of hafted weapons, some adapted from agricultural tools, were used by the infantry, including the vouge, glaive and gisarme. The cross-bow (arbalest) remained popular with foreign mercenary contingents, but during the twelfth century the power and accuracy of the Welsh longbow began to play an increasingly significant role on the battlefield. In the thirteenth century different styles of protective armour appeared, with the use of a shorter hauberk, the introduction of the great helm (a cylindrical headpiece with horizontal slits for vision) and the use of a broad-brimmed iron helmet by the infantry. During the second half of the thirteenth century armour made from plates of metal began to be worn as a supplement to mail, and gradually complete plate armour evolved. In the fourteenth century the great helm began to give way to the close-fitting bascinet for use in war. To

as cavalry. Hastings cannot be taken as demonstrating the innate superiority either of cavalry over infantry or the pre-conquest Norman military system over the Anglo-Scandinavian.

The Norman reliance on feudalism as the basis upon which to raise and equip armies was alien to English practice. William's introduction of feudalism should be seen as the result of his need to maintain a large force for the defence of his conquest rather than as a conscious intent to sweep away the Anglo-Scandinavian system of mobilization. Whereas the lordship of Anglo-Saxon England was a personal bond rooted firmly in the

Dover Castle. Built on a defensive position overlooking the harbour, Dover Castle was one of the strongest fortifications in England. Its main works were constructed during the reign of Henry II with the keep being completed in 1188.

increase their effectiveness against new forms of armour, sword blades were tapered to a sharp point and grips were lengthened to allow two-handed use.

If battlefield tactics were dominated by the mounted knight, strategy was increasingly subject to the powerful influence of the castle. William's trained knights were ideal troops for use against the scattered English risings but they were unsuited to the prolonged task of holding regions whose loyalty was suspect. In these areas fortified bases and strong-points were vital and this need was filled by an intensive programme of castle building. By 1100 there were at least 84 castles in England and there may have been as many as 400, whereas before the Conquest there had been only a few examples (in the Welsh marches and at Clavering in Essex) of castle building. Because the cost and speed of construction were important, most of the Norman castles were of the Motte and Bailey pattern and one such castle at York was built in only eight days in 1069. Castles were sited to defend the chief ports and estuaries of England, to guard border areas against incursion, to control river and road communications and to overawe centres of population. As time and resources allowed, the early timber and earth castles were replaced by stone structures and the spread of castles capable of withstanding a prolonged siege both dissipated and strengthened royal power. The conquest of any particular area was made more difficult by its network of castles, and although this could enable a baron to defy central authority the spread of regional rebellion was easier to control and isolate.

For much of this period English kings were attempting to extend their authority into Scotland and Wales, and this raised particular problems in waging war. Although support for the invader could often be found within these nations, the growing strength and feeling of nationality – particularly amongst the Scots – could be translated into a strength of resistance which went some way to compensate for a lack of arms, knights and mercenaries. War with France made it difficult for English kings to concentrate their available strength on one front and the repeated and widespread provision of military service by the feudal army could lead to antagonism between the monarch and his barons. In this respect mercenary forces raised at home or abroad were increasingly important, but their supply was dependent upon a healthy treasury. The topography of Scotland and Wales made the task of conquest extremely difficult and large English armies were alarmingly vulnerable to guerrilla warfare, at which the Welsh and the Scots were adept. Lack of adequate communications made it difficult to supply isolated castles and mobile operations had to be limited to the summer months, which gave the defenders the opportunity to recover their strength. New tactics such as the schiltron (a solid formation of pikemen affording all round defence) allowed the Scots to deal effectively with English cavalry until the technique of using archers in support of mounted troops was perfected. By the beginning of the fourteenth century the range, accuracy and rapidity of fire of the long bow were increasingly proving it to be a battle-winning weapon in the hands of the English and Welsh archers.

# England, Scandinavia and Normandy

During the tenth and early eleventh centuries the politics of England, Scandinavia and the Duchy of Normandy became increasingly intertwined. The Vikings had long regarded England and the maritime provinces of France as a common theatre of war in which campaigning fleets and armies could move from Channel coast to Channel coast as the need arose. England and Normandy were a prime focus of Scandinavian interest, both migratory and military. Viking

## THE BAYEUX TAPESTRY

The Bayeux tapestry presents a contemporary pictorial record of the events leading up to the Norman invasion of England in 1066, of the landing itself and of the decisive battle at Hastings. It was conceived, of course, as propaganda and it presents only the Norman version of the Conquest. Despite its bias and the historical inaccuracies which surround it, the tapestry remains a magnificent work of art.

It was almost certainly embroidered at the request of William's half-brother, Bishop Odo of Bayeux. It must have been commissioned soon after 1066 and was probably finished by 1070. Odo was made Earl of Kent in 1067 and the tapestry was worked by professional embroiderers and not, as tradition relates, by William's wife Matilda. The embroidery of the tapestry was undertaken in sections by several different workrooms, possibly in the Canterbury area, and its main stitches are couching and laid work. The statistics of the tapestry are staggering. It is 230 ft 10$\frac{1}{4}$ in (70.4 m) long, 19$\frac{3}{4}$ in (50cms) wide, and contains representations of 626 human figures, 190 horses, 541 other animals, 33 buildings and 37 ships.

The wear and tear of the centuries have taken their toll on the tapestry and it has come close to destruction on several occasions. During the French Revolution, for example, the tapestry was rescued by a Bayeux lawyer as it was about to be cut up to provide wagon covers for the local militia. When the Englishman, Charles Stothard, travelled to Bayeux to copy the tapestry in 1818–19 he found the edges torn and significant amounts of the embroidery worn away. Fortunately Stothard reconstructed the pattern of the stitches from the original needle holes, and his drawings provide a record of the tapestry as it appeared before it fell into the hands of nineteenth-century restorers.

Unfortunately, the tapestry was restored in a manner which would enable it to tell the traditional story of Harold's death rather than that shown in the original embroidery. Having been taught that Harold was killed by an arrow in the eye, the restorers ignored the line of the stitch holes and deliberately bent the arrow so that its point appeared to have found a mark in Harold's eye. In fact, in Stothard's drawing, the stitch holes for the arrow can be seen quite clearly to end in the actual helmet, several centimetres above the level of the eyes. Moreover, the figure plucking away the arrow is not even Harold. The English king is the figure to the right falling under a sword blow.

William's invasion fleet, complete with horses, sets sail.

King Harold drops his war axe as a Norman knight cuts him down with his sword.

# TOURNAMENT

The use of mock combats to prepare young men for battle is as old as war itself and formal skill-at-arms competitions can be traced back to at least the Roman Troy Game (*Ludus Trojae*). During the Middle Ages organized tournaments became a common feature of knightly life, and they were elevated from the level of private training into national and international contests waged before the public gaze. Because the tournaments of the eleventh and twelfth centuries were fought with ordinary armour and weapons a high casualty rate was normal, and the loss of life amongst knights who might be expending their energy on a crusade led to repeated Papal bans on this form of combat. Most English monarchs attempted to prohibit tournaments, for events which began as sport often developed into contests fought in deadly earnest to the detriment of the king's peace. Richard I, however, exploited the belligerence of his barons as a means of raising funds for his overseas campaigns, and he licensed the holding of tournaments in five areas of open country. The areas chosen were between Blythe in Nottinghamshire and Tickhill in Yorkshire; between Brackley in Northamptonshire and Mixbury in Oxfordshire; between Stamford and Wansford Bridge in Northamptonshire; between Warwick and Kenilworth in Warwickshire; and between Salisbury and Wilton in Wiltshire.

The main participants in these contests were the young men of the baronial class, who had little else to occupy their time, and those knights who had made warfare a way of life. The tournament itself was a contest between groups of warriors, either on foot or on horse while single combat was properly termed a joust. To reduce the risk of serious injury blunted lances and swords were introduced to tournaments in the thirteenth century, and in the fifteenth a barrier, known as a tilt, was placed down the centre of the lists to prevent mounted knights colliding as they charged.

A fifteenth-century joust with the contending knights separated by the barrier known as the tilt.

Surrounded by splintered lances, knights engage in foot combat with pollaxes.

# KNIGHT SERVICE

By the end of the eleventh century individual tenants often held land from more than one lord, with the consequent need to do homage to all those from whom they had accepted fiefs. To remove the possibility of conflicting loyalties the tenant acknowledged a principal lord to whom he owed liege homage, and commuted his personal service to his remaining lords by money payment or the provision of a deputy. From Henry I's reign contracts of vassalage reserved the tenant's principal allegiance to the king, and every knight was expected to serve the monarch at his own expense for forty days a year in peace and for two months in war. The main services expected of a knight were campaigning, castle guard, and escort duty, but during the twelfth century it became increasingly apparent that money payment (scutage) in lieu of personal military service was a far more efficient method of providing troops.

Scutage was normally paid at the rate of twenty shillings for each knight not providing personal service, and with the funds thus raised the king was able to hire men to serve for specified periods in peace or war, at home or overseas. By the close of the thirteenth century the majority of troops serving in Royal armies had contracted to fight for pay, and although the feudal host might still be summoned, a high proportion of its levies would be paid for their service.

The battle of Shrewsbury, showing the flight of Hotspur's army.

aids on Britain were launched from Norman ports and
t was the concern of successive English kings to
persuade the dukes of Normandy to prevent the use of
these harbours by marauding Viking fleets. Such an
agreement was concluded at Rouen in March 991 and
although it was not entirely successful it served to
foster the growing relationship between the dynasties
of England and Normandy.

In 1002 Emma, the sister of Duke Richard II, married
Ethelred II of England, and when the West Saxon royal
family sought refuge from Viking invasion in 1013
Emma and Ethelred, with their sons Edward (later King
Edward the Confessor) and Alfred, found sanctuary in
Normandy. This estrangement from the new Scandi-
navian dynasty of England did not last long, and
Ethelred's death in 1016 allowed Emma to marry his
supplanter, Cnut the Great. During the reign of Duke
Robert I (1027–35), relations between Cnut and Nor-
mandy deteriorated and the Duke lent his support to
the exiled West Saxon dynasty and the athelings
Edward and Alfred.

Cnut died at Shaftesbury on 12 November 1035,
leaving a problematical succession. Harthacnut, his son
by Emma, appears to have been his nominated heir, but
Harthacnut was in Denmark and his half-brother
Harold Harefoot was recognised as regent in England,
despite the opposition of Emma and Godwin, Earl of
Wessex. A compromise was reached whereby Emma
retained Winchester and Wessex, but this was a truce
which only temporarily checked the powerful factions.
While en route to visit Emma, Alfred was seized by
Godwin and placed at the mercy of Harold Harefoot.
Harefoot's followers blinded Alfred with a savagery
that caused his death. In the words of the *Chronicle*, 'No
more horrible deed was done in this land since the
Danes came' (Manuscript C), and Alfred's betrayal by
Godwin embittered relations between the Godwin
family and Alfred's brother, Edward the Confessor.
Emma was exiled and in 1037 Harold Harefoot became
King of England.

On his death in 1040 Harold was succeeded by
Harthacnut and both Emma and Edward returned to
Britain. When Harthacnut died in 1042, 'as he was
standing at his drink' (*Chronicle*, Manuscript C), Edward began a reign which was to last for nearly twenty-
five years. In general they were to be years of peace,
notwithstanding the threat of Scandinavian invasion
and the internecine power struggle between the earldoms of England. Instituted by Cnut as an administrative expedient, the earldoms had become the power

bases of the rival families of Godwin of Wessex, Siward
of Northumbria and Leofric of Mercia. Godwin emerged
as the most powerful and his authority was such that
exile in 1051–2, and Edward's hostility, could do little
to diminish it. As a counterbalance to the Godwin
family, Edward attempted to increase Norman influence in England. The King was childless and it
appears certain that by 1051 he had pledged the English
succession to William of Normandy. The following
year, however, Earl Godwin and his sons Harold and
Leofwine launched an invasion of England which
Edward was powerless to oppose. Royal authority was
humbled, the Norman connection severed, and the
house of Godwin established in an apparently unassail-
able position. Earl Godwin died in 1053 but his family's
influence was maintained and increased by his sons
Harold Godwinsson, Tostig, Leofwine and Gyrth. It
was clear that if William was to gain the throne of
England it could only be by force of arms.

There were others equally prepared to fight to obtain
the English crown. Scandinavian interest was never
long deflected from Britain and both the King of
Norway, Harold Hardrada, and the King of Denmark,
Sweyn Estrithsson, nurtured hopes of extending their
rule across the North Sea. When armed revolt ousted
the unyielding government of Tostig from Northumbria
in 1065, it was to Harold Hardrada that this errant
member of the Godwins turned for support. On 5
January 1066 Edward the Confessor died without heir.
Although Harold Godwinsson was crowned King in
Westminster Abbey, few of the leaders of northern
Europe believed that the question of the English
succession had been settled. Harold Hardrada and
William of Normandy, with Tostig waiting any chance
that came to hand, were preparing to make Harold
defend his right to the kingdom in battle. It was now
merely a question of which of the rival claimants would
be the first to arrive on the shores of England. The
traditional mobility and impetuousness of the Vikings
together with a timely north wind allowed Harold
Hardrada to stike the first blow.

OPPOSITE:
William I, William II, Henry I and Stephen from a fourteenth-
century manuscript.

# STAMFORD BRIDGE 25 September 1066

*A Gate Fulford   B Stamford Bridge*

The new English king would have been hard pressed to find two more formidable opponents in northern Europe than Harold Hardrada and William of Normandy. Even so, the scale of Hardrada's intervention in September 1066 must have come as a profound shock to Harold. Recruiting further men and ships in Shetland and Orkney to add to the fleet he had brought from Sogne Fiord near Bergen, Hardrada arrived off the north-east coast of England with 300 vessels and a force that was possibly as large as 12,000 men. After ravaging the coast at Cleveland and sacking Scarborough the Norwegians, accompanied by Tostig, sailed up the Humber estuary as far as Ricall on the River Ouse, nine miles from York. The northern earls, Morcar of Northumbria and his brother Edwin of Mercia, placed their army at Gate Fulford on the Ouse, between the Vikings and York. Knowing that Harold was preoccupied with the defence of the south against a landing by William they must have reasoned that nothing would be gained by delaying battle nor by risking a siege in York. Accordingly on 20 September 1066 they deployed across the road at Fulford with their right on the River Ouse and their left protected by a ditch and marshy ground near Heslington. The subsequent battle was long and bloody with the balance of fighting favouring first the English and then the Vikings. The decisive moment came when Hardrada, seeing the enemy centre and left heavily engaged, swung his own left inwards to roll up the English line. Pressed into the restricted and difficult ground near the marshes, the English army was cut to pieces and many of its troops drowned. Fulford deprived Harold of over 1000 fighting men who would be sorely missed in the campaign ahead. Hardrada and Tostig did not enter York immediately but began negotiations for the city's surrender. It was agreed that hostages would meet the Viking army at Stamford Bridge, eight miles east of York.

Harold had deployed his main strength of housecarls, supported by the southern fyrd, on the Channel coast to guard against a landing from Normandy. His army had been in the field for most of the summer and by early September he could no longer meet the demands of provisioning his troops and fleet. On 8 September he dispersed his army, the militia returning to their homes, the housecarls and the fleet to London. Ironically, news of the Viking landing in the north reached Harold in London a little over a week later. It presented Harold with a formidable strategic problem; could he risk a march to the north before the Normans landed? He accepted the challenge, marching from London between 18 and 20 September with the forces he had been able to recall. Reinforcements joined the English army as it made its way northwards and by 24 September Harold had reached Tadcaster, 185 miles (296 kilometres) north of London. His army was given no opportunity to rest after this remarkable march but at dawn on 25 September it pressed on through York to take the Viking host by surprise at Stamford Bridge.

Hardrada and his army were camped on the banks of the River Derwent where it was crossed by a wooden bridge and where four ancient roads converged. They knew nothing of Harold's progress northwards. Only as dust clouds rose over the road from York and the sun began to glint on the arms of approaching soldiers was their a stir in the Viking camp. By this time the English were just over a mile away and Hardrada and Tostig had little time to plan their defence. A number of warriors were left on the west bank of the Derwent to delay the enemy and gain time for the remainder of the army to deploy on the east bank. If Harold's troops were exhausted after their march from London, they now showed little sign of it as they drove in the Viking defence. Resistance crumbled, except for one warrior who held the bridge alone. Defying all attempts to dislodge him the Viking delayed the English deployment for vital minutes before he was struck down.

With the bridge clear, the English archers, foot and mounted troops rapidly crossed to the east bank where the Viking army was drawn up behind a shield wall 300 yards away on rising ground known today as 'Battle Flats'. The English launched a determined attack and in the ensuing mêlée both Hardrada and Tostig were killed. Late in the day Norwegian reinforcements led by Eystein Orre arrived from the ships at Riccall, but they were so exhausted after their approach march that although their intervention was fierce (Norse legend describes it as 'Orre's Storm') it was short lived. Harold's victory was complete and he allowed Hardrada's son Olaf to sail away with 24 ships, all that was necessary to carry the survivors of the Viking army. The English king had shown himself to be a formidable commander who could act quickly and decisively and who possessed the ability to inspire his troops to heroic efforts. Another searching test of Harold's military capacity awaited him to the south, in Sussex, where a Norman army was about to land.

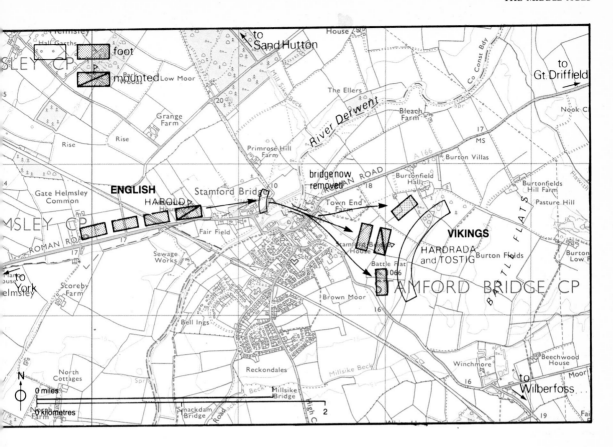

Stamford Bridge lies 8 miles (13 kilometres) east of York on the A166. The bridge of 1066 may have been the one which was demolished in 1727; the present bridge stands 400 yards (370 metres) downstream. There is not a great deal to see today but a memorial stone, with an inscription in English and Norwegian commemorating the battle, stands on an adjacent green.

Whether Anglo-Saxon armies, having ridden to the battlefield, habitually dismounted to fight, or whether they on occasion entered battle as cavalry, has been the subject of prolonged debate. The evidence for cavalry action at Stamford Bridge rests primarily with a thirteenth-century Icelandic saga composed by Snorre Sturlason, which describes a mounted assault by Harold's troops upon Hardrada and Tostig's position. His account of the battle is undeniably anachronistic and it does contain errors, but in favour of Snorre it can be argued that the ground and tactical situation at Stamford were ideally suited to a mounted assault. It is not impossible therefore that Harold's response was to keep a proportion of his housecarls mounted.

# HASTINGS 14 October 1066

Two days after Harold's victory at Stamford Bridge the north wind which had brought Hardrada to Britain and kept William of Normandy in harbour was replaced by a wind favourable to the Normans. In the evening of 27 September 1066 William's hastily-embarked troops set sail from St Valéry on the Somme estuary. The following morning the fleet made landfall at Pevensey on the south coast of Britain. William's invasion was his answer to the personal and political challenge inherent in Harold's assumption of the English crown. This act cut across Edward the Confessor's promise of 1051 that William should be his heir and was a violation of the oath of fealty to William extracted from Harold at Bonneville-sur-Touques in 1064. Harold's *coup d' état* of 6 January 1066 left William with no choice but to take up arms.

William's preparations for his invasion were thorough and on a massive scale. He lauched a three-fold diplomatic offensive designed to enlist the aid of his vassals, foster disunity amongst his enemies in

ance, and gain the support of European and Papal opinion. The success of this propaganda campaign was matched by the speed and organization of his military and naval preparations. His first requirement was a fleet capable of transporting an invasion force across the Channel. Between March and August 1066 the necessary ships were constructed in harbours and river estuaries along the Normandy coast and then assembled at the mouth of the River Dives. The majority of these vessels were similar to the Viking ships of the ninth and tenth centuries, but they probably incorporated special characteristics to facilitate the loading and unloading of the 2000 horses that accompanied the expedition. In total the invasion fleet may have numbered 3000 ships and it transported a European army of about 7000 fighting men, comprising Normans, Bretons, Frenchmen from other regions, Flemings, Italians and Sicilians. While Pevensey was an ideal site for William's initial landing, involving a voyage of only 60 miles (96 kilometres) from St Valéry, the uncertainties of the coming campaign dictated the need for a safe and large anchorage such as that at Hastings. William therefore moved his troops and ships to the port, ordered the construction of new defences, and proceeded to waste the surrounding countryside. It was vital for William's

plans that Harold should attack at the earliest opportunity.

It seems possible that Harold was already on the way south from York when news of the Norman landing reached him. He would have quickened his rate of march, probably pressing on to London with cavalry alone and leaving the infantry to make what progress they could. Arriving in London about 6 October, Harold began to muster the forces that were immediately available and it appears that he left the city before the majority of the archers and infantry who had fought at Stamford Bridge had rejoined. Although delay would have increased Harold's strength and attenuated William's, the English king, possibly driven by the need to defend his domaine against Norman marauding, decided to confront the enemy at the first opportunity. When he marched from London on 11 October Harold might have hoped that he could surprise the Norman army as he had the Vikings in the north. The English halted near the town of Battle during the night of 13–14 October after another march, this time of 58 miles (93 kilometres), which had taken a tremendous physical toll of the infantry.

Learning of his enemy's advance, William eagerly seized his chance and marched from Hastings early on

Norman knights crash to the ground during an attack on the English defenders of a hillock.

the morning of the 14th. By 8.30 am the Normans had reached Telham Hill opposite, but a mile away from, Harold's position on a ridge crossing a spur of the Downs running south from the forest of Andredsweald. The English troops were not yet deployed for battle and William's march must have taken Harold by surprise. Far from launching his own assault on William he was now obliged to adopt the defensive against a Norman attack. Fortunately the ridge Harold had chosen was a naturally strong position and offered several tactical advantages. Although the slope in front of the ridge was relatively gentle, the sides of the spur running out to the ridge were steep and virtually ruled out the prospect of flanking attacks. The Normans would thus have to launch a frontal assault across the wet and marshy ground between the Senlac ridge and Telham Hill. Harold drew up his men in a dense phalanx about 700 yards (640 metres) long on the crest of the ridge. His army, of approximately 7500 men, was composed of perhaps 2000 housecarls and the remainder of men of the hastily summoned fyrd, many poorly equipped and tactically inept. The housecarls were deployed on foot to stiffen the fyrd and each man was ordered to remain in his place and defend the spot on which he stood. As long as his army held its position and maintained a solid front it would be very difficult to dislodge.

William deployed his troops in three divisions. On the right stood the French, Flemings and Picards under Roger of Montgomery; in the centre the Normans under William; and on the left the Bretons under Alan of Brittany. The army was roughly equal in strength to the English but it numbered many more professional soldiers among its ranks and a strong contingent of archers. In the van of each division were the light troops armed with spears and slings supported by the archers; behind them the more heavily armed infantry, and at the very rear the mounted troops armed with javelins and swords. William ordered the first advance at about 9.30 am and the battle fell into four main stages, during each of which William held the initiative.

During the first phase the light troops drew close to the English position and discharged their missiles, receiving in return a hail of stones, spears and axes. This initial attack had little effect on the English shield wall and William next offered a full-scale infantry assault with cavalry in support. In ferocious hand-to-hand combat the Normans battered at the English line but failed to break its formation. Gradually the Bretons attacking on the left lost heart and began to waver under the ceaseless assault of the housecarls' axes.

Suddenly the Bretons streamed to the rear, their panic spreading quickly to the Normans as the cry went up that William had fallen. To stop the retreat before it became a rout William took off his helmet and rode amongst his troops so that they could see he still lived. As the Normans fell back some of the English rushed forward in pursuit, convinced that victory was theirs. William turned his cavalry against these isolated groups, annihilating them in full view of their comrades on the ridge. Harold had lost vital manpower and the Norman cavalry launched a sustained attack on the shield-wall. They failed to break into the English position, and as the horsemen once more recoiled down the slope a proportion of Harold's troops gave chase only to be cut down when they reached the valley. It has been claimed that the Norman retreat was a feigned flight intended to weaken the shield-wall by drawing men out in pursuit. It seems most unlikely that William would have risked such a deliberate manoeuvre, particularly as his army had already come close to a genuine rout earlier in the day, although it was used by the Normans in other battles.

The final phase of the battle came as the October evening drew in and William ordered a combined all-arms attack. While the Norman archers, re-equipped with arrows from the supply train, delivered high-angle covering fire, the infantry and cavalry closed with the now greatly reduced English line. By sheer weight of numbers the Normans broke into the position which had stood defiant for eight hours and Harold, his brothers Leofwine and Gyrth already dead, was cut down by the swords of Norman knights. The defenders of the ridge were overwhelmed and although a body of housecarls rallied to fight at a spot known thereafter as Malfosse, the outcome of the battle was no longer in doubt. Their king slain, the survivors of the fyrd left the field and the Normans pursued until nightfall.

William had won a battle but not yet a kingdom and his advance towards London was cautious and halting. By the end of November the Normans could count themselves masters of Kent, Sussex and parts of Hampshire and William turned his attention to the capital. It was unlikely that William would be able to storm London with the force at his disposal and he therefore chose to march across the southern, western and northern approaches to the city, laying waste the country as he went. As William reached Berk-hampstead the northern earls Edwin and Morcar with the Atheling Edgar and the leading men of the church and London offered submission. On Christmas Day

The ruins of Battle Abbey, Hastings. Tradition relates that the high altar of the Abbey marked the spot where Harold planted his standards, the Dragon of Wessex and the Fighting Man.

1066 William was crowned King of England in Westminster Abbey. Though he would still have to quell numerous English rebellions, particularly between 1067 and 1072, and safeguard his new kingdom against attacks from Scandinavia, William had established a Norman domination over England that would survive his death in 1087.

*The battlesite lies 6 miles (10 kilometres) north-west of Hastings where the A269 and A2100 meet at the town of Battle. New trees and later building have obscured some of the site and the ground level has risen considerably since 1066. The marshy land below the ridge has since been drained and new ponds formed. In recent years steps have been taken to provide a degree of interpretation of the battlefield for the visitor. Information panels and models marking walks across the battlefield are of considerable help in understanding the site and the action of 14 October 1066. The terrace and grounds of Battle Abbey School provide views of the western sector of the battlefield and of the field through which the Normans advanced to attack Harold's position. The Norman view of Senlac Ridge can be seen from Telham Hill which lies a mile (1.6 kilometres) to the south-east.*

# A THE BATTLE OF THE STANDARD 22 August
# B LINCOLN 1141

The fourth great seal of Henry I.

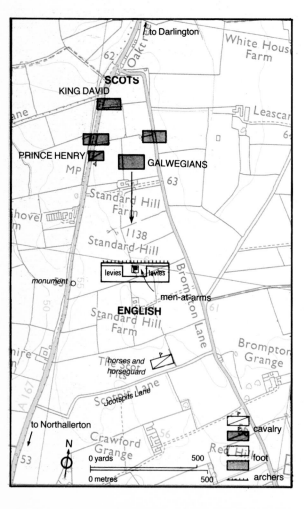

## THE BATTLE OF THE STANDARD

The death of Henry I in 1135 left a disputed succession in England. Prince William, Henry's only legitimate son and heir, had perished in the wreck of the White Ship in 1120 and Henry's second marriage to Adeliza, the daughter of Godfrey of Louvain, failed to provide a new male heir. In an attempt to secure the succession of his daughter, the Empress Matilda, Henry extracted an oath of allegiance to her from the English barons in December 1126. Matilda, however, remained an unpopular choice. Her marriage to Geoffrey, Count of Anjou, a traditional enemy of the Normans, provoked criticism from a number of English and Norman barons and the question of the succession was in reality far from settled. There were indeed a number of alternatives. The leading contenders were Robert, Earl of Gloucester, Henry's illegitimate son, and Henry's nephew, Stephen of Blois. A third, compromise, candidate reluctantly emerged in the person of Stephen's elder brother Theobald, Count of Blois. In the confusion following Henry's death Stephen acted quickly. He took ship to England, stopped briefly in London where the citizens received him as king, and hurried on to Winchester to secure the reins of government and the royal treasury. Although many of the barons immediately declared for Stephen, there was opposition both within England and from Scotland.

The Scottish king David I was the maternal uncle of the Empress Matilda and Stephen's accession provided a convenient justification for launching an invasion of northern England. Hoping to catch Stephen unprepared, the Scottish king led an army southwards during the Christmas season and rapidly occupied Carlisle, Wark, Alnwick, Norham and Newcastle. Stephen's arrival in the north with a large army at the beginning of February halted the Scottish advance, but his overgenerous concessions in the subsequent negotiations encouraged David to doubt the new king's resolution in pursuing affairs of state. A second Scottish invasion took place in 1137 and although a truce was arranged the Scots were back in January 1138. Stephen was forced to march northwards again. In a brief campaign, during which the Lowlands were to be ravaged as an object lesson to the rest of Scotland, Stephen's army disintegrated through maladministration and betrayal. King David again seized the initiative and while an army under his own command was advancing to Newcastle a column under his nephew William deeated an English blocking force at Clitheroe in Lancashire.

In the summer of 1138 the influential English baron Eustace fitz John went over to David, taking with him his castles at Alnwick and Malton. Thus encouraged, the Scots launched yet another and even greater offensive, with their army bolstered by reinforcements from the north and west. Stephen's attention was fully occupied by rebellions in the south and the defence of the north was organised by Archbishop Thurston of York. In allowing his troops from Galloway to plunder the countryside David overplayed his hand, and the northern barons united in a resolve to put an end to these repeated Scottish forays. Responding to Thurston's appeal for a crusade against the Scots, the armed strength of the north mustered at York. Proceeded by the banners of St Peter of York, St John of Beverley and St Wilfred of Ripon flying from a mast

mounted on a carriage, the army moved north to Thirsk. The Scots refused an offer of negotiations and the northern army advanced to intercept them at Northallerton.

Early in the morning of 22 August 1138 the English occupied the southernmost of two hillocks standing 600 yards (550 metres) apart on the right of the Darlington road. The carriage supporting the sacred standards was positioned on the summit of the hillock and the English troops deployed in its defence: They formed in three groups with a front rank comprising dismounted men-at-arms and archers, a solid body of knights around the standard, and shire-levies deployed at the rear and on each flank. Some distance to the rear a small number of mounted troops stood guard over the army's horses. The Scots drew up on the northern hillock with men-at-arms and archers to the fore and the poorly-equipped Gallwegians and Highlanders in the rear. The men of

Alnwick Castle, a vital bulwark against Scottish invasion.

Galloway were incensed by this deployment and demanded to be allowed their rightful position of honour at the front of the battleline. Reluctantly, and unwisely King David gave his assent and the unarmoured Gallwegians formed the highly vulnerable spearhead of the attack. The troops from Strathclyde and the eastern Lowlands formed on the right under David's son Prince Henry, who also commanded a body of mounted knights. The left was predominantly West Highlanders and to the rear stood a small reserve under the King with men from Moray and the East Highlands.

The men of Galloway opened the attack, charging through a hail of defensive fire from the English archers with such impetuosity that they temporarily broke the English front rank. The depth of the English formation, however, made further penetration impossible and the Gallwegians were gradually pushed back. Despite repeated assaults they were unable to make a decisive lodgement in the English position and Prince Henry attempted to break the stalemate with a mounted charge. Though many saddles were emptied this thrust was so successful that Henry and his knights crashed straight through the English line and disappeared in the direction of the tethered horses and Northallerton. Before the Scottish infantry could arrive to take advantage of the passage effected by their cavalry the English had closed ranks and the Scots again met a solid line of shields. Marooned to the rear of the English army, Prince Henry and his followers were forced to discard their insignia and mix with the enemy knights until they could break away to the north. The Scottish left and the King's reserve showed no enthusiasm for a renewal of the offensive and many of the infantry now began to leave the field. Admitting defeat, David and his bodyguard joined the retreat leaving only a small company of knights to cover the army's retirement.

The English deployment did not lend itself to the rapid exploitation of an enemy retreat and there seems to have been no attempt to harry or pursue the Scots. King David marched north to join the Scottish troops who had been attempting to reduce the castle at Wark since early June. Satisfied that the Scottish threat had been parried for the moment the English army dispersed, leaving only a baronial contingent in the field to besiege Eustace fitz John's castle at Malton. The ease with which the Scots were able to roam the northern counties demonstrated that the border country needed further fortification, and despite his defeat at Northallerton David I was able to advance the frontier of his domain to the rivers Tees and Eden.

*The battlefield lies just to the east of the A167, approximately 3 miles (5 kilometres) to the north of Northallerton in Yorkshire. A monument stands at the side of the road near to where the English left was positioned. Standard Hill Farm, although facing away from the battlefield, is built on or very close to the centre of the English line and may be taken as a marker when attempting to fix the position of the standard itself. Roughly 400 yards (370 metres) south of Standard Hill is Scotspit Lane which derives its name from the grave pits dug to accommodate the men killed in the fighting which swirled around Prince Henry's charge to the horse lines.*

## LINCOLN

Stephen's treaty concessions to the Scots, particularly the ceding of Northumbria, drove Ranulf, Earl of Chester, to rebellion as he considered the lordship of Carlisle and Cumberland to be part of his inheritance. Ranulf seized the castle of Lincoln and the town's citizens appealed to the King for aid. Stephen and his army arrived before Lincoln on 6 January 1141 and although the speed with which the King had acted took the defenders by surprise he was not able to prevent Earl Ranulf slipping away to Cheshire to raise troops. Ranulf also appealed for help to his father-in-law Robert, Earl of Gloucester, and promised loyalty to the Empress. Eager to exploit both the opportunity and the resources of his new ally, Robert quickly mustered his forces for a march on Lincoln. Earl Ranulf with an army of his Cheshire tenants and Welsh mercenaries joined Robert in Leicestershire and despite the restrictions on mobility imposed by the season they were before Lincoln by 1 February. Their immediate problem was the crossing of the waterways, the Fossdyke and the River Witham, which lay between the rebel army and the castle. It appears most likely that the rebels marched some way to the west of the city walls and stormed across a ford on the Fossdyke which was inadequately guarded by Stephen's troops. Once on the Lincoln side of the dyke the Earl's army deployed for battle.

The council of war summoned by Stephen to discuss the rebel threat was divided, the older nobles advising the king to garrison the city and withdraw to raise a large army, the younger barons urging immediate battle. Stephen chose the latter course and deployed his army from the West Gate of Lincoln on the slope leading down to the Fossdyke. Although we have no record of the size of either the allied or the royal army, their composition is known in some detail. Stephen formed his army in three divisions with mounted troops on either flank and infantry in the centre. On the right-hand side were the followers of Earls Waleran of Meulan, William de Warenne, Simon of Senlis, Gilbert of Hertford, Alan of Richmond, and Hugh Bigod, Earl of Norfolk. The left was commanded by Stephen's mercenary captain William of Ypres, who deployed a contingent of Flemish and Breton troops, and by William of Aumale. The centre comprised elements of the shire-levy provided by the citizens of Lincoln, and Stephen's own men-at-arms who fought on foot around the royal standard. The rebel army also deployed in three divisions with those nobles who had been disinherited by Stephen on the left, the infantry levies and dismounted knights in the centre under the Earl Ranulf, and cavalry under Earl Robert on the right. The lightly armed Welsh were deployed in front of the rebel right.

The rebels were the first to advance and it was soon clear that they were in earnest for they moved forward with swords drawn, intent on close quarter combat rather than a joust with lowered lances. Faced with the prospect of imminent butchery rather than mere capture, the royal right fled from the field in a *sauve qui peut*, everyman for himself. On the royal left events were initially more encouraging and a charge by William of Aumale and William of Ypres rode down the Welsh and crashed into Earl Robert's cavalry. At this crucial moment, however, the infantry of the rebel centre was able to intervene and the remaining royal cavalry recoiled in a panic which gave way to rout. Stephen's infantry of the centre were now isolated and faced the full strength of the rebel army. Though surrounded, the King and his men-at-arms fought on with Stephen himself prominent in the savage hand-to-hand combat which followed. Wielding his sword, and when that shattered a battleaxe, Stephen was the focus of resistance until struck down by a stone and captured by William de Cahaignes. The latter's cry of 'Here, everyone, here! I've got the King' brought the fighting to an end. It was total defeat for Stephen and fire and pillage for Lincoln whose citizens were slaughtered indiscriminately by the victorious rebels.

Stephen was conveyed as a prisoner to Bristol but although Matilda's coronation as Queen now appeared only a matter of time, her increasingly arrogant assumption of the prerogatives of state alienated the citizens of London and caused many of her supporters to reconsider their allegiance to her party. An army raised by Stephen's queen routed Matilda's forces at Winchester and by November 1141 Stephen had been freed.

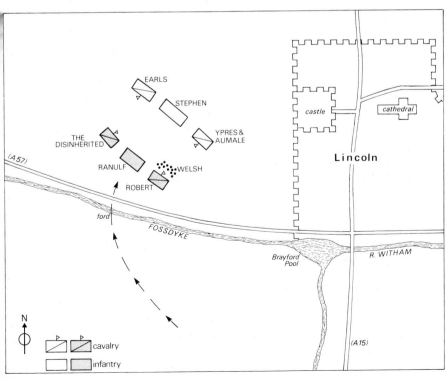

*The precise location of the battle is still in dispute. Some historians favour the heights to the north of the city near Newport, others the sloping ground to the west. The latter area appears the most probable site for as reported by Henry of Huntingdon the rebels fought with their backs to the Fossdyke and Stephen's defeated cavalry was able to effect an unimpeded escape northwards. The Fossdyke canal, built by the Romans to link the rivers Witham and Trent, is still in use and Brayford pool is now a pleasure area.*

# LEWES 14 May 1264

Henry III's acceptance of the crown of Sicily for his son Edmund raised an acute need for funds with which to underwrite the venture. This in turn provided those barons who were pressing for administrative reform with an opportunity to insist that their voice be heard in the government of England. Henry was forced to agree to a reforming committee composed of twelve barons and twelve members of his council. The results of their deliberations, issued in 1258, were known as the Provisions of Oxford and both King and barons swore an oath to uphold them. The King, however, devoted all his efforts to securing the nullification of the Provisions. The Papacy granted Henry an absolution from his oath and King Louis IX of France annulled the Provisions in his Mise of Amiens of 1264. Although many barons acquiesced in this annullment the faction led by Simon de Montfort, Earl of Leicester, refused, deciding that their commitment to the Provisions warranted a resort to arms.

In April 1264 Simon assembled his forces at St Albans before marching to relieve Northampton which was besieged by a royal army. Due to treachery the town fell before Simon could come to its aid and he turned in revenge against the royal castle at Rochester.

Here again Simon's plans were frustrated and he was forced to draw most of his army away from the siege on learning of an apparent march on London by the King. Henry had in fact only feinted at London and bypassing Simon's forces he speedily relieved Rochester. From there he moved westwards to draw support from a number of castles held by his supporters. Although Henry captured Tonbridge and Winchelsea, his army suffered greatly during its march across the Weald from ambushes sprung by parties of Welsh archers in Simon's employ. When the King's forces arrived at Lewes on 11 May they were in need of time in which to rest and recuperate before proceeding further with their campaign. Time was the very thing which Simon de Montfort sought to deny them, for it was imperative that he secure either peace or victory before the King's army was reinforced.

Simon had marched from London in pursuit of Henry and by the second week of May the barons were camped at Fletching, 8 miles (13 kilometres) to the north of Lewes. They were outnumbered by almost 2 to 1, for whereas Simon could muster perhaps 5000 men, of whom approximately 600 were mounted, the king could deploy 10,000 men, including perhaps as many as

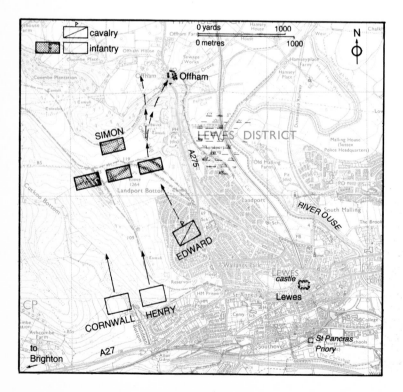

ABOVE:
The seal of Simon de Montfort.

OPPOSITE:
A view towards the town of Lewes.

1500 cavalry. Yet the morale of Simon's army was high and in the early morning of 14 May 1264 it marched towards Lewes and drew up in battle array on Offham Hill, a mile (1½ kilometres) to the north-west of the royal army. The royal troops under Prince Edward's command were billetted in the castle at Lewes, while the King's entourage was camped further to the south around St Pancras Priory. When the alarm was raised Prince Edward took the field in advance of Henry, and without waiting for the remainder of the royal army he charged the left of the baronial line where Simon had deployed the raw troops recruited in London. Before the other divisions of Simon's army or the Earl's own reserve could intervene the Londoners and their stiffening of mounted troops had broken and fled from the field with Edward and his cavalry in hot pursuit.

Henry, whose own troops had only now completed their deployment, had no alternative but to hurry to the attack, leading his centre division up the stiff climb to Simon's position on or near the hill-top. On the royal left the division led by the Earl of Cornwall joined the attack, but finding the defence too strong for its liking it was soon pushed back down the hill. In the centre Henry's division at first held its own but the commitment of Simon's reserve tipped the balance, and although still fighting strongly it too was forced to give ground. Simon's troops pursued the retreating royalists into Lewes and it was only with great difficulty that Henry extricated himself from the street fighting to take refuge in the priory. By the time Prince Edward returned with the residue of the royal left the battle was beyond redemption, and although the Prince wished to launch a fresh offensive his men settled the matter by riding off the field.

It seems probable that the casualties of both armies amounted to no more than 2800 men but it was a complete victory for Simon. The King was now under his control and Prince Edward was confined as a guarantor of his father's good behaviour.

---

*The general area of the battle to the north-west of Lewes and west of the A275 is not in dispute but the exact site of the fighting is open to argument. Did it occur on the summit of Offham Hill, or at the bottom of the slope leading to Lewes after a downhill charge by the whole of Simon's army? The former is the most probable for the advantage of a hill-top position to a numerically inferior force has been well-proven in the history of warfare. Offham Hill may be reached via a path running from opposite Offham Church on the A275, and an interesting view of the battlefield can be gained from Lewes Castle.*

---

# EVESHAM 4 August 1265

After the battle of Lewes, King Henry III was little more than a puppet ruler and the power of government lay with Simon de Montfort. Yet the forces arrayed against Simon were still formidable and the prospect of invasion from France and the reality of rebellion on the Welsh marches threatened the permanence of his rule. The defection of the Earl of Gloucester to the royalist camp was a heavy blow to Simon's cause, and Prince Edward's escape from his guards at Hereford at the end of May 1265 provided the opposition with both a leader and a developing soldier of outstanding ability.

With Simon at Hereford, Edward assembled his forces at Worcester before moving to capture Gloucester and the last available crossing over the River Severn. Simon marched to Pipton, near Hay, where he met Prince Llewellyn of Wales and concluded an agreement whereby the latter would supply 5000 spearmen for de Montfort's army. Moving to Newport to outstrip the Royalist pursuit, Simon attempted to take passage across the Severn but his transports were sunk by

warships from Gloucester. He was then forced to undertake a long and hungry march back to Hereford. Prince Edward turned his attention to the de Montfort stronghold at Kenilworth where the young Simon was preparing to come to his father's aid. In the early hours of 1 August Edward's army swooped on Kenilworth, catching most of the baronial force asleep. Simon escaped the subsequent slaughter by taking shelter in the castle but his army was no longer a force capable of intervening in the campaign. While Edward was absent from Worcester, Simon led his army away from Hereford to cross the Severn at Kempsey en route to Kenilworth by way of Pershore.

By 3 August Simon de Montfort had reached Evesham and Prince Edward was determined to intercept him before he could reach Kenilworth. A night march from Worcester brought Edward's army to the banks of the River Avon at Cleeve Prior. Detaching a cavalry column under Roger Mortimer to seal de Montfort's escape route over the Bengeworth Bridge,

The field of Evesham.

Edward deployed his own and Gloucester's troops on Green Hill to the north of Evesham. Simon's only chance was to attempt to fight his way out of the trap, even though he could muster only some 6000 men to the royalist 8000. He deployed his army as a single column with mailed horsemen in the van and English infantry and Welsh spearmen to the rear. He aimed this column at the junction between Gloucester's and Edward's troops and launched it forward at the charge as heavy rain began to fall. It was a desperate strategy devised by a veteran soldier and it might have succeeded had not the cavalry wings of the royal army swung in on de Montfort's flanks. Many of the Welsh spearmen had already slipped away and Simon's remaining troops were submerged in an avalanche of attacking royalists. Although the baronial army continued to resist for some hours the battle became a progressively bloody massacre, and both Simon and his son Henry were cut down with nearly 4000 of their soldiers. King Henry had been taken onto the battlefield by Simon and, quite anonymous, in his armour he repeatedly shouted 'I am Henry of Winchester your King! Do not harm me!', until someone in the royal army had the presence of mind to hoist him out of the carnage.

Their field army might have been destroyed, but the surviving barons still held their castles and the war dragged on until 1267. Complete reconciliation came only in 1275 when the best elements of the Provisions of Oxford were encapsulated in the Statute of Westminster.

*Evesham lies 15 miles (24 kilometres) to the south-east of Worcester. The site of the battle is now difficult for the visitor to see as it stands on private and heavily cultivated land. Most of the fighting took place near 'Battle Well' which, if the visitor is prepared to struggle through the encompassing vegetation, can be found approximately 65 yards (59 metres) south of the B4084 and some 40 yards (37 metres) west of the A435. The 'well' is today merely a shallow depression in the landscape.*

RIGHT:
Prince Edward came to the throne in 1272. He is shown here in Parliament flanked by Alexander III of Scotland and Llywelyn ap Gruffudd of Wales.

In 1286 Alexander III, the last king of the House of Canmore which had ruled in Scotland for more than two hundred years, fell from the cliff at Kinghorn and was killed. His own sons were already dead and his sole heir was his three-year-old grand-daughter Margaret, the Maid of Norway. In this sequence of dynastic events Edward I of England saw an opportunity to absorb Scotland within his rule. Six guardians were appointed to govern Scotland for Margaret who was still in Norway, and Edward set to work to secure a marriage contract between the Maid and his own son, the Prince of Wales. Although certain conditions were laid down to safeguard Margaret from Edward's domination, the marriage found favour in England, Norway and Scotland. In September 1290 Margaret died while en route to Scotland. Edward's carefully laid plans were brought to nought and the Scottish succession was thrown into the melting pot. No less than thirteen candidates came forward for the crown. Edward's hopes of imposing some form of suzerainty revived when he was asked to arbitrate over this confusion of would-be monarchs. He succeeded in extracting solemn recognition of his overlordship from nine of the principal claimants, and in November 1292 Edward judged John Balliol to be king of Scotland. Balliol became a vassal king expected to comply with all Edward's requests no matter how humiliating. By 1295 the Scots could stand no more and in open defiance of the English king they concluded a treaty with France. Edward marched north to sack Berwick while the Earl of Surrey defeated the Scottish nobles at Dunbar. Balliol made peace, Scotland was occupied and the Earl of Surrey became its Governor and Hugh de Cressingham its Treasurer.

A revolt against this government was not long delayed, and under the leadership of William Wallace and Andrew de Moray it made considerable military headway. The Earl of Surrey, lingering overlong at Berwick, at last saw that he must defeat the rebels if peace were to be restored. By September 1297 Surrey and Cressingham had reached Stirling where the Scots had taken up position on the far bank of the River Forth at Stirling Bridge. Surrey attempted to negotiate with the rebels but the latter, confident in their deployment on the slopes of Abbey Craig one mile (1½ kilometres) to the north-east of the bridge, rejected his appeals. At last on 11 September the English army moved forward and began to cross the river by the bridge which afforded passage for only two horsemen at a time. Two miles (3 kilometres) upriver lay a ford capable of accommodating upwards of sixty men simultaneously but Cressingham argued that even such a minor diversion would be an unnecessary compliment to the martial ability of the Scots.

Dutifully the English men-at-arms crossed two by two and once a reasonable proportion, but by no means their whole strength, had reached the far bank the Scots pounced. Surrey's force was cut in two, with one half vainly attempting to fight off the entire Scottish army while the other attempted to reinforce it, two men at a time. The majority of those who crossed the river, including Cressingham, were killed, and Surrey retreated to Berwick to await the advance of Edward. The victor, William Wallace, was knighted and made sole guardian of the kingdom.

The seal of John Balliol.

A statue of Wallace on the parish church of Lanark.

Edward assembled a force of 15,000 men, including 2500 cavalry, at York in the summer of 1298. At the end of the third week of July the English army, which was beginning to despair either of feeding itself or of running the Scots army to ground, encountered Wallace near Falkirk. Although his force was numerically inferior Wallace had to offer battle and he deployed in a strong position on the southern aspect of Callendar Wood. His troops were protected to their front by the Westquarter burn and an expanse of marshy ground.

The bridge, and the monument to Wallace built in 1861–9 at Abbey Craig in Stirlingshire.

Wallace organized his spearmen in four solid rings, which were later to become famous as the schiltron, and placed archers between the rings and cavalry to their rear. The English van was commanded by the Earls of Norfolk and Hereford, the second battle by Anthony Bek, Bishop of Durham, and the main battle under Edward formed the reserve.

Encountering the marshy ground, the van and the second battle moved respectively left and right before delivering their attack. As the English knights charged home, the Scottish cavalry retired from the field leaving the archers to be summarily ridden down. The English were, however, brought to a halt by the schiltrons and suffered some casualties. Edward thereupon ordered his archers forward and the dense formations of Scottish spearmen melted away under a hail of arrows. As huge gaps appeared in the schiltrons the English cavalry charged in amongst them, inflicting considerable slaughter on the Scottish rank and file. Wallace escaped through the forest, but his prestige gone he took ship to France, leaving Edward in control of southeast Scotland.

*The site of Stirling Bridge has been covered by subsequent building but the general area can be viewed from Stirling Castle. The exact site of the battle of Falkirk is uncertain but the probable site to the south of Callendar Wood can be examined from the high ground leading to Glen Village on the B8028.*

# BANNOCKBURN 23 June 1314

Robert Bruce (b. 1274) was elected a guardian of the kingdom of Scotland together with John Comyn shortly after the battle of Falkirk. Bruce had been born and raised a Scot but his family, originally Norman, had been traditional supporters of the English kings. His father remained pro-English and Bruce spent the years 1296–1306 in a confusion of loyalty and allegiance, offering his services first to one side, then to the other. But in 1306 his commitment to Scottish independence was dramatically illustrated by his assassination of John Comyn at Dumfries. Bruce hurried to Scone where on 25 March he was crowned King of Scotland. Edward I of England swore that he would capture Scotland and the Earl of Pembroke made an efficient start by dispersing Bruce's army at Methven Park in June 1306. Bruce retreated to the Highlands from where he proceeded to wage an increasingly successful guerrilla war against his enemies. On 10 May 1307 Bruce gained a signal victory over Pembroke at Loudoun Hill near Ayr, and the death two months later of Edward I, the 'Hammer of the Scots', provided a welcome breathing space for the Scottish leader. Edward II, although a soldier of some experience, did not possess his father's abilities and Bruce was able to consolidate and expand his hold on Scotland. Edward launched invasions in 1310 and 1312 but achieved little and failed to prevent Bruce from leading retaliatory raids into northern England. Gradually the English strongholds in Scotland were taken and by spring 1314 the only forward castle still holding out was at Stirling. The siege of Stirling had begun in 1313 and with the garrison's food supplies virtually exhausted the governor, Sir Philip de Mowbray, had made a covenant with Bruce's brother Edward whereby the castle would be surrendered if it had not been relieved within one year (by 24 June 1314).

This was a challenge that neither Bruce nor Edward II could ignore. The English king could not allow the castle to fall and Bruce could not allow an English army to advance to its relief without first bringing it to battle. Bruce was furious that the covenant had been made, for all along he had striven to avoid open battle with a large English force. Now invasion was a certainty. Although he had been given almost a year in which to prepare, Edward did little before the end of 1313 and final writs for service were not issued until 27 May 1314. These called for 21,540 men to join the King at Wark on 10 June, with 12,500 summoned from the northern counties, 5540 from Wales, 3000 from Lincoln, and 500 from Leicester and Warwick. It is doubtful whether all these contingents reached the assembly point before Edward marched on 17 June and it would seem reasonable to set the maximum size of the force which invaded Scotland at 18,000 men. It may, however, have been considerably less, since writs for service seldom produced the numbers required. Edward had called upon the Irish chieftains to supply 4000 infantry for service under Richard de Burgh, Earl of Ulster, but there is no evidence that any Irish troops fought with the English army at Bannockburn. Edward's cavalry was drawn from hired men-at-arms, the feudal levy and his own retainers, but as only 96 military tenants had been summoned, and not all had agreed to attend, the levy cannot have produced much more than 500–600 knights. It is difficult, therefore, to agree with estimates that Edward had 2500–3000 heavy cavalry at Bannockburn, particularly as he had written to the Sheriff of York on 27 May disclaiming the value of cavalry on the forthcoming campaign because of the unsuitability of the ground over which it was to be fought. It seems probably that Edward's cavalry strength was nearer 1000 knights than 2000.

The armies commanded by Bruce during his guerrilla operations seldom amounted to more than a few hundred men, and in order to assemble the maximum number of troops against Edward he ordered his forces to concentrate on the battlefield itself. This reduced the difficulty of provisioning a large force and allowed troops to serve for the short period covering the climax of the campaign. Even so, it is doubtful whether the Scottish infantry mustered more than 6000 men at Bannockburn and the cavalry more than 500. Approximately 3000 late reinforcements comprising contingents of townsmen, freemen and chiefs and their retainers joined the Scottish army just before the battle. Their military value was limited, as they were neither properly equipped nor trained for service in the schiltrons, but these 'small folk', as they were known, were kept at the rear ready to engage in the pursuit. The Scottish infantry were predominantly armed with 14 foot ($4\frac{1}{2}$ metre) pikes but most also carried an axe and a shield. Bruce began training and drilling those of his infantry that were available early in April, and as his forces assembled he ordered them in three battles under the Earl of Moray, Edward Bruce and Sir James Douglas, with a fourth battle in reserve under his own command.

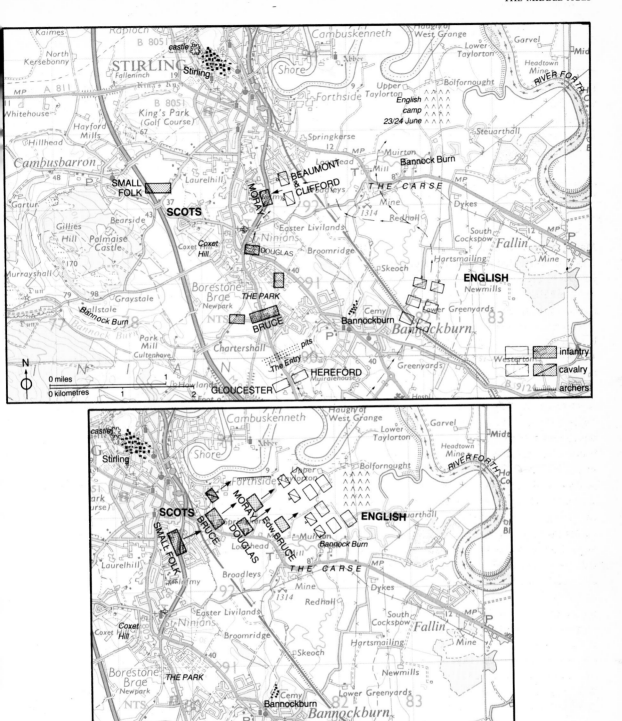

*A great deal of the battlefield has been covered by subsequent building, but the National Trust for Scotland has acquired significant portions of it. Few visitors to the site, which lies 2 miles (3 kilometres) south of Stirling, will lose their way for it is well signposted from the M9 and the Trust Visitor Centre stands alongside the rotunda and Robert Bruce statue.*

A statue of Robert the Bruce by C. d'O. Pilkington which was erected on the Borestone site at Bannockburn and unveiled on 24 June 1964.

The English king's need to relieve Stirling Castle before the deadline of 24 June dictated a fast pace on the march to Bannockburn, and by 22 June Edward's army had reached Falkirk, only 10 miles (16 kilometres) from its objective. The position in which Robert Bruce awaited the approaching English was a plateau of woodland, known as the 'Park', which stretched southwards for 2 miles (3 kilometres) from Stirling Castle. Where the Stirling to Edinburgh road emerged from the Park before crossing the Bannock burn lay an area of open ground known as the 'Entry'. This was suitable ground for cavalry, and to persuade the English against launching a charge from this direction Bruce ordered his troops to dig rows of pits on either side of the road. Each pit was about 12 inches (30 centimetres) across and 18 inches (45 centimetres) deep and camouflaged with turf. They would certainly have been a formidable obstacle to charging cavalry but in the event they played no part in the battle. To the east of the Scottish position beyond a 50 foot (15 metres) escarpment was a boggy plain known as the 'Carse', and although the plain passable for horsemen it was far, however, from ideal cavalry country. With the Bannock burn running east and south of his position Bruce had deployed his troops in an area which provided good natural defences against the power of an English cavalry charge.

On 23 June Edward organized his army in ten battles and advanced his troops to within 2 miles (3 kilometres) of the 'Park'. He detached Lords Clifford and Beaumont with 300 men-at-arms on a circuitous route eastwards, while the English vanguard closed with the southern edge of the 'Park'. Here the Earls of Hereford and Gloucester, having misinterpreted Scottish movement on the fringe of the trees as the precursor to a general retirement, pressed forward to catch the enemy before he could slip away. The commotion witnessed by the Earls was in fact the deployment of the troops under Bruce to resist the English advance. Sir Henry de Bohun rode at the head of the English column; as it approached the 'Entry' Sir Henry recognized the Scottish king, who was some way in front of his own troops and unprotected by retainers. Hoping to strike the blow that might end the campaign in an instant, Sir Henry spurred forward and levelled his lance at the King. Bruce was mounted on a palfrey and at the last moment he turned aside to avoid de Bohun's lance. As the English knight thundered past Robert Bruce rose in his stirrups, swung his axe and split Sir Henry's skull. The Scots rushed forward and the English, somewhat shaken by their comrade's fate, gave ground, retiring on the main body of their army.

The detached force under Clifford and Beaumont had meanwhile encountered the Earl of Moray's infan-

The castle of Stirling provided a residence for Scotland's kings until 1603. The present fifteenth-century castle is on the site of earlier fortifications begun in the reign of Alexander I (1107–24).

ry near St Ninian's Church. Despite repeated charges, the English cavalry were unable to break the Scottish schiltron and the enemy's pikes took a heavy toll of both men and horses. As the English saw the troops of Sir James Douglas approaching they broke away, some riding on to Stirling Castle, others falling back to the main army. The day had gone well for the Scots but as night fell Bruce contemplated retreat. The arrival of Sir Alexander Seton, a deserter from the English camp, with news that the enemy were discouraged and an easy prey to a Scottish advance, convinced Bruce to attack the next day.

Edward realized that he could not proceed to Stirling Castle via the road through the 'Park' and the English army marched eastwards, crossing the Bannock burn and camping for the night on the 'Carse' between the Forth and the Bannock. At daybreak the Scottish army advanced leaving the cover of the 'Park' and descending to the 'Carse', where they formed four schiltrons. The tired English awaited the Scots on the narrow ground of their own camp and as the range closed the archers of both sides opened fire. The English archers were gaining the upper hand in this exchange when their cavalry charged the schiltron of Edward Bruce, thereby screening it from the archers. The Earl of Moray's schiltron closed with the English right and was followed by the schiltron of Sir James Douglas, which

stormed the English centre. Faced by these solid formations of pikes and shields, the English cavalry failed to scatter the Scots and the archers were unable to intervene for fear of hitting their own knights. As each charge was repulsed, wounded and riderless horses ploughed through the English infantry causing further confusion. The English battles at the rear could not get forward through the mass of men in front and when Edward deployed his archers on the enemy left they were ridden down by the Scottish cavalry. Unable to find an effective answer to the schiltrons, the English were inexorably pressed backwards and the sight of 3000 'small folk' hastening to the attack broke the will of Edward's army. As men turned to flee, the Scottish schiltrons drove through the English line and the battle was won. Seeing their king riding for Stirling Castle the English army disintegrated in flight. Its losses were heavy, particularly in men-at-arms, and as a fighting force it had ceased to exist.

Although Bannockburn was a decisive victory, it did not end the war between the north and the south. Edward raided Scotland in 1322 but the Scots amassed an impressive series of victories, capturing Berwick in 1318 and defeating the English at Mytton in 1319 and Byland in 1322. In 1328 Edward III signed the Treaty of Northampton recognizing Robert Bruce as the king of an independent nation.

# A **OTTERBURN** 19 August 1388

# B **HOMILDON HILL** 14 September 1402

ABOVE:
Percy's Cross on the field of
Otterburn.

LEFT:
The battle of Otterburn, 1388.

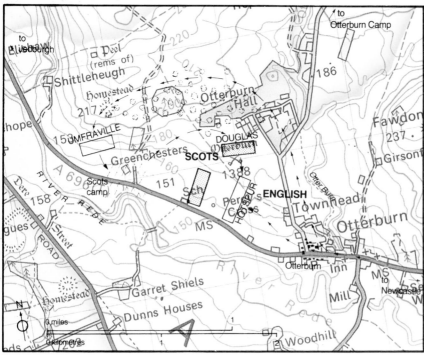

Despite the arrangement of truces between the English and Scottish kings, border warfare was endemic for much of the fourteenth century. While English rule extended to any part of Scotland, the inhabitants found it impossible to resist the temptation to harass the invader. Within the pattern of almost continual skirmishing, major expeditions involving armies of several thousand men were periodically mounted. The natural target for Scottish expeditions into England was the land held by the Earl of Northumberland and his son Henry Percy (known also as 'Hotspur'). The Percys were a campaigning family of the first order and Henry was the keeper of Berwick Castle and the warden of the East March. As such his authority represented a major barrier to the southward progress of the Scots and to the aggressive intent of the house of Douglas.

In the summer of 1388 James, the 2nd Earl of Douglas, led a raiding force into north-eastern England while Sir Archibald Douglas marched westward by Carlisle with a much stronger column. The force under James Douglas plundered County Durham, and in a skirmish at the gates of Newcastle Douglas captured Hotspur's lance pennon. This was a mortifying blow to the honour of the Percys and Hotspur swore to recapture it before the Scots recrossed the border. Douglas retorted that he would be delighted for Hotspur to try and that the pennon might be found displayed before his tent. Hotspur was restrained from launching an immediate attack by the English barons who feared that Douglas's force might be the bait in a Scottish ambush. Hotspur's army of between 7000 and 8000 men set out after the retiring Scots twenty-four hours later, and by 19 August the English knew that the enemy had made camp at Otterburn. Many of Douglas's commanders urged that the army should continue its retreat into Scotland, but he was determined to provide Hotspur with an opportunity to retake the pennon in battle. Douglas was camped across the road to the border with his army's right protected by the River Rede and its left on rising ground. Here he confidently awaited the arrival of the English. As the Scottish camp prepared for night on 19 August the English appeared to the east, and Hotspur, pausing only to dispatch Sir Thomas Umfraville with 3000 men on an outflanking march to the north, launched an immediate attack.

Douglas commanded 6000–7000 men. Forming them in two divisions, he appears to have sent one division forward to hold Hotspur, while he led the other against the enemy's right flank. It was by now quite dark and while the English were involved in a mêlée with the foremost Scottish division, Douglas and his troops crashed into their right, pressing the English line down the hill towards the river. In close-quarter combat at night the English longbows were useless and gradually the Scots began to gain the upper hand. At some point in the fighting Douglas was killed, but the English continued to give ground and both Hotspur and his brother Ralph were captured. Sir Thomas Umfraville meanwhile found the Scottish camp, overwhelmed its guard, and retreated by the route he had come, playing no further part in the battle. By morning the Scots were masters of the field, and finding that the retreating English were still capable of fighting off pursuit they resumed their march northwards.

The border raids continued and although a Scottish force was heavily defeated at Nesbit Moor on 22 June 1402, Archibald Douglas, taking advantage of the diversion of English arms to deal with the revolt of Owain Glyndwr in Wales, marched a second army as far as Newcastle. The Percys again reacted forcefully, blocking Douglas's retreat near Homildon (now Humbleton) Hill in Northumberland.

Though burdened with considerable loot, the Scottish army of just over 10,000 men was a formidable opponent, and the raiders were confident that their deployment on the slopes of the hill would be proof against an English advance. The Percys agreed and the English men-at-arms stood back while their archers proceeded to decimate the Scottish ranks from a safe distance. When they could endure this galling fire no longer the Scots charged down the hill, only to find that although the archers retreated their fire did not slacken. The Scots army disintegrated in flight, leaving seven prominent nobles killed and over eighty barons and knights captured. Douglas himself bore the marks of five arrow wounds despite his coat of mail.

---

*Although we cannot be certain of the exact deployment of the armies, the battle of Otterburn was fought on the slopes to the west of the village and north of the A696. A monument erected in 1777 employed the base of an earlier Battle Stone which stood some yards to the north-east as the foundation on which to erect Percy's Cross. The cross still stands at the side of the A696. In 1388 the ridge was covered in forest and the difficulty of spotting a flanking attack, particularly at dusk, would have been considerable. Humbleton Hill lies to the south of the A697 Wooler to Coldstream road about $1\frac{1}{4}$ (2 kilometres) to the north-west of Wooler.*

---

# SHREWSBURY 21 July 1403

When Henry Bolingbroke (later Henry IV) deposed Richard II in 1399 his leading supporters had been the Percy family. Henry's reign provoked hostility and rebellion from English nobles and witnessed border raids from Wales and Scotland. Much of the fighting against the Scots devolved on the Percys and in July 1403 Henry marched north with an army to help deal with the latest border raids. When the King reached Nottingham on 12 July he heard the news that the Percys had risen against him in alliance with the Welsh leader Owain Glyndwr. The Percys' change of allegiance was ostensibly due to Henry's failure to repay them in full for the expense of keeping out the Scots, and to his refusal to provide a ransom for Sir Henry Percy's brother-in-law, Edmund Mortimer, who had been captured by Glyndwr.

Sir Henry Percy had reached Chester on 9 July and was busy raising an army in the fertile recruiting ground of Cheshire. The King cancelled his march northwards and turned to the east, arriving at Lichfield on 16 July, where he issued warrants to raise the levies of the surrounding counties. By 19 July the royal army had reached Stafford and Henry appears to have received confirmation that Hotspur was advancing on Shrewsbury. The king's eldest son Prince Henry (later Henry V) commanded a small garrison at Shrewsbury but it was incapable of dealing with the rebels without reinforcement. The royal army made all speed to reach Shrewsbury before the Percys, and it covered the 32 miles (51 kilometres) from Stafford on 20 July. As Hotspur approached the city later the same day he found it already occupied by royal troops and drew back his own forces to the village of Berwick 3 miles (5 kilometres) to the north-west. The Percy resources were now dangerously dispersed for while Hotspur watched Shrewsbury the army raised by his father, the Earl of Northumberland was still in the north, and the forces of Owain Glyndwr were away to the south-west.

The King had been presented with the opportunity of defeating the rebels 'in detail' and on the morning of 21 July 1403 he advanced from Shrewsbury to confront Hotspur's army, which was drawn up on an east–west ridge on ground known today as 'Battlefield'. Both armies adopted a similar deployment with men-at-arms in the centre fronted by a rank of archers, and with further bowmen on the flanks. The rebel line appears to have been continuous but the royal army deployed in two divisons, with the left commanded by Prince Henry and the right by the King. Estimates for the size of the armies have ranged from 60,000 men for the King and 20,000 for the rebels, down to 5000 men for each side. An approximation of 14,000 royal troops and 10,000

rebels appears more justifiable and it does seem certain that the latter had the smaller force. The armies drew up out of range and there was a lengthy pause while last-minute negotiations were held in an attempt to resolve matters without bloodshed. When it seemed, however, as though the rebels were unnecessarily protracting the negotiations the King ordered his army to prepare to advance.

As the King's troops marched forward, with their van commanded by the Earl of Stafford, the enemy archers unleashed a hail of missiles and the royal bowmen immediately replied. There now began a furious fire-fight in which for the first time in a major battle on English soil longbow fought against longbow. The rebels gained the upper hand in this exchange and the King's archers recoiled on their men-at-arms. They were pursued by most of the rebel army. As the royal line fell back, Hotspur and the Earl of Douglas charged the royal standard in the hope that they could hack their way through the King's bodyguard and secure victory by Henry's death. They failed, but at least two decoys wearing the royal surcoat were cut down along with the standard-bearer, Sir Walter Blount.

While the King's division stemmed the rebel charge, Prince Henry's division advanced on the left, over-lapping the enemy's right. Although the Prince was wounded by an arrow, his men pressed inwards attacking the rebel line in both flank and rear. In the savage mêlée which followed Hotspur was killed, reputedly by an arrow striking him in the face while his visor was lifted. As word of his death spread, the rebel line gave way and Henry's troops turned the flight into a rout with a pursuit which lasted for 3 miles (5 kilometres). The victorious royal army had suffered heavily in the early stages of the battle and some chroniclers record their casualties as being higher than those of the defeated rebels. It may well be that casualties were comparatively even, with perhaps 3000 dead or wounded on each side.

Hotspur's body was quartered and a constituent part placed on display in London, Bristol, Chester and Newcastle, but his father, who was too ill to fight in the battle, was pardoned for his part in the rebellion.

*In 1408, five years after the battle, St Mary Magdalene Church, Battlefield, which stands to the west of the A49 Shrewsbury to Whitchurch road, just past its junction with the A53, was built on the general site of the battle. It does not, however, mark the location of the early fighting, which most probably took place on or near the low ridge to the north-west of the church. The Percys deployed on the ridge and the royal army on the level ground to the south. The church was established by royal charter of Henry IV and an effigy of the King can be seen on its east front.*

OPPOSITE:
The battlefield of Shrewsbury looking towards St Mary Magdalene Church.

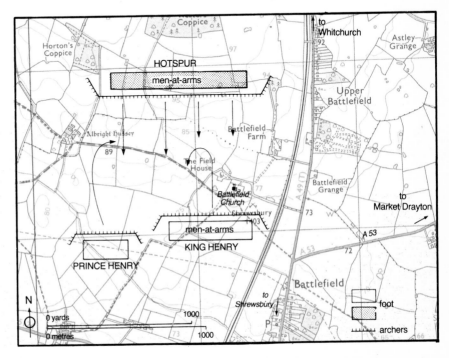

# THE AGE OF
# THE WARS OF THE ROSES
## 1450–1550

Medieval kingship and the wars which surrounded it have long been fertile ground for the development of myth and false tradition. In the case of the Wars of the Roses the embroiderers of history have worked overtime. Much of the responsibility lies with those Tudor propagandists who sought to enhance the position and prestige of the new dynasty, but some of our most famous literary figures must also share the blame. Shakespeare's symbolic identification of the Wars with the white and red roses plucked by York and Somerset in Part I of *Henry VI* (Act II, Scene iv) would have meant little to those who fought in them. There is no evidence that Henry VI used the red rose as a personal device and although Richard of York did employ a white rose, it was only one of the many badges used by his family. The spectacle of two warring armies bedecked in the uniforms of the white or red rose as they hastened into battle is totally misleading. Only the personal retinue of Henry, Richard or Edward would have worn their devices, and the soldiers of the miscellany of private forces which made up their armies would have worn the badges and livery of their own lords or captains. Only after the Wars had ended did the combined white and red rose come to prominence as a Tudor emblem, symbolizing the reconciliation implicit in the marriage of Henry VII to Elizabeth of York.

The historical label, 'The Wars of the Roses', which was first used in 1829 by Walter Scott in his novel *Anne of Geierstein* is undoubtedly convenient, but it has encouraged the growth of a number of misconceptions. The symbolism of the roses lends a degree of continuity and intensity to the Wars which it is difficult to justify. Scattered across three decades were three main periods of fighting, which in effect resolved themselves into three separate wars, with quite lengthy intervals of armed peace. Campaigning began in 1452 and although the prospect of serious conflict receded after 1487 the

threat of invasion and renewed fighting lingered until almost the end of the century. The first major battle was fought in 1455 but four years of peace followed, and the climax of the first war did not come until 1459–61. Thereafter intermittent fighting continued in the north until 1464, but the second war did not break out until 1469. With its conclusion in May 1471 England enjoyed twelve years of peace until the death of Edward IV opened the way to the third war between 1483 and 1487. During the thirty years from 1455 to 1485 the total time occupied by major campaigns was less than fifteen months, and it has been estimated that actual fighting occupied less than twelve weeks. In European terms, the Wars of the Roses were warfare in miniature.

The symbolism of the white and the red rose, with its emphasis upon the dynastic success or failure of the houses of York and Lancaster, has led many writers to view the Wars purely as a struggle for the crown. Behind the enmity of York and Lancaster they see the entrenched interests of a belligerent aristocracy, playing out the final hours of a decadent chivalry in an attempt to put their candidate on the throne. In fact a dynastic interpretation of the Wars cannot stand alone. York did not become an overt claimant for the throne until 1460 and although, once raised, this dynastic challenge was to be a major factor in the recurrence of the Wars, it was not their initial cause. Similarly the nation did not split into two armed camps committed to the support of either York or Lancaster's hereditary right to the crown. Throughout, the Wars were characterized by a shifting pattern of loyalty and allegiance. Relatively few contemporaries were indissolubly committed to one particular faction, and most experienced little difficulty in allowing personal advantage to dictate their allegiance to either lord or king. Richard, Earl of Warwick, the most powerful of the Yorkist supporters, adopted the Lancastrian cause in 1469, and lesser subjects by the score were prepared to discard Lancaster in favour of York once Edward had emerged victorious. The limitations of the tags 'Yorkist' and 'Lancastrian' should always be borne in mind.

Although the cause of the Wars of the Roses cannot be found in a dynastic competition between York and Lancaster, it can be seen in a wider competition which affected society as a whole in the mid fifteenth century.

The peace of England was dependent upon the hereditary system of monarchy providing a king who possessed the ability to govern well. He must preserve justice and the laws of the land, but above all he had to be capable of gaining the respect and loyalty of his subjects. Should there be doubts concerning the monarch's claim to the throne or should he lack the personal and institutional stature to make the machin-

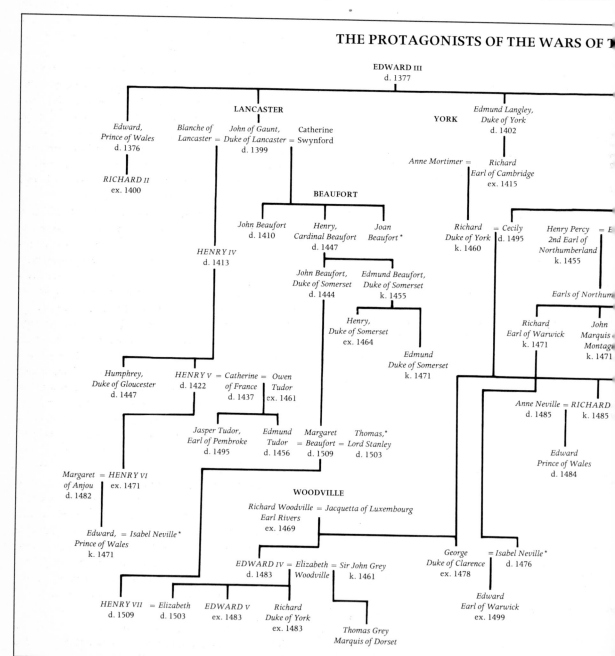

THE PROTAGONISTS OF THE WARS OF T

ery of government work, then the internal peace of his kingdom could collapse rapidly. In the absence of a standing army, a key element in the monarch's success was his relationship with the peerage. If he could command their duty by providing sound leadership in war and justice and honour in peace, then a preponderance of the lords would support his government against both external and internal threat. If this relationship failed, the king and his lords would become rivals for the effective control of power.

The lords' struggle would centre upon control of the king's council, for the government of the land was vested in this body. After his usurpation of the throne in 1399, Henry IV's council was dominated by the men who had helped him gain the crown. The tension thus created was eased by the strong rule of Henry V and by his popular policy of conquest in France. With his death in 1422 the long minority of Henry VI began, and monarchical restraint of the lords disappeared. An aristocratic council wielded power for nearly fifteen years and disputes among its members led to the rise of factions determined to gain for themselves the lucrative rewards of government. While the council might still take steps to control disputes at a national level, it did little to interfere with the working-out of feuds in local affairs. In the absence of strong central government, corruption and lawlessness spread through the land and to ensure their local dominance many peers increased their retinues to the size of small armies.

Henry VI's assumption of power in 1436 should have checked the growth of this anarchy but he possessed none of the personal qualities necessary to restore order. The power of the monarchy was not re-asserted, and Henry allowed the council to be controlled by a small baronial faction who used the King's name to further their disputes. Unable to secure the King's justice through his council, the lords and gentry sought the protection of powerful magnates against their local enemies. In return, the gentry supported their patrons in disputes with their fellow peers. Baronial aggression translated itself into private wars with the respective sides aligning themselves with the opposing factions in council. Many of those out of favour at court joined the opposition led by Richard, Duke of York, providing him with the armed strength to attempt to resolve matters by force. Because of his vast holding of land – he had estates throughout England and held large areas in central and southern Wales and in Ireland – Richard was able to sustain a widely-based war effort which encouraged men to adopt his banner. The Duke of Norfolk saw him as a useful ally in his struggle with the Duke of Suffolk, and the Earl of Devon sought his support against the Earl of Wiltshire. The failure of the King to govern thus promoted a growth of faction at court which was reflected at the local level of society. Henry VI's inability to extend impartial justice to the solution of local disputes fostered anarchy and armed rivalry which escalated to civil war.

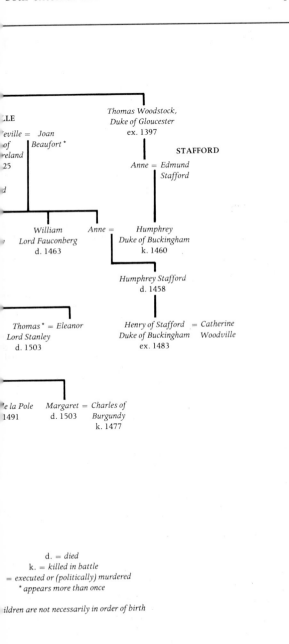

Thomas Woodstock, Duke of Gloucester ex. 1397

LE

eville = Joan of Beaufort* reland 25

STAFFORD

Anne = Edmund Stafford

William Lord Fauconberg d. 1463

Anne = Humphrey Duke of Buckingham k. 1460

Humphrey Stafford d. 1458

Thomas* = Eleanor Lord Stanley d. 1503

Henry of Stafford = Catherine Duke of Buckingham    Woodville ex. 1483

e la Pole 1491

Margaret = Charles of d. 1503    Burgundy k. 1477

d. = died
k. = killed in battle
= executed or (politically) murdered
* appears more than once

ildren are not necessarily in order of birth

Henry VI is crowned King of England at Westminster.

The outbreak of war implies an ability on the part of the combatants to raise armies. The growth of political violence in society had compelled many influential men to increase the size of their company of retainers purely in the interests of self-defence. Although of great importance, these forces could not alone provide the manpower needed to prosecute a national war. Moreover, by no means all members of the nobility took an active part in the Wars of the Roses. Only eighteen secular peers were present at the battle of St Albans in 1455, and although it has been calculated that fifty-six out of the total of seventy peers in the land did participate in the fighting between 1459 and 1461, not all of them took the field at once. The highest total in one campaign appears to have been in 1462 when thirty-eight peers accompanied Edward to the north of England. A growing casualty list (at least thirty-eight peers died violently at the hands of their enemies between 1455 and 1487) and the spread of indifference led to notably less participation in the later campaigns. Only ten peers, for example, took part in the Bosworth campaign. Once in the field, nobles expected appointment to commands which they considered equal to their

A Victorian interpretation of the symbolism of the Wars of the Roses. The supporters of the Houses of York and Lancaster pick roses in the Temple Garden, London. Painting by John Pettie (1839–93).

status, and it was traditional that armies, and particularly the 'battles' from which they were formed, should be commanded by peers. It was also obligatory for the king and his rival to take the field with the armies fighting to uphold their causes. The monarch's presence on campaign stamped an official seal of approval on the mayhem that was unleashed, and he could be a great stimulus to recruiting and to zeal in battle. To combat the bad press he received for waging war in Henry VI's presence, Richard of York issued proclamations declaring his loyalty to Henry and explaining his resort to arms as a measure of self-defence against the traitors surrounding the King. The risk of accidental injury to the monarch in battle was something neither side took lightly and the frequency of battlefield negotiations can be partly attributed to this fear.

Although the king needed to be seen with his army it

A bascinet with visor, and a mail aventail to protect the throat and neck. North Italian c. 1380–1400.

A sallet, the light helmet which in the fifteenth century replaced the bascinet.

was not necessary for him to exercise strategic or tactical command, unless he was particularly fitted for the task and wished to undertake it. Edward IV and Richard III were sound strategists and had keen tactical minds, but the relatively inexperienced Henry VI and Henry VII usually left such matters to their professional commanders. There were many such professionals available for duty and most members of the high command up to 1460 had already learned the art of war in battle against the French. Of these the most impressive was probably the Yorkist commander William Neville, Lord Fauconberg, who played a key role at Calais in 1459, at Sandwich in 1460 and at Towton in 1461. The Wars of the Roses provided a useful boost to the employment market for professional soldiers at a time when their usual job opportunities in France were severely restricted. The customary practice for raising men to fight in foreign wars was for the crown to raise companies of men through contracted captains. In return for an indenture from the king setting out rates of pay and other terms of service, a captain issued an indenture of his own to men willing to serve with him. Thereafter he paid them the king's wages, looked to their training, and led them in battle. Although this system was used to recruit foreign troops during the Wars of the Roses, it was too elaborate and time-consuming to be used extensively for the recruitment of armies at home. The sudden emergencies and wildly varying fortunes of civil war meant that the crown, and indeed the rebels, had to rely largely upon a general summons to arms of those who had supported them in peace. The certainty of reward from a grateful monarch after the campaign was over formed the basis of incentive, rather than the remote prospect of steady wages. As Richard of Gloucester wrote to Lord Neville when seeking his military support in June 1483: 'And, my lord, do me now service, as ye have always before done, and I trust now so to remember you as shall be the making of you and yours' (*Paston Letters*).

The major towns of England were an important source of recruits and in general they took care to see that their citizens went off to war under a capable commander. Such precautions were necessary since the levies pressed into Lancastrian or Yorkist service often lacked experience of war, particularly if they came from the south. The shires and towns receiving commissions of array to produce men for service were also expected to provide some of the necessary finance, and on occasion to supply at least a proportion of the weapons required. The ideal complement of arms appears to have

A detail from the east window of East Harling church of St Peter and St Paul, Norfolk.

ABOVE:

Mons Meg on the ramparts of Edinburgh Castle. Although by no means the largest cannon of its type Meg's barrel is nearly $14\frac{1}{2}$ feet long (4.4 metres) and weighs approximately 7 tons (7110 kilograms). Her bore is 20 inches (50 centimetres) in diameter and a charge of 105 pounds (47 kilograms) of powder, at 45 degrees elevation, could project a stone cannon ball weighing 340 pounds (154 kilograms) 2876 yards (2630 metres). Meg was made for the Duke of Burgundy in 1449 and presented to James II of Scotland in the late 1450s.

LEFT:

The siege of a town showing the use of cannon in the bombardment. A scene from a manuscript by the contemporary chronicler Jean de Waurin.

een a helmet (sallet), leather tunic (jack), bow, sword, ircular shield (buckler) and dagger. Probably only ten o twenty per cent of the arrayed men from areas which id not formally face the risk of border raiders, would ossess the full complement of weapons and equip-ient. Many improvised, and eccentric forms of veaponry, in addition to poleaxes, glaives, handguns, xes and spears, would have been used by a large force. ull plate-armour was usually purchased from abroad nd would normally only be worn by the higher ranks f society. It afforded considerable protection to the night in battle and was not, as is traditionally uggested, so heavy as to make it necessary for him to be ifted into the saddle with a crane. Full armour weighed n the region of 50 pounds (23 kilograms) and although t did not reduce the wearer to immobility, it was hot nd uncomfortable to wear in battle for long periods. The knight's horse was armoured to reduce its vulnera-bility but the knight would often fight on foot to take advantage of ground and field fortifications, or simply o encourage the levies by his presence among them. In :lose-quarter fighting the man-at-arms relied primarily upon his sword, though he might also use a battleaxe and very occasionally his lance. The appearance of the handgun on the battlefield already pointed to the demise of the sight of rider and mount in full armour.

The tactics employed by armies during the Wars of the Roses were primarily conditioned by experience gained during the Hundred Years War in France. For ease of manoeuvre and tactical strength armies were divided into all-arm formations known as 'battles'. Three 'battles' would normally be used and they would fulfill the functions of vanguard, main battle and rearguard. This division might take place immediately prior to an engagement, or it could be put into effect at the start of a campaign as a convenient way of speeding the army's march to an agreed rendezvous. By employ-ing separate but converging routes a commander could alleviate bottlenecks while crossing rivers or traversing broken country, and ease problems of supply and billeting. The 'battle' forming the vanguard might be given an independent role during the approach to action. It could be used for a reconnaissance in force or for the seizure and defence of an important town or river crossing. As its name implies it was usually the first section of an army to be engaged on the battlefield and its morale, equipment and deployment needed careful monitoring. Archers would normally be sta-tioned in front and on the flanks of the vanguard for additional support.

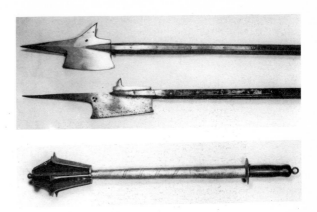

TOP:
The mace; a weapon used by cavalry for close combat.

ABOVE:
The halberd; a staff weapon used with great success by the Swiss and adopted by the English in the late fifteenth century.

Archers usually dominated the opening stage of a battle when they would fire volleys of arrows in an attempt to inflict casualties and disorganize the enemy array. As both Lancastrian and Yorkist armies were able to recruit archers relatively freely, the longbow seldom achieved the dramatic tactical breakthroughs which we associate with its performance against the French and Scots. Where one side lacked sufficient numbers or quality of bowmen, as for example at St Albans in 1455, Edgcote in 1469, and Tewkesbury in 1471, the archer tended to play a more decisive part in the battle. The tactical stalemate of archer against archer encouraged commanders to employ artillery and handguns on the battlefield. The technical development of ordnance had been accelerated by the Hundred Years War, and from early in the fifteenth century cannon were considered an essential feature of the defence of fortified towns such as Calais. The weight and lack of manoeuvrability of heavy siege artillery meant that its use in the field was seldom successful, and the tactical use of artillery only gained momentum with the introduction of lighter and less expensive pieces during the fifteenth century.

The chroniclers of the Wars of the Roses seldom attempted to assess the effectiveness of artillery and they often failed to mention its presence at a particular battle. Two exceptions were the engagements at North-ampton in 1460 and at St Albans in 1461 when the dangers of placing too much reliance on artillery were underlined. At Northampton the Lancastrians, entren-ched behind extensive field fortifications and well equipped with artillery, felt little need to negotiate with the surrounding Yorkists; but when the latter attacked during a rainstorm, the gunners were unable to fire their pieces. At St Albans, Warwick's impressive array of artillery and handguns, the latter manned by Burgundian experts, was completely defeated by wind and snow and it appears to have inflicted far more casualties upon his own men than upon the enemy. Thus while the tactical application of artillery was still at an elementary stage, it does seem that cannon could exert a psychological effect on the course of a battle. Their sheer size and the drama of their detonation was reassuring to inexperienced recruits and, conversely, discouraging to the enemy. Edward's decisive victory at Losecoat field may have been due in no small measure to the moral effect of his artillery upon the hastily recruited rebels. Edward and Warwick certainly valued artillery, for they made strenuous efforts to ensure that a train would be available for their operations. In practice, however, many of their campaigns had to be mounted at such speed that the artillery found itself hopelessly outdistanced by the rest of the army.

The campaigns of the Hundred Years War had shown the effectiveness of English men-at-arms fighting as infantry. They continued to fight in this manner during the Wars of the Roses, riding to the battlefield and then dismounting for action. Very few of the Lancastrian or Yorkist levies would have been trained to fight from horseback and even fewer would have actually owned a horse. The battles between 1455 and 1487 were thus to a very large degree dominated by infantry tactics, and they took place on ground which suited the fighting qualities of the foot soldier. Defensive positions were chosen because of the advantage they afforded through natural obstacles such as woods, ditches, hedges, streams, marsh and rising ground. Where the terrain failed to provide sufficient impediment to the enemy, field fortifications were prepared using pits, carts, stakes and entrenchments. Henry VI fortified his position at Northampton, and at Ludford Bridge Richard placed his infantry behind a series of elaborate defences which in the event were not tested by assault. Despite the importance of infantry, horsemen did play a role in the Wars, particularly as light cavalry for scouting, flank protection while on the march, and pursuit after battle.

The Wars of the Roses were essentially wars of movement and their outcome depended upon a decision in open battle rather than upon the prosecution of siege warfare. Towns and castles were important strategi-

Edward IV in a contemporary portrait by an unknown artist. Edward was an exceptional soldier and powerful ruler, but his was a complex character which made him at once intelligent and dissolute, resourceful and indolent.

cally as sources of raw materials, finance, and man power, and they could provide a convenient haven for an outmanoeuvred commander and his army. There was only one major assault on a defended city (against London in May 1471) and by comparison with earlier wars in Britain few castles found themselves under siege. Successful campaigns in the Wars of the Roses depended so greatly upon speed of action; whether aimed at the suppression of a rising before it could develop into full-scale rebellion, or the seizure of a king before he could deploy his full strength, that the logistical intricacies of a major siege were a burden which neither side could risk nor maintain for long.

# THE HOUSE OF YORK IN REBELLION 1452

By 1450 the manifest inability of Henry VI either to administer his own kingdom or to hold onto England's possessions in France had strained the loyalty of his subjects to breaking point. At the beginning of May some of them translated their resentment into action when they executed Henry's favourite, William de la Pole, Duke of Suffolk, while he was en route to France. Later that month rebellion broke out in Kent and a large force of armed rebels under the leadership of Jack Cade camped on Blackheath outside London. When the rebels were ordered to disperse they ambushed the vanguard of the royal forces at Sevenoaks. Henry withdrew to Kenilworth, his government collapsed, and Cade's men were admitted to London. Other risings took place in Wiltshire, the Isle of Wight and Essex, and in many towns men connected with the Lancastrian government were threatened by angry mobs. One of the rebel demands was that Richard of York should be recalled from his appointment to the lieutenancy of Ireland. His tenure of office had been set at ten years and virtually amounted to the exile which the Duke of Suffolk had sought to arrange for him.

In 1450 York was ready to return to England to assume the political leadership of the government's opponents. His motives were partly financial – the crown still owed him over £30,000 of the money which he had dispensed on its behalf in Normandy and Ireland; and partly the result of his enmity towards Edmund Beaufort, Duke of Somerset, around whom a new court faction had gathered. On his return to England York joined forces with the commons in Parliament who were pressing for reform. By so doing he had hoped to ensure the removal of his enemies from positions of influence, but this adoption of constitutional means failed completely. York now began to plan rebellion and he launched a propaganda campaign to raise support for a coup against the Duke of Somerset. In February 1452 York marched on London to join forces with his southern allies, Lord Cobham and the Earl of Devon. Evading the royal army sent to oppose him, York deployed his followers for battle at Dartford in north-west Kent. Although isolated risings took place in other parts of England the men of Kent did not rally to York's standard, and it became obvious that he had seriously overestimated the strength of his cause among the people of the south-east.

By 1 March the royal army had retraced its steps southwards and pitched camp on Blackheath. The opposing armies were roughly equal in strength and neither side was now anxious to resolve matters in battle. Negotiations were opened and terms agreed whereby in return for the disbandment of York's army Somerset would be placed under arrest. In the event it was York and not Somerset who found himself a prisoner, and it was only after he had sworn an oath against future rebellion that he was allowed to return to Ludlow to brood on his defeat and humiliation.

BELOW:
A view of Blackheath across Mount's Pond looking towards Hollyhedge Lodge and with Shooters Hill in the distance.

# FIRST BATTLE OF ST ALBANS 22 May 1455

Richard of York's political isolation after the failure of his military revolt lasted until the autumn of 1453. In August Henry VI suffered a mental breakdown which left him in a catatonic state, and he was to remain deprived of speech and movement for the next eighteen months. Although the Queen and her advisers tried to conceal the King's illness, the birth of her son, the heir to the throne, on 13 October necessitated the summoning of a great council. Somerset sought to exclude York, but he was belatedly summoned to attend and once present at the council began to rally support amongst his peers. By January 1454 the Earls of Warwick, Salisbury, Worcester, Pembroke and Richmond, together with the Duke of Norfolk, had aligned themselves with York. Forced to choose between appointing the Queen as regent during the King's illness or installing one of their number as protector and defender of the realm, the Lords adopted the latter course. On 27 March 1454 York was nominated as chief councillor to the King with a specific responsibility for the suppression of treason and the maintenance of the nation's defence.

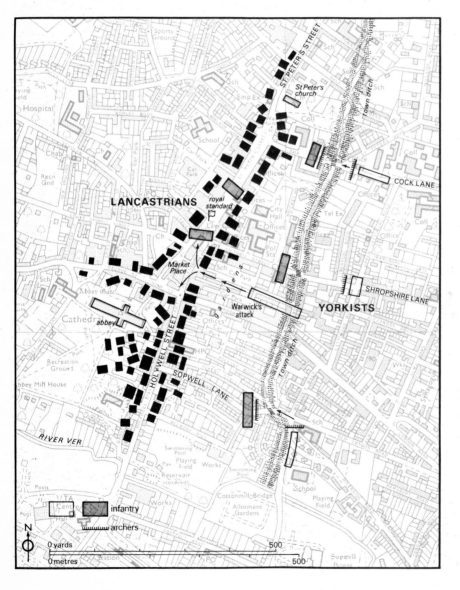

OPPOSITE:
An aerial view of modern St Albans showing the Abbey (left centre) and in the (right) centre St Peter's Street and the market place. The Yorkist attack was delivered from the right of the photograph.

York's position at the centre of power was not, however, to last. In the first days of 1455 Henry regained his senses, York's commission lapsed, and Somerset was freed from arrest (he was committed to the Tower in 1454) and reinstated in his position of favour at court. Fearing their imminent destruction at the hands of Somerset, York and the Neville Earls, Warwick and Salisbury, withdrew from London to prepare to uphold their position by force. As Henry and Somerset progressed northwards towards Leicester, York's forces hastened south in a series of forced marches. By 21 May the King's army had reached Watford, and York had turned westwards from Ware and was marching on St Albans. Pressed to take decisive action by the Duke of Buckingham, Henry reached St Albans ahead of York and prepared the town for defence. As the King's army began to establish their position around the market place, York pitched camp in Key Field to the east of St Peter's Street and Holywell Street.

St Albans stands on the south-western edge of a ridge rising approximately 100 feet (30 metres) above the surrounding plain. The ground to the south of the town slopes steeply down to the River Ver and to the west the approaches were dominated by the abbey. On the east, however, the ground was more open, particularly at the northern end of St Peter's Street. The only vestige of formal defences around the town was the remains of a ditch dug in the thirteenth century to link wooden barriers that could be swung across the streets leading to the market place. On the King's eastern flank the ditch ran parallel to St Peter's Street and approximately 200 yards (183 metres) in front of it. It had been occupied by royal troops early on 22 May, but once Buckingham entered into a parley with York's emissary many of its defenders fell back to refresh themselves in the town.

The Yorkist army was roughly 3000 strong and the King's force was slightly inferior with somewhere between 2000 and 3000 men. If advantage could be won through negotiation it was obviously in Henry's interest to maintain a dialogue with York, but he could not accept the latter's demand that Somerset be imprisoned and tried. York thereupon resolved to take Somerset by force and at 10 am he launched his army against the eastern boundary of the town in an attempt to break into St Peter's Street. York would have wished to seal both ends of the street, and it seems probable that in addition to an advance along Sopwell Lane he also launched a probing attack against the barrier in Cock Lane to the north. Both attacks were held and it was left

A plaque on a building on the corner of St Peter's Street and Victoria Street, St Albans.

to Warwick to break the deadlock by attacking unexpectedly through the houses and gardens between Shropshire and Sopwell Lanes. He was able to clear the southern defences from the rear and lead the Yorkists into the market place, where they found the Lancastrian leaders unarmoured and their men unprepared for battle. Pressed in upon itself the Lancastrian force was an ideal target for the Yorkist archers whose arrows wounded both Henry and Buckingham.

A short but savage mêlée followed, during which Somerset, Northumberland and Clifford were cut down and Buckingham and the King captured. Casualties among the lesser folk were, however, light and only some 100 soldiers fell, most of them Lancastrian. York treated Henry with the respect that was his due and escorted him to London on the day after the battle, there to reaffirm his allegiance.

*The street plan of the cathedral city of St Albans in Hertfordshire has altered considerably since the fifteenth century. However, sufficient roads have retained their 1455 alignment to allow the visitor to trace the course of the battle from the top of the Clock Tower. Holywell Street is now Holywell Hill, and Shropshire Lane is now Victoria Street, but St Peter's Street occupies the same position and still bears its original name.*

# BLORE HEATH 23 September 1459

The first battle of St Albans was followed by an uneasy four-year truce, during which the rival factions manoeuvred and intrigued for positions of advantage. After his victory York had assumed Somerset's old title of Constable of England, and Warwick was appointed captain of the Calais garrison. In February 1456 the King revoked York's commission as protector, but he continued to attend the council. The most potent threat to York's position came not from Henry but from his queen, Margaret, who was determined to seize the reins of power herself. Gradually Margaret gathered supporters from amongst the enemies of York and the Nevilles, and began to advance them to positions of influence. Attempts to defuse the tension which was increasing between the court and the Yorkists had apparently achieved a measure of success by the spring of 1458, but in the following year Margaret presented indictments against York and his followers, and demanded the arrest of Warwick. By April 1459 both sides were preparing for war.

The Yorkist mobilization was hampered by the dispersion of the forces of York, Salisbury and Warwick. Richard was at Ludlow, the elder Neville at Middleham Castle in Yorkshire, and Warwick was still in Calais. By contrast, Henry's forces were remarkably well concentrated around Coventry and in Cheshire. After recruiting at Nottingham, the King's army marched westwards to Staffordshire in the hope of intercepting Salisbury before he could join forces with Richard of York at Ludlow. It was, however, the young Prince of Wales's army, recently recruited in his earldom of Chester and under the command of James Tuchet, Lord Audley, which was to bring Salisbury to battle.

As the Lancastrian force under Audley marched east along the road from Market Drayton, its scouts encountered the Yorkist advance guard near a small stream known today as Hempmill Brook. By the time the Yorkists had negotiated the wood to the east, Audley had deployed his men across the road on a shallow ridge

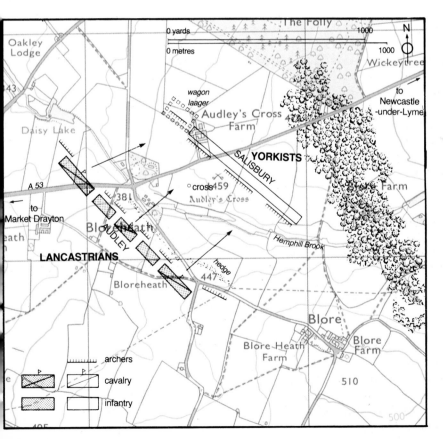

ABOVE:
Margaret of Anjou, Queen of Henry VI, seated with the King surrounded by members of his court, from a fifteenth-century manuscript.

## WALES

The eventual unification of the smaller kingdoms of Wales into the principalities of Deheubarth, Gwynedd and Powys, provided rulers such as Rhys ap Gruffudd (d.1197) and Llywelyn ap Gruffudd (d.1282) with the resources to recapture land that had fallen to the Normans. In the Treaty of Montgomery in 1267 Henry III acknowledged Llywelyn's territorial conquests and his title of 'Prince of Wales', but this success proved transitory for within twenty years Wales had fallen to Edward I in two decisive campaigns (1277 and 1282 to 1283). Resentment at English dominance flared into rebellion under Owain Glyndwr but despite his defeat of Edmund Mortimer at Pilleth in June 1402, Glyndwr's skill at guerilla warfare brought no lasting triumph. Although the accession of a Welshman, Henry Tudor, in 1485 again raised hopes of greater freedom his reign produced little of substance for Wales.

running down to the brook. The 9000 to 10,000 Lancastrians were in a strong defensive position, with their whole front protected by the brook and their right additionally strengthened by a hedge of bushes and trees. Salisbury reconnoitred the enemy position and wisley decided against an assault by his army, which was outnumbered by at least 2 to 1. He ordered his men to prepare an equally strong defence, with stakes planted in front of the Yorkist line and a trench dug to their rear. He anchored the left of his line on the wood and drew up his wagons in laager to the north of the road to protect his exposed right. With his defence established, Salisbury's problem was to persuade Audley to advance to the attack. We do not know for certain what stratagem Salisbury employed, but it is possible that he simulated the start of a Yorkist retreat by ordering that the draught-horses be re-harnessed to the wagons. Audley, who had been charged by Margaret with Salisbury's capture, would be unlikely to let such an opportunity pass, and the fact that he attacked with his troops mounted, ready for pursuit, suggests that he believed the enemy to be retreating.

As the Lancastrians charged across the brook, Salisbury's archers shot their horses from under them and the Yorkist infantry rushed in to finish the winded and disorganized cavalrymen. A second mounted attack met the same fate and for his third assault Audley changed his tactics, leading 4000 infantry forward as the main thrust of his attack with cavalry in support. A furious and bloody mêlée took place on the slopes of the Yorkist position, during which Audley was cut down and killed. His cavalry, their morale already low after their earlier defeats, now withdrew entirely, some riding off the battlefield, others deserting to the Yorkists. Unable to make progress against the enemy fortifications, with their commander dead and their cavalry defeated, the Lancastrian infantry broke and fled. The Yorkists, whose casualties had been minimal, harried the enemy to the banks of the River Tern. As many as 2000 Lancastrians may have fallen during the battle and pursuit.

Salisbury pressed on to complete the Yorkist concentration at Ludlow, where Richard had already been joined by Warwick. As Henry marched southwards he was confronted by the Yorkist army between Kidderminster and Worcester, but when the King's force prepared to give battle York ordered his men to retreat. Henry resumed his advance and York, reluctant to initiate action against troops under the King's direct command, fell back to Tewkesbury and then to Ludlow. York camped near Ludford Bridge on the River Teme. Although he had chosen a good defensive position, the morale of his army was dangerously low in consequence of the superior numbers of the King's force and the demoralizing Yorkist retreat. At midnight on 12 October York deserted his army and took ship to Ireland, while Salisbury, Warwick, and Edward Earl of March fled to Calais. The following morning the Yorkist army surrendered to the king.

*The battlefield spans the A53 Market Drayton to Newcastle-under-Lyme road approximately 2¼ miles (4 kms) to the east of Market Drayton. The ground between Audley Cross Farm and the junction of the A53 with the minor road to Hales was the site of most of the fighting. The cross erected to commemorate the battle and mark the spot on which Audley met his death stands in this area just to the south of the A53 and roughly half way up the slope to Salisbury's position. There is evidence to suggest that the road in 1459 did not follow the modern route straight across the heath, but diverged southwards along the line of the brook before swinging back to its present course.*

# A NORTHAMPTON 10 July 1460
# B WAKEFIELD 30 December 1460

Henry VI's victory at Ludford Bridge had been extensive though not decisive, for the Yorkist leaders could still strike from their exile overseas. Lancastrian attempts to capture Calais failed and Warwick's men struck back across the channel in a raid on royal forces at Sandwich. Encouraged by their success, they returned six months later in June 1460 and established a Yorkist garrison in the town. The occupation of Sandwich gave the rebels a bridgehead in England which they put to good purpose, landing an invasion force of 2000 troops under March, Salisbury and Warwick. At the beginning of July a greatly-enlarged Yorkist army took London, and Henry, who had been organizing the defence of the Midlands against a possible landing by York in Wales, moved southwards to Northampton. While the royal army dug itself in on the approaches to the town, a Yorkist force under March and Warwick hurried north, leaving Salisbury to deal with the garrison in the Tower of London.

The Lancastrian position in the fields immediately to the south of the River Nene was strongly entrenched

ABOVE:
Edward, Earl of March at the battle of Northampton. From the *Chronicles of Edward*.

RIGHT:
The battle of Wakefield, 1460.

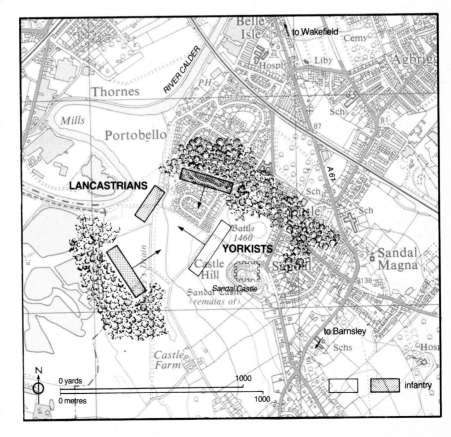

and well-supplied with artillery. The defenders were, however, outnumbered by the Yorkists, who divided their army into three 'battles' under March, Warwick and Lord Fauconberg. The three 'battles' launched a simultaneous assault on 10 July 1460, while pouring rain prevented the Lancastrians from discharging their guns. The sodden ground and slippery entrenchments hampered Yorkist progress until the troops of Lord Grey, whose command of the Lancastrian vanguard had not prevented him from coming to an arrangement with Warwick, helped the attackers to gain entry. Within thirty minutes the royal army had collapsed, Buckingham, Egremont, Beaumont and Shrewsbury had been killed, and the King was once more a prisoner.

York returned to England and on 10 October the Act of Settlement recognised him as Henry VI's heir. This exclusion of Henry's son, Edward, Prince of Wales, was completely unacceptable to his mother, Queen Margaret, and she immediately summoned the forces of Exeter, Devon and Somerset, and of Clifford, Roos, Greystoke, Neville and Latimer to join her in the north. This concentration of Lancastrian forces in Yorkshire was a threat which York and Salisbury could not afford to ignore. In the second week of December they left London and marched north to Wakefield, recruiting as they went. At Worksop a Lancastrian force surprised and severely handled the Yorkist vanguard, but the main body of York's army reached his castle at Sandal outside Wakefield. Contemporary estimates of the size of the force York had been able to recruit varied between 5000 and 12,000, but he was almost certainly outnumbered by the Lancastrians assembled at Pontefract. Whatever the exact size of York's force, he was unable to provision it from the resources of Sandal Castle and was obliged to disperse his strength on foraging expeditions. He must therefore have welcomed the Lancastrian suggestion that a truce be concluded until after Epiphany, and the approach of the Christmas festivities appears to have blinded the Yorkists to the possibility of an early enemy attack.

By acting quickly and decisively the Lancastrians had deployed more men than York at a time of year when few commanders would normally consider venturing on campaign, but their present dominance could easily be eroded if they delayed and allowed the enemy to gather his full strength. They lacked the necessary siege train to batter Sandal Castle into submission and their hope of success lay with the adoption of a stratagem which would draw York from its defences. The Lancastrians appear to have used a number of methods of deception, including the introduction of 400 of their most able soldiers into the garrison in the guise of reinforcements. On the following day, 30 December, while the truce was officially still in being, more Lancastrian 'reinforcements' under Sir Andrew Trollope arrived before the castle. Whether York sallied from the Castle to greet them or to attack them after seeing through their pretence is open to question. Whatever the reason, the Yorkists were now in the open and Somerset's men charged out of the surrounding woodland to overwhelm their startled enemy. York and over 2000 of his men fell in the battle. His young son Edmund, Earl of Rutland, was killed by Lord Clifford on Wakefield Bridge, and next day Salisbury, dragged from his captivity at Pontefract, was executed.

*Sandal Castle stands 2 miles (3 kilometres) south of Wakefield in West Yorkshire and can be reached from the A61 Wakefield to Barnsley road. Turn off the A61 at the signposted castle road and then left at the first crossroads. The battle took place on the ground immediately to the north and west of the castle; an area which today is very much an urban and industrial landscape.*

Troops scale the walls of a town. From a late fourteenth-century manuscript.

# A MORTIMER'S CROSS 2 February 1461
# B SECOND BATTLE OF ST ALBANS 17 February 1461

York's eldest son Edward, Earl of March, heard the news of his father's defeat and death in the battle of Wakefield while celebrating Christmas at Shrewsbury. He immediately began to recruit a force to advance against the Queen's army, but before he could begin his campaign news arrived that the Lancastrian Earls of Wiltshire and Pembroke had landed in Wales. Edward was determined to intercept them and he deployed his army in a blocking position at Mortimer's Cross on the River Lugg. The Yorkist force outnumbered the enemy, who lacked experienced commanders, and the battle was decided by the collapse of the Lancastrian centre. Yorkist losses were light but over 3000 Lancastrians fell during the battle and subsequent pursuit, including the Earl of Pembroke's father, Owen Tudor, who was beheaded at Hereford.

While Edward was destroying the Lancastrian forces in Wales, the army of Queen Margaret, fresh from its triumph at Wakefield, had advanced southwards towards London, reaching Dunstable on 16 February

ABOVE:
The inn at Mortimer's Cross.

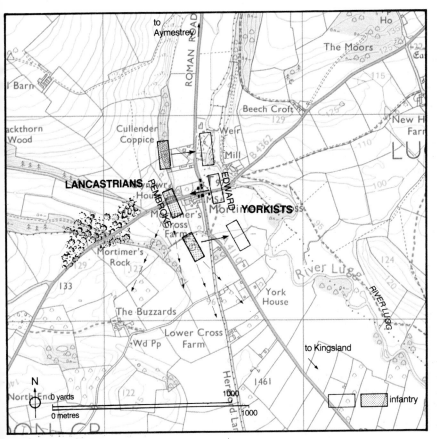

105

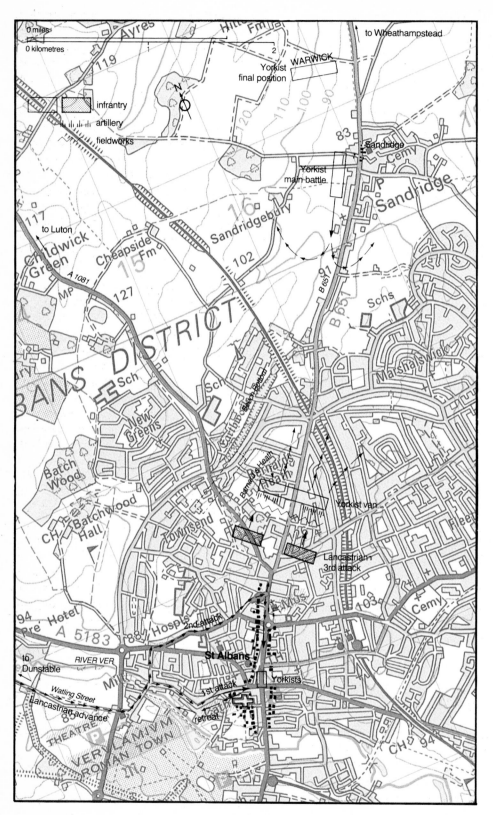

The chronicles recording the second battle of St Albans are singularly unhelpful concerning the deployment of Warwick's forces. That they covered a wide area seems certain, and the battle developed into a running fight that eventually embraced Barnard's Heath, Sandridge and Nomansland Common. All three are accessible by road but Barnard's Heath is now a built-up area.

1461. Warwick had recruited a large Yorkist army in London, Kent and East Anglia, and in the second week of February he marched to St Albans to meet the Lancastrian advance. Perhaps because of the memory of the way he had trapped the Lancastrian forces in the streets of St Albans in 1455, Warwick extended his deployment 1½ miles (2 kilometres) to the north-east of St Albans on Nomansland Common near Sandridge. This position would allow the Yorkists to intercept a Lancastrian advance down either the road from Wheathampstead or the road from Luton. Unfortunately for Warwick, Margaret and her army approached along the Dunstable road during the night of 16/17 February, thus marching across the rear of the Yorkist position. As dawn broke, the Lancastrian advance guard crossed the River Ver and burst into St Albans from the south. The Yorkist garrison of archers reacted quickly, blocking the enemy's approach in the narrow confines of what is now George Street, and pouring deadly volleys of arrows into the packed Lancastrian ranks. Faced by this steadfast defence, Margaret's troops fell back across the river to regroup and rethink their strategy.

It was obviously essential for the Lancastrians to find another route into the town which would enable them to outflank the Yorkist archers. Sir Andrew Trollope, commanding the Lancastrian advance guard, led his men forward again through the unguarded lanes of the north of Romeland, and succeeded in reaching St Peter's Street at a point above the Yorkist barricade. The archers, attacked in front and rear, continued to resist at the southern end of St Peter's Street and inflicted heavy casualties on the Lancastrians. The breathing space won by his archers enabled Warwick to redeploy his vanguard across Barnard's Heath, ready to confront this unexpected attack from the south. By the time the Lancastrians had overcome the last Yorkist defenders of the town and reconnoitred the enemy position to the north it was almost noon.

Warwick's new line was a formidable one with his right resting on the extensive ditch known as Beech Bottom, and his heavily fortified centre and left on the ridge astride the Sandridge road. The Yorkists' field fortifications consisted of numerous devices such as caltrops (two pieces of iron twisted together to form needle-sharp points which were strewn on the ground to impede the advance of both enemy horse and foot), and wooden pavises covered with nails which when stood upright provided archers with a protective screen from which to shoot. Warwick's front was further reinforced by artillery and handguns and it was these weapons which opened the battle as the Lancastrian vanguard approached. Behind Trollope's forward troops came a main 'battle' under Somerset and there may have been a small Lancastrian rearguard in St Albans. The Yorkist bombardment proved largely ineffective since it was delivered into the wind and during a snowstorm. Arrows fell short of their targets, the matches needed to fire the handguns were extinguished, and several pieces of artillery exploded as they were fired. Even so, the Lancastrians were at first unable to make any impression on the Yorkist line; only as Warwick's men began to wonder why the earl had not arrived to reinforce them with the Yorkist main 'battle' did their defence falter.

Warwick's essential problem was the difficulty he experienced in imposing effective control over the raw levies who formed most of his army. As Warwick attempted to march his main force south to the battlefield, he was opposed by many subordinate commanders who argued that the Yorkists should cut their losses and retreat on London. Rumours of treason were already in the air and a Kentish captain named Lovelace may have sent details of Warwick's deployment to Margaret while her army was at Dunstable. During the battle itself Lovelace and his men changed sides, and by the time Warwick had got his main force moving, his men on Barnard's Heath were leaving the field. At the sight of their comrades streaming away in retreat with the Lancastrians in pursuit, Warwick's troops broke and fled. The Earl rode off to bring up whatever men he could gather together at Sandridge, and he succeeded in forming a new line approximately 4000 strong. Just to the south of Nomansland Common Warwick fought on until dusk, when he was able to make a more-or-less orderly retreat to join the Earl of March at Chipping Norton in Oxfordshire. Henry VI, who had been with Warwick throughout the campaign, was re-united with his Queen and son on the field of battle.

*Mortimer's Cross is to be found at the junction of the A4110 and the B4363 roads approximately 17 miles (27 kilometres) north of Hereford and 5 miles (8 kilometres) north-west of Leominster. The monument commemorating the battle stands to the south-east of Mortimer's Cross at Kingsland.*

# TOWTON 29 March 1461

After his victory at Mortimer's Cross Edward, Earl of March, made rapidly for London where he was acclaimed as King Edward IV on 4 March 1461. Margaret, who even after St Albans did not feel strong enough to risk a battle for London, had retired northwards towards York. She had effectively surrendered the initiative to the battered Yorkists, and Edward was determined to act before she could regain it. On 5 March the Duke of Norfolk left London to raise men in East Anglia. Next day Warwick marched off to recruit in the Midlands. A week later Edward began his advance in pursuit of the Lancastrians, and by 22 March he had reached Nottingham. From there he pressed on to Ferrybridge on the River Aire, a line which the Lancastrians had chosen to defend with a considerable force under Somerset and Rivers. In a fierce encounter on 28 March the Yorkists fought their way across the river, despite the fact that the Lancastrians had wrecked the bridge.

With his army's morale high Edward deployed for battle on the following morning at Towton, 6 miles (10 kilometres) north of Ferrybridge. A Lancastrian army of over 30,000 men under the command of the 24-year-old Duke of Somerset was waiting for the 19-year-old Edward and his army of approximately equal strength. Somerset had drawn up his troops on the heath land of a ridge between Saxton and Towton which rises over 100 feet (30 metres) above the surrounding York plain. The slopes to the ridge were slight on all sides except the west, where the ground fell sharply to the River Cock. The top of the ridge was broken by a gentle east–west depression known as Towton Dale. Again to the west, the character of the depression became more formidable as it dropped in a gulley down to the river. No record of the exact location or order of battle of either army has survived, but it seems probable that each was drawn up in at least two divisions, with the Lancastrians north of Towton Dale and the Yorkists to the south. The deployment of the armies left little scope for tactical enterprise, although it does appear that the Lancastrians took advantage of the proximity of Castle Hill Wood to the enemy's left flank, by concealing an ambush party within its leafy confines.

At 11 am as snow began to fall, the Yorkists started the battle with a ruse which was to reduce the offensive power of the Lancastrian army. The foremost ranks of both armies were composed almost entirely of archers. Lord Fauconberg, commanding the Yorkist van, ordered his archers to fire a single volley of heavy-shafted arrows and then withdraw a number of paces. Assisted by a following wind, these arrows carried to the Lancastrian ranks. The latter now believing the Yorkists to be closer than they supposed, fired repeated volleys of arrows. As these missiles were fired into the wind and driving snow they fell short on empty ground. When the Lancastrian fire slackened, Fauconberg ordered his men forward to collect the spent arrows, a proportion of which were used to rearm the Yorkist bowmen while the remaining were left where they had fallen as a rudimentary barricade.

There seems little doubt that the Lancastrians were the first to advance, although whether in accordance with a plan involving the ambush party or simply to rid themselves of the fire of the Yorkist archers is not known. Somerset's men appear to have made some progress against the Yorkist line but the Lancastrian troops under the Earl of Northumberland were slow to engage, giving Edward time to repair the damage done by Somerset. The predominant movement in each of the battle lines was from rear to front as fresh troops replaced the dead, the injured and the exhausted. The infantry battle was fought with an intensity and slaughter seldom seen in battles in England. Edward, it was true, had ordered that no quarter should be offered or accepted, but with such large forces engaged in a relatively-confined area it was perhaps inevitable that casualties would be heavy on both sides. The turning point in this bloody contest came with the arrival on the Lancastrian left flank of Yorkist reinforcements under the Duke of Norfolk. Gradually Lancastrian resistance was worn down and at last as night fell Henry VI's army broke and fled. Flight was difficult, for most of the survivors made for Tadcaster by way of the bridge or ford across the River Cock. The ensuing bottleneck rendered the Lancastrians an easy prey to the pursuing Yorkist cavalry and for many escape proved impossible. Several heroes of earlier Lancastrian battles now lay dead, including Sir Andrew Trollope, and the total number of casualties was computed by the Yorkist heralds at 28,000, of which John Paston believed the Yorkist share to be 8000.

Next day Edward entered York, where yet more Lancastrian fugitives were rounded up, but Henry, Margaret, the Prince of Wales and Somerset had already escaped to Newcastle. Edward briefly took up the pursuit before returning to London and his coronation.

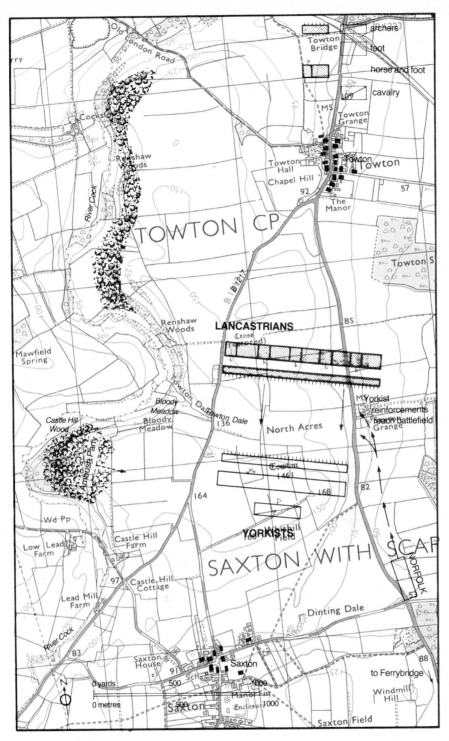

*The village of Towton stands on the A162 Pontefract to Tadcaster road in North Yorkshire. From Towton the B1217 leads, after approximately 1300 yards (1190 metres), past the cross erected to commemorate the death of the Lancastrian Lord Dacre during the battle. The cross marks the right flank of the Lancastrian line and most of the battlefield is visible from this point.*

# A HEDGELEY MOOR 25 April 1464

# B HEXHAM 15 May 1464

Although their field army had been destroyed at the Battle of Towton, the surviving Lancastrian supporters continued to launch minor military operations, usually with the aim of capturing a specific town or castle. They were particularly active in the northern border areas of England, and Henry VI concluded an offensive alliance with the government of James III of Scotland. In June 1461 the Lancastrians and Scots besieged Carlisle before moving on to threaten Durham. As the Yorkists recovered ground in the north the Lancastrians switched their attention to Wales, but here also fortune favoured Edward's forces and Lancastrian castles (with the exception of Harlech) fell with monotonous regularity. The Lancastrians also negotiated for foreign military aid and their prospects brightened substantially as the result of a diplomatic offensive launched by Queen Margaret. In June 1462 she persuaded Louis XI to allow Lancastrian agents to recruit in France and to grant a subsidy to support her war effort.

These resources were used in an attempt to establish Lancastrian control of Northumberland, which was judged to be far enough from London to be defensible against Edward. In the face of an unimpressive campaign by Edward and despite French and Scots support, the Lancastrians failed. They did, howver, maintain their hold on several castles and fighting continued intermittently for nearly two years. In the spring of 1464 the Lancastrians felt confident enough to push southwards into Yorkshire, where they captured Skipton Castle. They also laid ambush near Newcastle for John Neville, Marquess of Montagu, and his escort, who were riding to Norham to conduct Scottish ambassadors to York. The ambush failed but Montagu clashed with a Lancastrian force under Somerset, Lords Roos and Hungerford, and Sir Ralph Percy at Hedgeley Moor near Alnwick on 25 April 1464. A number of Lancastrian troops along with Roos and Hungerford, perhaps realising that the odds were not in their favour, quickly drew off, but Sir Ralph stayed to contest the field, for which he paid with his life and with those of most of his followers.

Somerset regrouped and enlisted additional support but the force which he deployed at Hexham on 14 May was still inferior in numbers to the Yorkists. When Montagu attacked next day he had a superiority which one chronicler estimated at 8 to 1, and Somerset's force quickly gave way to panic and flight. Most of the Lancastrian leaders were taken and the Yorkists'

executioners dispatched Somerset, Roos and Hungerford. Margaret had failed to secure a base from which she could seriously threaten Edward's crown.

*Hedgeley Moor is approximately 6 miles (10 kilometres) south-east of Wooler in Northumberland. The battlesite is east of the A697 just to the south of its junction with the B6346 Alnwick to Wooperton road.*

*The battlefield of Hexham is to be found in a field known as Hexham Levels, 2 miles (3 kilometres) south-east of the town along the B6306.*

# EDGCOTE 26 July 1469

After the Battle of Hexham in 1464 the Lancastrian cause in England was virtually extinguished. Henry VI was captured in Lancashire and imprisoned in the Tower of London, while his Queen and son were forced to accept exile in France. Edmund Beaufort, Somerset's brother and heir, went to fight in the service of Burgundy, and only Jasper Tudor was able to light a brief spark of revolt in Wales in the summer of 1468. The most potent threat to Edward IV came not from his Lancastrian enemies but from his own Yorkist supporters, who were growing weary of the exacting demands made by some of the royal favourites. Such discontent was encouraged by Edward's brother George, Duke of Clarence, and by Warwick, who both wished to oust rivals at court. Warwick and Edward had clashed bitterly on a number of policy issues and Warwick resorted to arms in an attempt to restore his declining influence in government. A Yorkist rising in May 1461 under 'Robin of Redesdale' (probably a pseudonym of Sir John Conyers, who was related to the Neville family by marriage) gave Warwick his chance.

Edward's campaign to crush the rebels began lethargically and reinforcements for the royal army were slow to come in. In July the King, who had reached Newark, found himself heavily outnumbered by the northern insurgents and was forced to retreat to Nottingham. The rebels were not yet prepared for a direct confrontation with the King and they bypassed the royal army and headed south to link up with Warwick. Clarence, Archbishop Neville and Warwick had crossed from Calais on 16 July to a joyous reception in Kent, and had then moved on to London. Their northern allies were in fact to settle the outcome of the campaign without them, for on 26 July the Yorkishmen made contact with Welsh reinforcements under the Earl of Pembroke hurrying to join Edward. The encounter took place at Edgcote near Banbury, with much of the fighting centred on a river crossing-point; presumably the tributary of the River Cherwell which flows through the valley of Danes Moor.

The armies camped on either side of the stream on the night of 25/26 July 1469 and at dawn advanced to the crossing. The exact composition of Pembroke's force is uncertain, for although English chroniclers state that the Earl of Devon and his archers had left Pembroke's command before the battle, the Burgundian Jean de Waurin, who provides the fullest account of the engagement, maintain that Devon withdrew during the fighting when he learned of the approach of rebel reinforcements. Pembroke was certainly outnumbered and although he repulsed the first attack launched by the northerners, Devon's absence made it difficult for him to maintain a continuous battle line, and eventually both he had his brother, Sir Richard Herbert, were captured. Welsh resistance collapsed and 4000 of Pembroke's troops died on the moor. Pembroke and Herbert were executed next day in Banbury, and Devon was captured in Somerset and beheaded at Bridgwater.

---

*The main area of the battle lies on Danes Moor, to the south-east of Edgcote, an Oxfordshire village some 6 miles (10 kilometres) north-east of Banbury off the A361 Banbury to Chipping Warden road.*

---

## HERALDRY

Heraldry in Western Europe originated in the twelfth century when individual knights and later, families, adopted specific devices as a form of identification in warfare. The development of tournaments and the internationalism of the crusades encouraged this practice to the point at which heraldry became an essential mark of knightly status, and by the middle of the fifteenth century an important aspect of state ceremonial. A knight might display his device on a banner or pennant, on a shield, as a crest or figure on his helmet, or as part of an embroidered surcoat worn over mail, hence the phrase 'coat' of arms. The interpretation and creation of such armorial bearings became the province of heralds who had first appeared as announcers at tournaments, but who developed into marshals of chivalric pageantry and plenipotentiaries in war. As coats of arms became more numerous a complex language of description arose, at first embracing French and Latin terms but gradually allowing the introduction of English.

LEFT:
Brass-rubbing showing Sir Nicholas Dagworthy (1401) from Blickling, Norfolk.

# WARWICK THE 'KINGMAKER'

After the defeat of Pembroke at Edgcote, the majority of the troops supporting Edward in Bedfordshire deserted and he was forced to surrender to the Nevilles. With Edward under restraint at Middleham Castle, Warwick attempted to direct the government of the realm, but he quickly found that with only the shadow of royal authority to support his actions the country was uncontrollable. Local rivalry flared anew and many nobles and gentry took the King's absence as an opportunity to settle old scores. Warwick was only able to begin to restore order by releasing Edward from his confinement. Once at liberty the King quickly gathered support, returned to London, and resumed control of the state.

Unable to extract any advantage from their victory in 1469, Warwick and Clarence resolved to try again in 1470. They planned to use a northern rebellion centred on Yorkshire and Lincolnshire to release a groundswell of discontent which would allow them to defeat and possibly depose Edward. On this occasion, however, Edward moved quickly to stamp out the rebellion in its early stages, and on 12 March he dispersed the forces (reported by Waurin to be 30,000 strong) of Sir Robert Welles at Losecoat Field near Empingham. Papers found on the battlefield provided clear evidence of the involvement of Warwick and Clarence in the rebellion. Edward summoned the errant magnates to his presence but they marched northwards in the hope of fomenting further risings. Edward pursued them through the north of England and then southwards to Exeter from where, with their remaining supporters quickly withdrawing from what was now obviously a lost cause, Warwick and Clarence took ship to Normandy. There they were urged by Louis XI of France to join forces with Queen Margaret and the Prince of Wales in a united attempt to remove Edward. The prospect of French military support must have overcome any doubts Warwick may have had at the prospect of an alliance with his former enemy, and he renewed his allegiance to Henry VI.

Heartened by news of an impending Lancastrian invasion with Warwick at its head, his supporters in Yorkshire once more took up arms. Their enthusiasm was premature for the invasion fleet was held in port by a naval blockade maintained by Edward's Burgundian ally, Charles the Bold. It was not until the middle of September 1470 that Warwick and Clarence made landfall in the West Country, far from their followers in the north and in Kent. They advanced steadily into the Midlands gathering support as they went, while Edward marched south to confront the insurgents. The King's force still numbered fewer than 2000 men, while Warwick was reported to have 30,000 under arms when he passed through Coventry. Warwick's brother John Neville, Marquess of Montagu, was also now marching against the King with 6000 men. Edward decided that he could not muster sufficient military support in time to meet the Nevilles in battle, and on 2 October the King and his young brother Richard of Gloucester sailed to the Continent to seek sanctuary with Charles the Bold. On 6 October 1470 Warwick and Clarence released Henry VI from the Tower of London and restored him to the throne.

Within six months Edward was back in England at the head of an invasion force underwritten by Charles. Edward's ships had been forced to run before the wind and he had landed in the north-east rather than near his support in the south. By the end of March 1471, however, the Yorkist forces had reached Coventry where the Earl of Warwick had taken refuge within the city walls. Warwick declined battle, and Edward and Gloucester took advantage of this pause in operations to effect a reconciliation with their brother Clarence, then advancing from Bristol to join his fellow conspirator at Coventry.

Reinforced by Clarence, Edward withdraw from the Midlands and marched south to tackle London. Edward occupied his capital on 12 April and two days later turned northwards again to deal with Warwick.

A representation of Warwick the King Maker from *The Pageant of the Birth, Life and Death of Richard Beauchamp, Earl of Warwick*, by John Rous.

# A BARNET 14 April 1471

# B TEWKESBURY 4 May 1471

## BARNET

After Edward's withdrawl from Coventry the Earl of Warwick had followed the Yorkist army southwards to London, probably in the hope that he would find an advantageous moment to attack while the King's troops were establishing themselves in the capital. The speed with which Edward had consolidated his hold on the city, and deployed his army in its defence, confounded Warwick's plans. As night fell on 13 April 1471 the Earl's outposts around Barnet were driven in by Edward's vanguard and the King made camp in line of battle across the road leading into the north of the town. The Yorkist army was 9000–10,000 strong while Warwick, who had deployed his army on the plateau running southwards from Hadley Green to Barnet, commanded in the region of 15,000 men. The two armies spent the night within earshot of each other, so close that when Warwick ordered a night bombardment of Edward's position his guns overshot their target.

On 14 April Edward's army advanced to the attack between 4 am and 5 am, while the ground was still obscured by a heavy mist. Edward's deployment on the previous evening had left his troops slightly out of alignment with the enemy, and the Yorkist right flank in the east overlapped Warwick's left flank, and vice versa in the west. Each army was deployed in three 'battles', with the Yorkist 'battles' under Richard, Edward and Lord Hastings, and the Lancastrian 'battles' under Warwick, Somerset and Oxford. The morning mist and the speed with which Edward advanced gave little opportunity for the misalignment of the armies to be corrected, and though the King's right effectively took Warwick's left in flank, Edward's own left under Hastings was driven back through the town by Oxford's attack. This was Oxford's undoing, for while a proportion of his men disappeared in pursuit of the beaten Yorkists, the rest fell to looting Barnet. When Oxford had gathered together the remnants of his force he retraced his steps northwards, and since he was

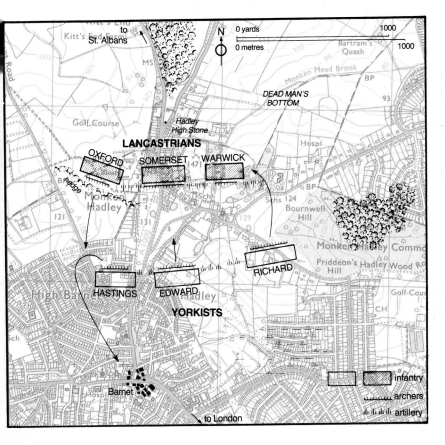

ABOVE:
The battle of Barnet from the *Historie of the Arrival of Edward IV.*

approaching the fighting from the direction of the Yorkist position, was promptly fired upon by Somerset's men. This was too much for Oxford's troops and many of them, putting up a cry of treason, fled from the field.

In the centre, where the battle was being conducted at close quarters by a mass of struggling men, their vision of events on the battlefield still obscured by the mist, the cry of treason was quickly taken up. Somerset's troops, now believing that Oxford had gone over to Edward, began to attack the survivors of the Earl's force with gusto. The Lancastrian battle-line quickly degenerated into chaos and Edward, seizing his moment perfectly, launched his reserve in an attack on Warwick's centre. After a brief but hectic mêlée the Lancastrians broke and fled, and Warwick, struggling to regain his charger at the rear of his army, was caught and killed. Casualties on both sides were comparatively heavy, the Lancastrians alone losing over 1000 men, and although the total Yorkist loss was probably only 500 many of Edward's most constant supporters were numbered amongst the casualties.

---

*Barnet lies only some 10 miles (16 kilometres) to the north of the centre of London and it can be reached easily by train or road. Take the A1000 northwards out of the town towards Hadley Green and the road junction leading to Kitts End. A monument, known as Hadley High Stone (erected by Sir Joseph Sambroke in 1740), stands at the junction and commemorates the battle. Warwick's deployment was some distance to the south of the High Stone where the plateau widens appreciably. Edward's line was approximately 300 yards (274 metres) south of the Lancastrian position.*

---

# TEWKESBURY

In the evening of 14 April 1471 Queen Margaret and her son landed at Weymouth, accompanied by a force of French troops. That same day Lancastrian hopes had been dashed at Barnet and Henry VI remained in Edward's custody. An immediate challenge to Edward on the battlefield was obviously unwise and Margaret, accompanied by Somerset and John Courtenay, Earl of Devon, set out for the north-west to recruit the skilled English troops they so desperately needed. Edward anticipated their plan and on 24 April advanced from London in the hope of intercepting Margaret at one of the crossings of the River Severn. The King narrowly missed the Lancastrians at Bath on 30 April and the

enemy gained the temporary security of Bristol. Although Edward again had hopes of an early battle, this time at Sodbury, Margaret and her army slipped away by night march for Gloucester. There they found the castle firmly held for Edward by Sir Richard Beauchamp and we were forced to march on to the crossing at Tewkesbury.

By the time they reached the town on 3 May the Lancastrian troops were exhausted and Edward was now near Tredington only 3 miles (5 kilometres) away. The following morning the Yorkists advanced against a strong Lancastrian position on a hill close to Tewkesbury Abbey. Somerset may have ordered the construction of field works but it seems more likely, in view of the condition of his men, that the Lancastrian deployment gained its strength from the natural obstacles of hedge, ditch, brook and tree. Margaret's army was deployed in three 'battles' with Somerset commanding the right, Lord Wenlock the centre, and Devon the left. The Yorkist 'battles', from left to right, were led by Gloucester, Edward and Hastings and they drew up about 400 yards (366 metres) from the Lancastrian line. Edward took the precaution of placing 200 spearmen on the edge of Tewkesbury Park to protect his left flank.

The action began with a largely ineffective artillery duel in which Edward, by virtue of his larger train, probably gained an advantage. The Yorkist archers joined in the bombardment giving Somerset's battle their particular attention. The Lancastrian commander now led the majority of the troops in his 'battle' out of range on a flanking march directed against the Yorkist left. This was almost certainly part of a prepared plan based upon a reconnaissance of the ground the previous day, and it would take advantage of an approach particularly concealed by trees and rising ground. Once the flank attack began, the intention must have been for the Lancastrian centre under Wenlock to advance against Edward's 'battle'.

Unfortunately for Somerset the approach march brought his force into contact with the left centre of the Yorkist line rather than with its open flank. Somerset's flank was now exposed to attack by Gloucester's 'battle' and by the concealed spearmen. The situation might have been retrieved had Wenlock now joined the action, but apart from some desultory skirmishing he took no part in the battle. Edward was free to attack Somerset with his own troops, supported by those of his brother Gloucester. The Lancastrians were gradually driven back until they suddenly broke and fled through the appropriately-named 'Bloody Meadow'.

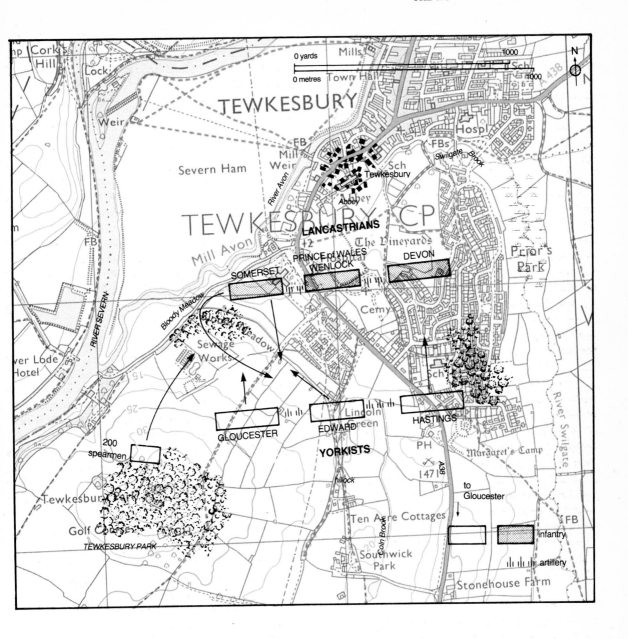

Somerset managed to regain the temporary safety of the main Lancastrian line where he is reported to have declared Wenlock a traitor and dashed out his brains with a battle-axe. Wenlock was certainly killed during the battle but whether by Somerset's hand is doubtful.

Edward left the pursuit of Somerset's broken right to his brother and turned his own troops against the Lancastrian centre. Despite their inferior numbers, the Yorkists made rapid progress against the enemy already disarrayed by the fate of Somerset's 'battle', and after a short mêlée the Lancastrian army disintegrated in flight. Probably 2000 Lancastrians fell during the battle and pursuit and amongst them was Edward, Prince of Wales. The long resistance of Henry, Margaret and their son was at an end. Somerset was executed two days after the battle, Margaret was captured and remained a prisoner for the next four years until ransomed by the King of France, and Henry was put to death in the Tower of London. Apart from a brief and bloodless advance against the rebels of Kent, Edward was never again to campaign on English soil. At last his throne was thoroughly secure.

ABOVE:
Tewkesbury Abbey rising from the mists.

RIGHT:
The execution of the Duke of Somerset after the battle of
Tewkesbury, from a late fifteenth-century manuscript.

*The battlefield is just to the south of Tewkesbury and to the
west of the A38 Gloucester road. Modern development has
changed the face of the battle-site but it is still a rewarding
field to visit. The turning to Tewkesbury Park (now a golf
club) from A38 is signposted to Bloody Meadow, and the
public park to the south of the Abbey, known as 'the
Vineyards', has a monument to the battle.*

# BOSWORTH FIELD 22 August 1485

The discontent aroused by Richard III's seizure of the throne and by his imprisonment of Edward IV's sons prompted a rebellion inspired by Edward's widow, Elizabeth Woodeville, and Lord Stanley's wife, Margaret Beaufort. The object of the conspiracy was to depose Richard and place Margaret's son Henry Tudor, then an exile in Brittany, on the throne. The Duke of Buckingham was to launch a revolt in south Wales in preparation for a landing by Henry. However, Richard's spies discovered the plot, counter-measures were set in train, and no sooner did Buckingham take up arms than his rebellion collapsed. Henry Tudor's invasion fleet bearing 5000 men was scattered by a storm and made landfall in Normandy rather than in Wales. Richard was still on the throne, but the methods by which he had gained the crown had led to a resurgence of dynastic conflict. The fact that a strong alternative candidate had taken the field, however briefly, encouraged the growth of opposition at home and abroad. The way had been prepared for Henry to

LEFT:
Richard III, painting by an unknown artist.

A view of Bosworth Field from Richard's position on the top of Ambion Hill.

try again and on 1 August 1485 he set sail from the Seine estuary with men, money and ships provided by Charles VIII of France.

The probability of invasion had been in Richard's mind since the spring of 1484 and he had taken what steps he could to guard against it. The supreme difficulty, as with most invasions, was trying to predict where his enemy would land. Would it be in Wales, where there was strong support for the Tudors, or in the Solent, only a few days' march from London, or on the coast of northern England? To improve his chances of intercepting the enemy force wherever it might land, Richard established his headquarters in the Midlands, at Nottingham Castle.

Henry Tudor, with a force of 2000 French mercenaries, landed in Wales, at Milford Haven, on 7 August 1485. Richard must quickly have learned of Henry's progress towards Shrewsbury for on the 11th he summoned his principal supporters, the Duke of Norfolk, the Earls of Surrey and Northumberland, and Sir Robert Brackenbury, Keeper of the Tower of London, to meet him at Leicester.

The attitude of one of Richard's nominal supporters was to be crucial to the course of the campaign and to the subsequent history of the crown of England. Lord Thomas Stanley, the Steward of the Royal Household, was a reluctant member of the Yorkist entourage and his brother Sir William Stanley was already secretly attached to the Tudor cause. Richard must still have hoped that the Stanleys with their considerable following in Lancashire and north Wales would destroy Henry Tudor before he set foot in England, but when summoned by Richard to come to his aid Thomas Stanley excused himself, on the grounds that he was ill with the 'sweating sickness'. Thomas's son, Lord Strange, who had been detained by Richard in London as a hostage to his father's loyalty, confessed that the Stanleys were contemplating a change of allegiance. With his son a prisoner, Thomas Stanley could not afford to ignore Richard's threats, but neither was he prepared to commit himself before the outcome of the campaign was more certain.

After crossing the River Severn at Shrewsbury, Henry and his army advanced towards Stafford and then by way of Lichfield and Tamworth to Atherstone. Sir William Stanley, with a force of 2000 men, was following a route parallel to that of Henry's army and Lord Stanley was apparently retreating before the invader towards Leicester. On 19 August the King, accompanied by just under 8000 men, set out from Nottingham for Leicester. The vanguard of his army, consisting of 1200 archers and 200 cavalry, was commanded by Lord Norfolk; the King followed with the mainguard of 2000 pikes and 1000 billmen; and the rearguard of 2000 billmen flanked by 1500 cavalry was commanded by the Earl of Northumberland. On the 21st the armies drew closer, as Henry continued his march eastward along Watling Street and the Roman Road through Fenney Drayton, and Richard advanced westwards from Leicester to the village of Sutton Cheney. The armies were now on a collision course, and with under 2 miles (3 kilometres) separating them, the forces of Tudor and Plantagenet camped for the night; Henry at Whitemoors and Richard on the summit of Ambion Hill. Neither can have viewed the approaching battle with equanimity.

The strength of the royal army has been variously estimated at between 7500 and 12,000 men, and that of the rebels at between 5000 and 8000. For both armies the lower figures appear more realistic, although it is impossible to be precise since Richard was gradually losing men through desertion and Henry accordingly gaining them. What is certain is that Stanley support was now of crucial importance to both armies.

Without aid from the Stanleys, Henry would be fighting a skilful opponent at a serious numerical disadvantage. With the Stanleys on his side, however, he would comfortably outnumber the King. Although the royal army was superior to Henry's even without the Stanleys, Richard was rightly doubtful of the loyalty of many of those he commanded. The Earl of Northumberland for one had shown little enthusiasm for a fight, but Richard knew that with the Stanleys in his battle-line many of the waverers would rally to the Plantagenet cause.

Initially, at least, Richard occupied the most advantageous position, since Ambion Hill dominated the ground leading from Henry's camp. Moreover the western end and the southern slopes of the hill were protected by marshy ground which was impassable to an army. There is no trace of the marsh today, but the site of the spring which fed it, and which became known as 'Richard's Well' is marked by a stone pyramid. Most of the marsh area of 1485 is now covered by Ambion Wood.

The Stanleys mustered approximately 4000 men and local tradition asserts that William took position to the north of the rival armies and Thomas to the south. The evidence for this division of force is slight, but even if the Stanleys concentrated to the north of the battlefield, they were well-placed to intervene on the side of whichever force appeared to be gaining the upper hand.

On the morning of 22 August the royal army was first on the move, marching to occupy the western crest of Ambion Hill soon after dawn. From there they would have seen the assembled might of the Stanleys drawn up for battle. There was still no indication of which army would benefit from their presence and Richard had to be content with a battle-line composed of the Duke of Norfolk's vanguard of men-at-arms and archers deployed on the crest, his own cavalry to the north, and the Earl of Northumberland defending the army's rear along the north-eastern slopes of the hill.

Henry's confidence in Lord Stanley was obviously greater than the King's, for the Tudor battle array was drawn up on the assumption that the Stanleys would occupy the left of the line. It says a good deal for the morale of Henry and his commanders that they pressed on to the attack even though Thomas Stanley declined to move to their support. Henry's troops advanced north-eastwards from their camp until they came to the edge of the marsh, where they changed direction to the north-west to pass across the front of the royal army. As the weakened left wing commanded by Henry, the vanguard under the Earl of Oxford, and the right wing under Gilbert Talbot, came abreast of Richard's men, they swung into line to face them up the slope of Ambion Hill. While they were performing this manoeuvre Richard gave orders for the execution of Lord Strange and for his archers to open the battle. In the ensuing confusion the execution order was never carried out.

Henry's army completed their deployment under a hail of arrows but they were ready for the charge which Norfolk led against them. As Richard's men crashed into the vanguard, the Earl of Oxford ordered his troops to concentrate round his standard. Faced by a solid wedge of archers and men-at-arms, the Yorkists drew back to re-form. Both vanguards then joined in fierce hand-to-hand combat, during which the Earl of Norfolk was killed. As the forward ranks of both armies began to thin, more and more men were sent from the rear to reinforce them. The Duke of Northumberland's rearguard, however, made no move to come to the King's support.

It will never be known precisely where or by whose hand Richard III met his death. Sixteenth-century chroniclers, and of course Shakespeare, insist that Richard rode out from his lines seeking to strike down Henry in personal combat. It seems improbable that he would have been able to pinpoint Henry amidst the dust and confusion of battle, let alone fight his way through to him, and a more acceptable explanation is that Richard was unhorsed and killed while leading an attack upon the forces of the treacherous Stanleys. With his death there was little left for his soldiers to fight for and many quickly laid down their arms and surrendered. The royal troops were now at their most vulnerable and although the pursuit of those who took flight was not prolonged, Richard's men sustained approximately 1000 casualties to Henry's 200.

Tradition claims that Richard's crown which he had worn on his helmet during the battle was found hanging from the branches of a hawthorn bush. Retrieved by a soldier, it was placed on Henry Tudor's head to shouts of 'Long live King Henry VII'. This episode is commemorated in the stained glass windows of the Henry VII Chapel in Westminster Abbey, where the crown can be seen on a hawthorn bush surmounted by a Tudor rose.

Although Bosworth Field was not the final conflict of the Wars of the Roses – the Battle of Stoke was still to be fought two years later – it was the decisive battle. The Tudors had secured the throne of England and no amount of Yorkist intrigue and conspiracy was able to wrest it from them.

A processional cross found on the field of Bosworth.

*The site of this, the climactic battle of the Wars of the Roses, is one of the very few in England to provide facilities specifically for the visitor. Situated on farm land between the A444 and A447 11 miles (17 kilometres) to the west of Leicester and 2 miles (3½ kilometres) south of Market Bosworth, the battlefield is now part of a country park. A diorama of the battle, excerpts from the film* Richard III, *and weapons and artefacts associated with the Wars of the Roses are displayed in a visitor centre which is open every afternoon from Easter to October. Battle trails which guide the visitor to the main positions and scenes of action are open all the year round.*

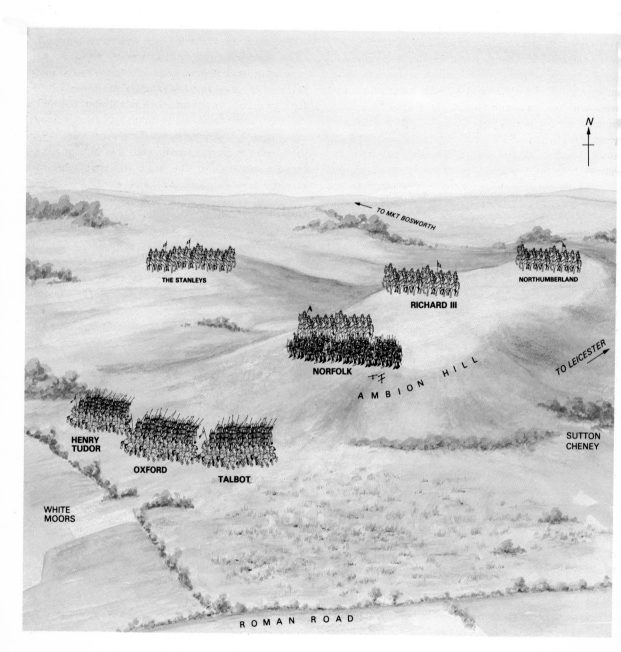

# STOKE FIELD 16 June 1487

Henry Tudor's victory at Bosworth gave him the crown of England but it by no means guaranteed that he would retain it. The dynastic struggle which had lain dormant since 1471 was again at the forefront of politics, and Henry's declaration of his marriage to the Yorkist daughter of Edward IV was a recognition of the need to reduce the shock of a violent change of monarchy. For those Yorkists so abruptly deprived of the power of royal patronage in local and national affairs, the dynastic claim of Clarence's son Edward, Earl of Warwick, held a strong appeal. The north of England was a particular danger area and Henry moved quickly to discourage opposition. Warwick was taken into custody while at Sheriff Hutton Castle in Yorkshire and was then escorted to the Tower. The Earl of Northumberland was temporarily imprisoned, and the Stanleys were ordered to prepare the North for defence against any Scottish attempt to exploit the prospect of rebellion.

In the spring of 1486 Henry rode northwards amidst rumours that rebellion had broken out in Yorkshire and Worcestershire. At York Henry received news that a large force of rebels under Francis, Viscount Lovell had assembled near Middleham Castle, and although the King could muster only some 3000 troops he deployed them against the enemy camp. The rebellion collapsed; Lovell took to his heels in the direction of France, and his men came to terms. With the defeat of the Yorkshire rising Lovell's co-conspirator, Humphrey Stafford, abandoned his revolt in Worcestershire, but failed to secure sanctuary and was executed. As Henry's aim was to reduce tension rather than instigate confrontation, he was on the whole generous in his issue of pardons during 1486, and many rebels took advantage of his clemency. The north-west, however, remained a focal point of discontent, providing the fertile ground in which the seeds of Yorkist rebellion could quickly take root. That rebellion was not long in coming.

With Edward confined in the Tower of London, a major obstacle to the success of a Yorkist rising was the lack of a suitable royal figurehead to take into the field. In 1487 such a figurehead presented himself in the form of Lambert Simnel, an Oxford artisan's son, who had been tutored by a local priest, Richard Symonds, in the manners and speech of a Yorkist prince. Here was someone who could be used to impersonate Edward during the course of a campaign in the hope that a royal presence would draw support to the rebels. Symonds

took Lambert to Ireland where he was declared to be Edward lately escaped from the Tower. This subterfuge was accepted by the pro-Yorkist nobles and gentry, and the Irish offered Lambert their aid in his quest for the throne. The conspiracy rapidly gained momentum and it received the additional support of Margaret, Duchess of Burgundy, Charles the Bold's widow and Edward IV's sister. The plotters gathering at her court in the Low Countries included Lovell, Sir Thomas Broughton and John de la Pole, Earl of Lincoln who had been designated as heir to the throne by Richard III.

The very extent of the conspiracy meant that its existence could not be kept secret and Henry set counter-measures in motion. He first looked to the defence of East Anglia and then established himself at Coventry from where he could quickly march north or south. The first destination of the Yorkist fleet which sailed from Flanders in May 1487 was not, however, England but Dublin. The immediate emergency was over and Henry stood down many of his troops while calling together his closest advisers to discuss a possible invasion of Ireland. The rebels now moved with considerable speed, crowning Lambert Simnel as 'Edward VI' in Dublin on 24 May. Eleven days later the Yorkist armada made landfall at Piel Castle on the Isle of Foudray in Lancashire, where Sir Thomas Broughton had a considerable holding of land. The military strength of the invasion lay in 2000 Swiss and German mercenaries supplied by Margaret and commanded by the highly professional Swiss soldier, Martin Schwarz. The Earl of Kildare had raised 4000 Irishmen to accompany the expedition but both their equipment and their discipline left a good deal to be desired.

The rebels marched across the Pennines gathering some support as they went, most notably that of John Lord Scrope of Bolton and Thomas Lord Scrope of Masham. While at Masham 'Edward VI' summoned York to admit him and his troops, but the city had at last been reinforced in the Tudor interest by Henry, Lord Clifford with 400 men, and the Earl of Northumberland was also moving to its aid. The rebels therefore changed direction southwards and on 10 June Clifford sallied out of York in pursuit. He halted for the night at Tadcaster unaware that the Yorkists were close by on Bramham Moor. A night attack by the rebels swept through Clifford's camp, capturing his baggage and supplies, and scattering his men. Undeterred, Clifford and Northumberland, intent on joining forces with the King, marched out of York with 6000 men on 12 June. They had been gone for little more than four hours when an assault was launched against the city by the Scropes. The attack was beaten off by the inhabitants but Clifford and Northumberland made a hasty retreat to York and remained in the North. By now the rebel army probably numbered some 8000 men and it appears that a royal vanguard under Sir Edward Wydeville retreated before the Yorkists as they approached Doncaster.

Henry, whose main forces had concentrated at Kenilworth, moved north-eastwards via Leicester towards Nottingham where, just to the south of the city, he joined forces with George Stanley, Lord Strange, bringing the strength of the royal army to 12,000 men. Morale appears to have been fragile in the King's army and desertions took place as he paralleled the Yorkists' march towards Newark. On 16 June, however, Henry's troops were early on the move and they encountered the rebel army drawn up astride a ridge near the village of Stoke. The Yorkists had deployed in a strong position, with the River Trent covering their right flank and part of their rear. The Earl of Lincoln appears to have placed his own 'battle' on the right, with the foreign mercenaries in the centre and the Irish on the left. As the royal army marched up from the south the Earl of Oxford, commanding the vanguard, outdistanced the remainder of Henry's force and at first confronted the rebels alone. Lincoln, seeing this detached portion of the enemy, and knowing himself to be outnumbered, led his troops forward to attack Oxford before the odds became overwhelming.

There are few recorded details of the fighting, but it seems that Oxford's vanguard fell into confusion when it tried to correct its deployment, which was out of alignment with that of the rebels. Lincoln's attack struck home while Oxford's troops were still in some disorder, and as a result the royal vanguard suffered heavy casualties and a proportion of its troops fled in panic from the battlefield. Only the arrival of Henry's main and rear 'battles' stopped a rout. Lincon's troops were dismayed to find that victory had been snatched from their grasp and the Irish contingent in particular was no match for the fresh and well-armed royal troops who now surged into the action. The German and Swiss mercenaries stood and fought it out, while the broken Irish tried to escape across the river. The congestion at 'Red Gutter' was ably exploited by Henry's pursuing troops, and over 4000 rebels died in the vicinity of the battle. The Earl of Lincoln and Martin Schwarz were killed, but Lambert Simnel, although captured, sur-

vived as a gastronomic adornment at Henry's court where he was employed as a cook in the royal kitchens. Lovell is reputed to have escaped by swimming the River Trent, only to die of starvation, trapped in a secret room at Minster Lovell in Oxfordshire. The royal army lost between 2000 to 3000 men, most of them from Oxford's rearguard.

Henry had secured his throne in battle amidst considerable doubts across the country, and particularly in London, of his ability to do so. He had still to weather further rebellions, in 1489 and 1491–2, but neither these nor later risings were to make the headway that had been achieved in 1487. In the summer of 1495 Perkin Warbeck, aided by Duchess Margaret, sailed from Flanders with an invasion fleet bearing over 1000 troops. His attempted landings in Kent met local resistance and he returned to the Continent, from where he placed his hopes on a Scottish invasion of northern England in 1496. When that failed, he landed in Cornwall in September 1497 and although he assaulted Exeter, Henry's massive counter-measures forced Warbeck to abandon his men and surrender.

---

*The village of East Stoke stands astride the A46 Leicester to Newark road 3 miles (5 kilometres) south of Newark. Take the route to Stoke Hall from the village crossroads, and then turn first left onto a road which leads almost to the top of the ridge on which Lincoln deployed his army.*

---

# FLODDEN 9 September 1513

Henry VIII's accession to the throne of England in April 1509 brought no fundamental departure from the nation's traditional foreign policy. Henry, a young man just short of his eighteenth birthday, was anxious to prove himself a redoubtable monarch both at home and in international affairs, and he adopted as a means to this end the time-honoured stance of hostility to France and her ally Scotland. During the first months of his reign, Henry renewed his father's treaties with both the Scots and the French, but relations with Scotland were quickly jeopardized by Henry's flexing of his growing military and naval muscle. Though incensed at the provocations inspired by Henry, James IV of Scotland was reluctant to start a war which would further undermine the Christian unity of Europe. France, already fully occupied with war in Italy, also worked to maintain peace between the three nations. Henry, however, was determined upon martial exploits and towards the end of 1511 he joined the Holy League against France formed by Ferdinand of Spain, the Pope and Venice.

Beset by the English on land and at sea, Louis XII of France invoked the terms of his treaty of alliance with Scotland to bring James into the struggle against Henry. The Scottish king still hoped for peace but Henry maintained the cadre of an army in the north throughout the autumn of 1512 while he intrigued against Louis. In May 1513 Henry invaded France with an army of 25,000 men and James was left with little alternative but to issue an ultimatum. Either Henry withdrew immediately from France or a Scottish army would descend on the north of England. Henry's answer was predictably contemptuous and James set to work preparing an invasion force.

The king of Scotland did not possess a standing army but it was a comparatively simple matter to raise men for duty in war – the male population between the ages of sixteen and sixty was under an obligation to provide military service at eight days' notice for a maximum period of forty days in any one year. The provision of an adequate store of weapons and equipment was monitored by holding quarterly 'wapinschawings', at which sheriffs and other officers were empowered to fine those who failed to produce the minimum requirement of weapons laid down by Parliament. Since each man provided both his weapons and his service at his own expense, the monarch was able to assemble a large army at very little cost to his exchequer. Though the system provided men and weapons it did not ensure that the army was trained for war and gradually the 'wapinschawings' assumed the character and purpose of drill sessions. Skill at archery was tested, and in an attempt to encourage the pursuit of martial arts, football and golf were proscribed by the Scottish Parliament. Less care was taken in the provision of cavalry, for most of the gentry were mounted and the Border contingents produced a large force of efficient light cavalry. The only regular element of the Scottish forces was formed by the artillery which was maintained in both war and peace at the king's expense. Mobilization orders for the campaign of 1513 were issued for infantry and cavalry in the last week of July, and the stated assembly point was Edinburgh. James's artillery train left the capital on 18 August a month after a cannon had been dispatched to Glasgow for use in a planned diversionary expedition to Ireland.

When James crossed into England at Coldstream on 22 August his army probably numbered around 40,000 men. It was accompanied by a contingent of French soldiers who had been serving as military advisers to the Scots, improving their tactics and teaching the use of the 18 foot (5.5 metres) Swiss pike. In addition, a field force of 5000 French troops was present under the command of the Comte d'Aussi. James's artillery had caught up with the army by 23 August and it was immediately brought into action against Norham Castle, which duly fell five days later. The Scots then proceeded to attack the castles of Wark, Etal and Ford. During the fourteen days which the army spent in siege operations there was a steady reduction in its strength through desertion and sickness. Although well-equipped, James's forces were very diverse in character comprising, in addition to the French, Highlanders, men from the Isles, Lowlanders and Borderers. There had not yet been time to weld it into a cohesive fighting force able to stand the strains of battle.

Henry VIII had left the north of England in the charge of the septuagenarian Thomas Howard, Earl of Surrey, and preparations for its defence had been under way since the end of June. Surrey had made his first headquarters at Pontefract Castle, where he spent most of August preparing the way for the eventual mobilization of his troops. On 25 August he received the news of the Scottish invasion and ordered a general muster at Newcastle for 1 September. Nearly 26,000 men assembled, and Surrey marched them northwards to Alnwick

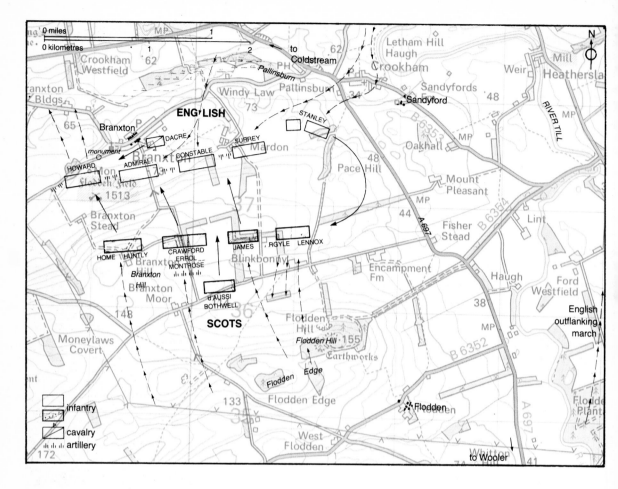

where he was joined by his son Thomas, the Lord Admiral, with 1200 men from the English fleet. At Alnwick Surrey organized his bowmen and billmen into an effective command structure and summoned a council of war to discuss the coming campaign. The English were particularly concerned that the Scots might retreat prematurely across the border, and in an attempt to detain James, Surrey issued a challenge in which he offered battle by Friday 9 September at the latest. James accepted, and the English army moved confidently forward expecting to meet the Scots on the plain of Milfield on 7 September.

As he prepared for action, however, Surrey received the disturbing intelligence that the Scots had marched westwards and deployed in a formidable position on Flodden Edge. The hill they occupied rose to a height of 500 feet (152 metres) and was over a mile (1.6 kilometres) in length, with its right flank protected by marshy ground and its left by a precipitous slope. The only feasible approach along the road which traversed

the centre of the hill was covered by Scottish artillery. If the English attacked such a position they invited certain defeat; yet attack they must, for Surrey had issued a challenge. Suggestions that the Scots might care to move to more suitable ground for a battle met curt refusal, and the English once more went into council to find an answer to the tactical impasse they now faced. Their solution was the daring one of undertaking a march past the eastern flank of the enemy position with the object of enveloping the Scots and attacking them from the rear.

At dawn on 8 September the English army marched north for 8 miles (13 kilometres) in lashing rain until they came to Barmoor Wood. The Admiral reconnoitred the enemy position from the higher ground to the east of the River Till, and next day the army pushed on towards the bridge at Twizel. Just before noon the English vanguard under the Admiral crossed to the west bank of the Till via the bridge, while the rearguard under Surrey forded the river at Milford. The Scots

The field of Flodden, looking towards the English position and the memorial on Piper's Hill.

were puzzled by this English manoeuvre and at first they did nothing to counter it. On the 9th, however, they received firm intelligence that the enemy had crossed the Till at Twizel, and a stormy council of war finally decided that the army should move to Branxton Hill, a mile (1.6 kilometres) to the north of Flodden Edge. With some difficulty James turned his army around and marched north to the new position, luckily arriving there before the English who had more difficult ground to cross. As the English army entered the small valley formed by the Pallin's Burn, they encountered a bog which extended for nearly a mile (1.6 kilometres), and contained only two practical crossing points for an army. Its progress supervised by a local guide, the Admiral's division crossed the bog to the west at Branx Brig while Surrey's division crossed to the east near Sandyford. All the English artillery crossed by the latter route.

As the Admiral's men ascended the ridge to the south of Pallin's Burn they saw the Scots deploying in four divisions on the top of Branxton Hill along a frontage of nearly 1500 yards (1371 metres). An urgent plea was sent to the rear to urge Surrey's division forward into line, but it was to be a further two hours before the entire English army was deployed for battle. During this time the Scots watched and waited. The English conformed to the enemy's deployment and their right was taken by Surrey's younger son, Sir Edmund Howard, their centre by the Admiral and Sir Marmaduke Constable, and their left by Surrey himself. A mounted reserve under Lord Dacre was formed behind the centre of the English line. The Scottish left

A stained-glass window at the Church of St Leonard, Middleton, Manchester, showing some of the archers who fought with Sir Richard Assheton at the battle of Flodden.

the casualties inflicted must have been few the bombardment unsettled the Scottish infantry, particularly on the left wing. Here the Borderers suddenly swept forward down the hill and crashed into the Cheshire levies under Howard who gave way after a short resistance. The Scottish troops in the centre were ordered forward to support the Borderers and as they closed on the English line they were raked by cannon and volleys of arrows. The division under Errol, Crawford and Montrose made little impression on the English defence, but the King's column pushed Surrey's men back for over 300 yards (274 metres). While the English centre was fighting to maintain its position, Lord Dacre led 1500 cavalry against the victorious Borderers, who were busy plundering the dead. The English right was stabilized, and fighting almost ceased in this part of the field, but on the extreme left Sir Edward Stanley was about to take the battle by the throat.

The Scottish right under Argyll and Lennox was still on top of the hill, and Stanley led part of his force round the Scots' flank while the remainder of his men maintained a front to hold the enemy's attention. Approaching through dead ground, Stanley's men swarmed up the eastern slope of the hill and his archers poured a devastating fire into the Scots from their flank. Few of the Highlanders waited for the English to charge and the Scottish right disappeared from the field. At the foot of the hill the Scottish centre, although reinforced by d'Aussi's and Bothwell's troops, was being gradually crushed by weight of numbers as the English closed in from the flanks. Suddenly Stanley's men, their business on the crest of the hill now over, crashed into the rear of the King's division. The Scots formation disintegrated and James, still fighting strongly, was cut down. Besides her King, Scotland lost twelve earls, fourteen lords, a member from almost every leading family in the land, and 10,000 of her soldiers. The English loss probably amounted to no more than 1500. The bill had proved a more effective weapon than the pike and Scottish power had, for the moment, been broken.

*Branxton Hill in Northumberland lies to the south-east of the village of Branxton which stands roughly 2000 yards (1830 metres) to the west of the A697 Wooler to Coldstream road. The battlefield is signposted from the main road and the marked route leads to the monument erected on the English position on Piper's Hill.*

was formed by the Borderers and Highlanders under Lord Home and the Earl of Huntly, the centre by the troops of the Earls of Errol, Crawford and Montrose, with the King's column to their right, and on the extreme right the Highlanders and Islanders under the Earls of Argyll and Lennox. The Scots also had a reserve formed by the French troops under Comte d'Aussi and the men of Lothian under the Earl of Bothwell.

The action began with an artillery duel in which the English established a clear superiority, and although

# PINKIE 10 September 1547

Scotland was not in serious danger of invasion after Flodden, for the Earl of Surrey's army was exhausted and short of supplies. James IV's Queen was appointed as Regent within two weeks of the battle and the infant king was crowned as James V at Stirling. In 1514 Henry III concluded a peace with France in which Scotland was also included, but the English King could not afford to ignore developments north of the border. Henry's diplomatic position in Europe made him determined to detach Scotland from its traditional alliance with France. When the francophile Duke of Albany was appointed as Regent of Scotland in 1515, Henry attempted to have him intercepted while on the journey from France to take up office. In the summer of 1522 Albany tried to mount an invasion of England, but the Scottish lords refused to cross the border, arguing that they would be fighting merely for the interest of France. In 1523 Henry offered his daughter Mary in marriage to James V if the Scots would remove Albany, and when they refused he dispatched the Duke of Norfolk on a successful raid across the border. Ironically, a year later Albany returned to France of his own accord.

James was kept within the power of contending factions in Scotland until 1528 when he was at last able to exercise his personal rule. Offered brides by England, the Emperor and France, James chose Madeleine, the eldest daughter of the King of France, whom he married in January 1537. Her death in Scotland only six months later left James free to marry Mary of Guise in June 1538, an act which roused Henry VIII to a fury of indignation. Swallowing a good deal of his pride, Henry offered to meet James at York in September 1541 to discuss their differences. James, despite prior agreement, failed to appear and Henry now determined to teach him the power of an English king. In August 1542 Sir Robert Bowes mounted a raid into Teviotdale which came to grief at Hadden Rig near Berwick, where he was routed by a Scottish force under the Earl of Huntly. An expedition under the Duke of Norfolk was more successful, and James retaliated with an invasion of England which was defeated at Solway Moss on 24 November 1542. Within a month of the battle, and only a week after the birth of his daughter Mary, James was dead.

Henry moved quickly, and by August 1543 Mary, Queen of Scots, was betrothed to his six-year-old son, the Prince of Wales. When the Scots later repudiated the marriage treaty Henry sent his troops northwards to raid and burn the border country. Tremendous devastation was inflicted by the English, but the Scots gained a measure of revenge at Ancrum Moor on 27 February 1545 when the Earl of Angus destroyed a raiding force led by Sir Ralph Evers and Sir Brian Latoun. Henry VIII's death in January 1547 left an uneasy truce with Scotland and brought a nine-year-old boy to the throne of England. The Duke of Somerset, as Protector of the Realm, was determined to force the Scots to agree to the marriage of Mary and Edward VI. On 1 September 1547 an English army again crossed the border, and nine days later it encountered a superior Scottish force on the banks of the River Esk 7 miles (11 kilometres) east of Edinburgh.

Somerset deployed his force of 16,000 troops to the east of the river, in an extended position on the forward slopes of Falside and Carberry Hills. Somerset's force included 4000 cavalry, an artillery train of 80 cannon, and it was supported offshore by an English fleet under Lord Clinton. Opposing Somerset was the Earl of Arran with an army of 25,000 men deployed behind the Esk, and with the only bridge across the river strongly guarded by the Earl of Huntly. Arran's left, close to the sea, was protected by an entrenchment constructed to give protection against the cannon of the English fleet, while his right was anchored on difficult, marshy ground. It was not a position which would fall easily to frontal assault, particularly when attacked by a numerically-inferior force.

Somerset decided that if he were to break the Scots line he must occupy the hill on the enemy left on which St Michael's Church stood. This ground would allow the English fire to dominate much of the Scottish position and Somerset strengthened his right for the task of taking the hill. In this he was aided by the recklessness of the Scottish cavalry, which on 9 September crossed to the English side of the river and proceeded to taunt the enemy to attack. The English heavy cavalry obliged, and in a brief but fierce action the Scots were destroyed as an effective fighting force. Later that day Arran opened negotiations offering the English a safe conduct home and, if that were refused, the choice of personal combat between Somerset and Huntly, with each supported by twenty men. These overtures were rejected, and at 8 am on 10 September the English moved forward to the assault.

As he prepared to attack Somerset witnessed the

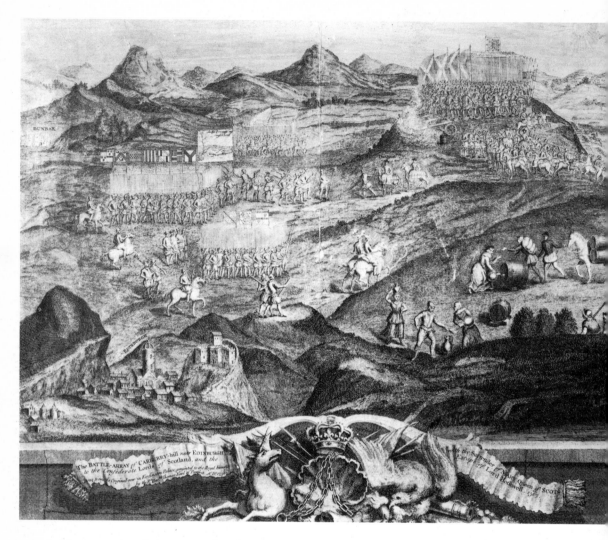

remarkable spectacle of the Scots abandoning their position and beginning to cross the river to the English bank. Why they did so is still a mystery; it may have been through sheer impetuosity or as a result of the realization that the English were about to take St Michael's hill. Whatever their motives the Scots, once across the river, found themselves in a very dangerous position. Somerset was superior in cavalry and artillery and the open ground now occupied by the armies was ideal for the application of both. Argyll's Highlanders on the left of the Scottish line fled from the field after coming under fire from the English fleet, and the remains of the Scots cavalry on the right stood off from the battle. As a result both Scottish flanks were in the air. Lord Grey's cavalry charged the Scots pikemen but could make little impression on the schiltron until the English artillery proceeded to rake the enemy forma-

tion. Pounded by cannon, handguns and archers, the schiltron disintegrated and the English cavalry seized its chance to deliver a charge which broke the Scot army. The pursuit became a massacre as nearly 10,000 of the Scots were cut down. The English loss was little more than 500. Somerset, however, failed to exploit his victory politically and by August 1548 Mary, Queen of Scots, was in France awaiting marriage with the Dauphin.

*Pinkie was fought near Musselburgh which stands on the A1 approximately 7 miles (11 kilometres) to the east of Edinburgh. Much of the battlefield is now covered by the town itself but Falside Hill is still open ground, and it provides an ideal view towards the plain on which the main action took place.*

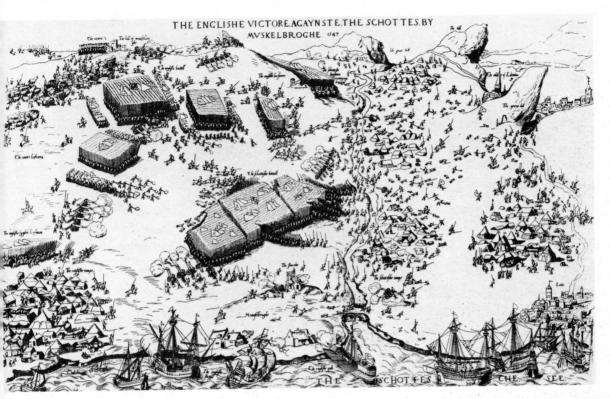

ABOVE:
The battle of Pinkie represented in one of the earliest contemporary engravings of a British battle.

OPPOSITE:
Carberry Hill, near Musselburgh, where on 15 June 1567 the forces of Mary Queen of Scots under James Hepburn, 4th Earl of Bothwell, surrendered to the Confederate Lords.

Mary Queen of Scots, painting by an unknown artist.

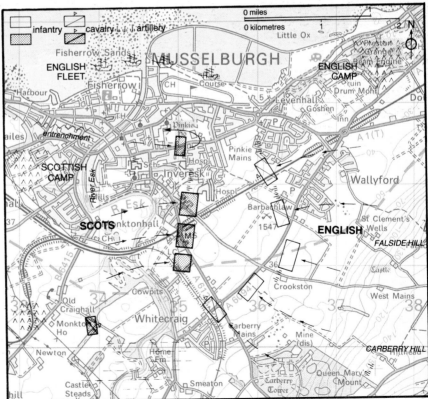

# THE
# ENGLISH CIVIL WARS
## 1642–51

That civil war would occur in England was a prospect which few men welcomed and even fewer understood. The nation slid into war amidst a confusion of political and religious mistrust and economic and diplomatic mismanagement. Opposition to the King in the Long Parliament, which assembled on 3 November 1640 and was dissolved on 16 March 1660, centred not upon demands for the removal of the King or his prerogative, but for the reform of Stuart government. Despite Charles's acceptance of many of the proposed reforms and his repeated pledge to uphold the established Church, the legacy of forty years of Stuart incompetence, of the failure of foreign and financial policies and of the King's evident willingness to seek help from abroad against his enemies at home, served to reduce his credibility and prestige. A rift had opened between the monarchy and many of its subjects, and Charles's ambivalent policy of conciliation and aggression did nothing to convince his political opponents that viable political solutions could be found. Charles's public reaction to the successive crises of the National Covenant in Scotland, the Catholic uprising in Ulster and the impeachment of the 'five members', led men to doubt his capacity for responsibility and sincerity. The degree to which Charles believed he could rightfully ignore the concerns of his subjects lent respectability to the accusations levelled by the extremists in Parliament. To men who had seen the King destroy the religious unity of England, it now seemed but a short step to his destruction of the law and of their liberty.

For his part, Charles I had long harboured a fundamental suspicion of parliaments and particularly of the malign influences which he believed dominated their opposition to his personal rule. He was convinced that the Puritans were one such influence and he declared that their goal was nothing less than the destruction of his 'person and crown, the laws of the land and the present government both of Church and state'. Supported by his belief that he ruled through divine right, Charles found it impossible to accept that Parliament should share in the interpretation and definition of that right. When the King's natural deviousness and penchant for intrigue and the Puritans' talent for propaganda were added to the constitutional impasse, the intense mistrust which allowed the nation to slide into civil war was born.

A natural prerequisite of civil war, of course, was the ability of the combatants to raise armies and secure munitions. Though the nation possessed a regular navy it had no standing army, and the responsibility for defence on land fell upon the trained bands established during the reign of Elizabeth I. The bands were formed of men selected from the militia in each county for training and drill in the use of weapons and in basic tactics. The number of men thus produced was not inconsiderable and it has been estimated that the total available for service through the trained bands in 1623 was 160,000. The difficulty of employing the trained bands in place of a standing army lay not with their quantity but rather with the extent of their training and the nature of the service they were prepared to render. The training requirement for the bands was that they should muster on one day a month during the summer to perfect their drill with pike and musket. The training days were condemned by contemporary military observers for the ease and regularity with which drill sessions became drinking sessions. For lack of a serious attitude to training, the bands were dismissed as being militarily irrelevant, with the exception, that is, of those raised in London. The trained bands of the capital took their role more seriously and their preparedness was tested when they were called out to provide aid to the civil power as an anti-riot squad. In 1642 the London bands were reorganized as 40 companies of 200

An Elizabethan matchlockman.

men each in 6 regiments which were designated by the colour of their ensigns as the Red, White, Yellow, Blue, Orange and Green Regiments. Their drill benefited from the supervision of hired professional officers and they would indeed render signal service to Parliament during the civil war. They were not the only trained bands who proved to be effective soldiers. The bands from Cornwall and the north of England fought with skill and courage for the cause they espoused. They could not, however, fulfill the role of professional soldiers, for they remained essentially trained civilians who served outside their own counties only with extreme reluctance and who objected to enlistment for an indeterminate period.

Once war became a probability both King and Parliament had little alternative but to summon the trained bands, despite their manifest inadequacy for the task before them. Charles began raising men by issuing commissions of array. This was an obsolete statutory instrument which allowed the King to empower selected notables of county or city to secure control of the trained bands, and to raise men for service with a field army. Although the local reaction to these commissions provided an indication of where Charles might find support, they produced little in the way of manpower. In some areas many of the gentry were happy to be associated with general expressions of loyalty to the King, but they were not prepared to take up arms. The

twin appeal of self preservation and local harmony was greater than that of a Royalist war effort. A number of counties and cities were determined that the only issue on which they were prepared to be militant was their own neutrality. Truces and peace pacts were negotiated between local Royalists and local Parliamentarians and in many instances partisan minorities were stifled by local indifference. The only areas where the King's commissions of array met with marked success were Herefordshire and Wales.

The King then sought to create a mobile army through the issue of commissions to individual Royalist supporters. These empowered the holder to raise regiments of volunteers who would serve for pay. The recipient took rank as colonel of the regiment and in turn provided commissions for the required number of senior and junior officers. The strength of both Royalist and Parliamentarian regiments of foot raised in this manner was set at 1200 men, while the establishment of Royalist cavalry regiments was fixed at 500 and that of Parliamentarian troops of horse at 60. Initially volunteers were plentiful, with young courtiers and the students of Oxford rallying to the King and the London apprentices and tradesmen to Parliament. Many volunteers joined the respective field armies because of the strength of their religious views, the Royalist supporters wishing to aid the King in his defence of the Church, and many on Parliament's side responding to the appeal of Puritan ideology. By turning volunteers into regular soldiers willing to fight anywhere in England, both sides broke the ties of local community which had so inhibited their attempts to use existing county channels of recruitment. As a result they were able by September 1642 to assemble armies which could contest the issues between King and Parliament on the battlefield.

Having raised armies which were predominantly amateur in their outlook and training, both combatants were faced with the need to inject a leavening of experienced officers and battleworthy soldiery. During the sixteenth and early seventeenth centuries English troops did the bulk of their fighting on the Continent of Europe, nearly always in small numbers and as the auxiliaries of foreign armies. A proportion were dispatched as part of official expeditions but the vast majority went as soldiers of fortune. Such men were trained in a Continental style of warfare which had superceded the English practice of arms and they experienced the innovations of commanders such as Gustavus Adolphus of Sweden at first hand. Convinced

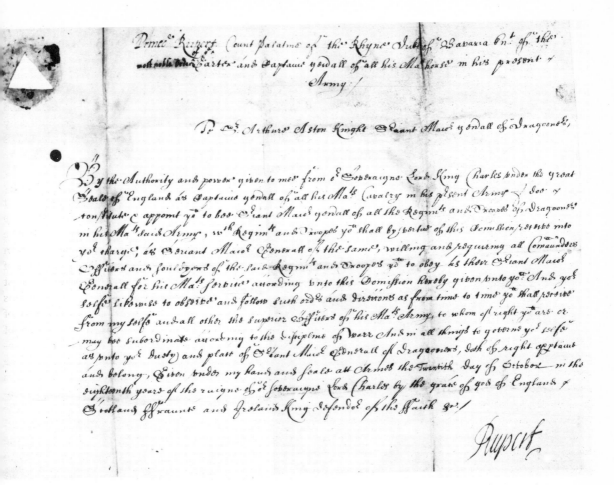

A commission to Sir Arthur Aston as Sergeant Major General of Dragoons in the Royalist Army, signed by Prince Rupert and dated 20 October 1642.

that England could never rest secure in a Europe dominated by Spain some veterans attempted to disseminate the new lessons of warfare by means of the printing press. In books such as *The Theorike and Practike of Modern Warres* by Robert Barret and *Five Decades of Epistles of Warre* by Francis Markham, the more literary of these soldier adventurers set out the precepts of a military awareness schooled on the battlefields of France, Germany, Italy and the Low Countries. With war in Britain imminent there was a rush to secure the services of such professionals, and Parliament adopted the expedient of providing half-pay for unemployed officers. Many of the senior commanders in both the Royalist and the Parliamentarian armies had experience of service overseas, although not all of it recent, and men such as the Earl of Essex, Lord Forth, Prince Rupert, Sir William Waller,

Philip Skippon, Prince Maurice, Sir Jacob Astley, Sir Marmaduke Langdale, and Sir Ralph Hopton, attempted to instil the fruits of their experience in the raw recruits.

The King was Captain-General of the royal forces and commanded his army in person. His military experience was limited to the abortive wars against the Scots (1638 and 1640) and he had never witnessed a battle, but he could call upon a more experienced group of general officers than Parliament. In Prince Rupert he had the services of an impetuous but outstanding soldier whose strength of leadership welded the Royalist horse into a military unit worthy of the battlefield, and in Sir Ralph Hopton one of the foremost generals to emerge during the early years of the war. On the Parliamentary side the Earl of Essex, although Captain-General, was a soldier of moderate ability and he lacked the support of outstanding officers. The talents that did emerge as the war progressed were undoubtedly Sir William Waller, who, although he lost a number of battles was a master tactician; Sir Thomas Fairfax, a commander who combined immense popularity with his troops with a verve and energy on the battlefield that went some way to matching Rupert; Oliver Cromwell, whose grasp of the reality of the war and tenacious pursuit of victory were probably unequalled; and Henry Ireton, John Lambert and Philip Skippon. While the Royalist command structure was often fractured by the petty jealousies of senior officers, Parliament's chain of command suffered from the lack of a centre of power such as that provided by the person of the King.

Both sides had to ensure a supply of equipment and weapons for their recruits. In terms of immediate access to military stores, Parliament began the war with a marked advantage since it secured the arsenals at Hull and the Tower of London. The King relied initially upon weapons from the private armouries of his supporters, though a large proportion were of sporting design and lacked the robustness of military patterns. Charles ordered the disarming of the trained bands to provide weapons for his volunteers, but this could be little more than a temporary expedient. The quality of the weapons held by the bands varied considerably, and in those counties anxious to provide for their own defence the royal agents were refused access to the magazines. The Royalists were therefore increasingly dependent upon arms shipments from Europe, but for this source to be used successfully there were two prerequisites: finance and a safe passage by sea. Charles was extremely pragmatic in his approach to the problem of raising funds. The crown jewels were pawned abroad, peerages bestowed in return for hard cash, donations of money or plate accepted and receipts issued, confiscations exacted upon known and supposed Parliamentarians, and Cornish tin was exported in return for arms.

Once munitions had been purchased on the Continent the difficulty of shipping them to England had to be surmounted. Immediately after the King's attempt to seize the 'five members', the seamen of the navy offered their services to Parliament. The loss of the majority of

Oliver Cromwell by Robert Walker, c. 1649.

Charles I by Sir Anthony van Dyck, c. 1639.

he fleet, although not fatal to the Royalist war effort, vas to have far-reaching consequences. Most of the najor harbours in the land, particularly the strategically important ones of Plymouth, Portsmouth, Milford Iaven and Hull, were secured for Parliament. On the ast coast the Royalists were forced to use the smaller nd more remote ports such as Scarborough, from vhich munitions had to be transported overland on long and often dangerous journeys. The limited number of available ports made it easier for Parliamentarian warships to intercept the gun-running vessels and redressed to some extent the advantages of the latter's superior sea-going qualities. The navy thus acted as a vast Parliamentarian cordon around the cockpit of the war, keeping the Royalists within and those sympathetic to their cause without. While the navy was at sea no

## CIVIL WAR WEAPONS

The main Civil War infantry weapons were the musket and the pike; in battle pikemen were deployed in the centre and musketeers on either wing. As the pike could be as long as 18 feet (5.5 metres) only the fittest recruits were selected as pikemen. Although, while reloading, the musketeer still needed the pikes' protection, the proportion of musketeers to pikemen steadily increased during the Wars. The main firearm in use was the cumbersome muzzle-loading matchlock musket with a barrel length of 4½ feet (1.4 metres), and a bore of 12 bullets to the pound 'rowleing in'. Its killing range was between 40 to 100 yards (37 to 91 metres) and it could be loaded and fired up to once a minute. It was simple and cheap but its tactical usefulness was limited because the firing charge was ignited by a match whose glow and smoke could disclose a surprise attack, and in wet or windy weather it was difficult to load and fire. Cavalry were normally equipped with wheellock and occasionally flintlock arms because the matchlock was an impossible weapon for a man on horseback. The wheellock's ignition was more intricate but more certain. A serrated wheel powered by a spring revolved against iron pyrites held in the jaws of the cock, causing a stream of sparks to ignite the firing powder. As the wheellock mechanism was costly to produce, numbers were limited.

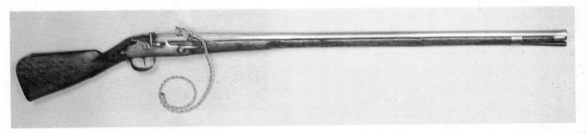

ABOVE:
A Danish matchlock musket of a type which postdates the Civil Wars. Matchlocks almost identical to this were used by British infantry from the Restoration to the reign of Queen Anne.

BELOW:
A wheellock pistol of the type commonly used by cavalry. It is unlikely that any of the wheellocks issued during the Civil Wars were of English manufacture. This example was made in Brescia, Northern Italy, between 1625 and 1650.

foreign power was prepared to risk armed intervention on Charles's behalf. The navy also formed a vital logistical and communication link for isolated Parliamentarian garrisons, conveying artillery, men and supplies to threatened areas. On occasion the system failed, as when the prevailing westerly winds prevented the seaborne evacuation of Essex's force from Lostwithiel, but in general the navy under its Lord High Admiral the Earl of Warwick was essential to Parliament's war effort.

The strategic conduct of the First Civil War (1642–6) centred upon the need to capture and hold areas of population and the resources they controlled. At the start of the campaigning season of 1643, for example, the King's underlying military position was stronger than it had been the year before, largely because he held more ground. Charles controlled much of the north including Yorkshire (with the exception of Hull and the West Riding), Lancashire, Chester and most of Wales. Cornwall was Royalist but isolated, and the King exercised a measure of control in the country around Oxford. Parliament held the important centres of London, Bristol, Plymouth and Hull and controlled most of the West Country and South Wales, the Home Counties, the Midlands and East Anglia. It was essential for both sides that they maintain their territorial integrity as far as possible during the campaigning season. Only by controlling the ports, towns and countryside could they levy the revenue and muster the recruits upon which their military strength depended. It was thus an enormous undertaking for either side to channel its resource into a decisive strategy based upon a single, large army. Regional forces supported by a myriad of garrisons were seen to be essential, simply to retain a territorial base from which to prosecute the war.

By 1644 it had become clear that the side which could organize and support an effective army, capable of operating as a strategic force anywhere in Britain, would win the war. The influx of volunteers which had provided the armies of 1642 and early 1643 had been exhausted, and both the King and Parliament were forced to resort to impressing the manpower they needed. By August 1643 Parliament was issuing instructions for the impressment of 22,000 men in London and the east of England, and it is probable that both sides raised over 60,000 men in this way. Yet because of regional and local garrisons, sickness and desertion, it was exceptional for either side to have more than 18,000–20,000 men available at what should have been

## JAMES GRAHAM, MARQUESS OF MONTROSE

Montrose by Gerrit van Honthorst (1590–1656).

decisive battles. Indeed, more often than not Charles was fortunate if he could field more than 12,000–14,000 men at the critical moment of a campaign. The failure of both sides to concentrate sufficient trained and committed soldiers in any single army led to a series of indecisive campaigns in which victory on the battlefield provided little prospect of victory in the war.

Before an effective army and a decisive strategy were possible a successful war administration capable of translating resources into men, weapons and supplies was required. The financial strength and expertise of the City of London provided Parliament with an early advantage, but like the Royalists they quickly found that single counties were inadequate units from which to organise an army. Parliament therefore sought to

In 1638 Montrose subscribed to the Covenant in opposition to Charles I's arbitrary rule over Scotland, and for the next three years he fought with the Covenanter army commanded by Alexander Leslie. The increasing influence of extremists amongst the Covenanters alienated Montrose from their cause and in 1642 he changed allegiance to Charles I. Over a year passed before Charles came to appreciate the military and intellectual capabilities of his new disciple, but on 28 August 1644 Montrose raised the Royal Standard at Blair Atholl. With an army of Macdonalds and men of Atholl which was scarcely 3000 strong, Montrose took the offensive against the Covenanters and routed them at Tippermuir (1 September 1644), Aberdeen (13 September), and Inverlochy (2 February 1645). With less than 2000 men Montrose outmanoeuvred and destroyed an army of 4000 under Sir John Hurry on 1 May 1645 at Auldearn, two miles east of Nairn. On 2 July the Royal army defeated the Covenanters in a fiercely contested battle at Alford, although not without the loss of Lord Gordon, one of Montrose's ablest commanders. At Kilsyth on 15 August Montrose destroyed a Covenanter force of 7000 which rashly attempted to manoeuvre across the front of the Royalist army, and little more than 100 of the 6000 enemy foot escaped. Decisive measures were obviously needed to deal with Montrose and the Earl of Leven detached David Leslie from the Scottish army campaigning in England to track him down. On 13 September 1645 Leslie surprised and bloodily defeated Montrose's force of 1500 men while they were encamped at Philiphaugh. Montrose, having left Scotland on Charles I's orders in 1646, returned in the service of Charles II in 1650 but was defeated at Carbisdale on 27 April and executed in Edinburgh.

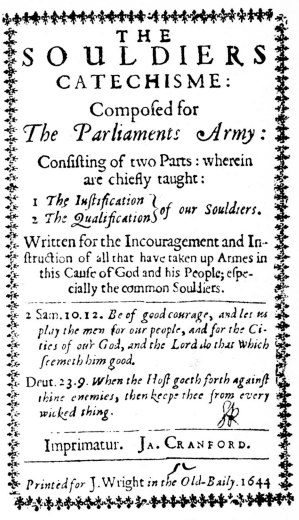

Published by Robert Ram, minister of Spalding, the *Catechism* sought to justify the profession of arms and the waging of war.

group a number of counties together to provide a more viable basis for raising funds and men. At the end of 1643 a Midland Association of the counties of Leicester, Rutland, Nottingham, Derby, Northampton, Huntingdon, Buckingham and Bedford was formed, together with an Eastern Association comprising Norfolk, Suffolk, Essex, Cambridge and Hertford. Royalist attempts to administer their counties were bedevilled by the military vulnerability of many of the areas they controlled. Raising taxes was at best extremely difficult in regions threatened by Parliamentarian garrisons and raids, and Royalist financing was often in a state of emergency far greater than that experienced by Parliament. The Eastern Association was the most solid of the Parliamentarian organizations and once its administration had overcome the initial disturbance of the war it formed a successful logistical base for Parliament. The success of the New Model Army was to be heavily dependent upon the resources of the Association.

After two years of indecisive campaigning a number of voices were raised in an attempt to persuade Parliament to establish a standing army under central direction. Sir William Waller had stressed to Parliament in June 1644 that 'till you have an army merely your own, that you may command, it is impossible to do anything of importance'. Cromwell realised that it was a question not merely of centralized control but also of discipline, regular pay and commitment to Parliament's cause. In an oft-quoted letter dated 29 August 1643, Cromwell outlined his criteria for selecting officers: 'I

Sir Thomas (later third Lord) Fairfax. Painted by E. Bowers, engraved by W. Marshall and used as the frontispiece to *Anglia Rediviva* (1647) by Joshua Sprigge.

Henry Ireton, who rose from the command of one of Cromwell's troops of horse at the start of the Civil Wars, to the rank of Commissary-General and command of the Parliamentary cavalry on the left at Naseby. Ireton fought in Ireland during 1650 and died there of plague on 26 November 1651.

would rather have a plain russet-coated captain that knows what he fights for and loves what he knows . . .' It was just this sort of man that Cromwell wished to see Parliament employ in a new army, in place of the usual jumble of discontented peasantry, deserters, prisoners and pressed men indifferent to the cause for which they fought.

In January 1645 the Committee of Both Kingdoms recommended the formation of a new army of 22,000 men, to be supported by a levy of £6000 per month on a number of the districts controlled by Parliament. The establishment of this New Model Army was set at 12 regiments of foot each of 1200 men, 11 regiments of horse of 600 men each, and one regiment of 1000 dragoons. The senior officers of the army were selected on 21 January, and Sir Thomas Fairfax was appointed as Commander-in-Chief (on a salary of £10 per day) and Philip Skippon as Sergeant Major General (£2 per day). Cromwell was only nominated as Lieutenant-General of the Horse (£2 per day) on the eve of Naseby, and he was not appointed as Commander-in-Chief until 26 June

1650. The New Model was to be formed from the existing units of the armies of Essex, Manchester and Waller but these had been so roughly used during the campaigns of 1644 that they could supply only 7000 of the required establishment of 14,400 infantry. It was intended that the balance should be provided by impressment in London and the south-east, but when the New Model set forth on its first campaign it was still 4000 men short. It was nevertheless an instrument which by its professionalism, courage and discipline would bring Parliament victory.

OPPOSITE, ABOVE:
The trial of Charles I before a High Court of Justice established by the Rump of the House of Commons. By refusing to plead, Charles played into the hands of the regicides, who were able to conclude his trial in a week and execute him three days later on 30 January 1649.

OPPOSITE, BELOW:
The execution of Charles I in Whitehall. The dignity and courage with which he met his death added greatly to Charles's prestige.

## The Tryal of the King.

The Army having purg'd the House of Commons and left none but their own Creatures to sit there, appointed a Committee for y
Kings Tryal wᶜʰ began 20 Jan: 1648, on which day 67 Commissioners were present and when Genˡ Fairfax's Name was called over, his
Lady cryed out He has more Wit than to be here, and when he was Indited in the Name of all the good People of England she also Cry
ed out, no nor one hundred part of them, his Gold Head dropt from his Cane, this day without any visible cause, on the 2ᵈ 70 Commiſ
ſioners were present, as were 71 on the 3ᵈ day. and 66 on the 4ᵗʰ when Bradshaw pronounced the Sentence.

# EDGEHILL 23 October 1642

In the early spring of 1642, as the division between the King and his parliament appeared irreconcilable, both sides recognized the probability that they must either fight or surrender. Although attempts at negotiation would still be made, attitudes hardened quickly and the contestants prepared to support their arguments with armed force. A vital preliminary for both Charles and Parliament was the need to secure the weapons and ammunition which had been stockpiled for use against the Scots. These were held at Hull, and on 29 April Charles appeared before the city and demanded entry from the governor, Sir John Hotham. Sir John refused to comply and Charles, lacking the necessary troops and artillery to enforce his demand, withdrew. The contents of the magazine were quickly loaded onto waiting Parliamentarian vessels and shipped to London. Henceforth the Royalist war effort was bedevilled by a crippling dependence on munitions from abroad; a dependence which it was almost impossible to satisfy in the face of Parliament's control of the navy. The first round in the as-yet-undeclared civil war had gone to Parliament.

After an intensive propaganda campaign, Charles issued commissions of array to the cities and counties of England from York in June 1642. He formally raised his standard at Nottingham on 22 August and his infantry strength, if not that of his cavalry, grew steadily. By 20 September Charles had reached Shrewsbury and contingents had joined him from Derbyshire, Lincolnshire, Bedfordshire, Cheshire and Wales, and more were to come from Staffordshire and Somerset. As the Royalist army began its march on London on 12 October, it totalled nearly 10,000 men formed as 13 regiments of infantry, 10 of cavalry and 3 of dragoons. The army was accompanied by 20 pieces of artillery. Charles was well supplied with officers, including many such as Prince Rupert who had fought in European wars, but his troops were still woefully short of weapons and equipment. Despite a redoubling of efforts to secure weapons from the private armouries of the gentry and from the local militia, many of the infantry marched to battle with little more than clubs and pitch-forks to wield in their defence.

Parliament had begun to raise an army early in June and on 13 July Robert Devereux, Earl of Essex, was appointed as Captain-General. When Essex concentrated his forces at Northampton in the second week of September he mustered 20 regiments of infantry, over 60 troops of cavalry and 5 of dragoons, together with 46 pieces of ordnance. On paper the 20,000 men of Essex's army posed a considerable threat to the Royalists, but in reality the Parliamentarian troops were untrained, ill-disciplined and morose. Yet Essex now had the raw material upon which his few experienced officers could work and he felt confident enough to push westwards in pursuit of the King. Essex marched on Worcester, which had been occupied by Royalist troops on 19 September. Prince Rupert had already decided that the town should be evacuated and he deployed a covering force of 1000 horse and dragoons $1\frac{1}{2}$ miles ($2\frac{1}{2}$ kilometres) to the south of Worcester at Powick Bridge. On 23 September a detached force of horse and dragoons from Essex's army under Colonel John Brown made contact with Rupert's squadrons and rashly attempted to cut their way through to Worcester. The Royalists were deployed in a shallow depression to the north of where the main Gloucester road crossed the River Teme. Rupert's dismounted dragoons lined the hedges and when the Parliamentarians advanced across the bridge they were met by steady musketry at point-blank range. Seizing his moment, Rupert charged with the Royalist horse. Though the troop commanded by Nathaniel Fiennes fought well, the rest of the Parliamentarian force quickly broke and fled, spreading panic among Essex's advance guard which was approaching from Pershore. The casualties at Powick Bridge were relatively few but the Cavaliers had achieved a notable moral victory which did much to hearten Charles's army and to fuel the Royalist propaganda machine.

The King turned for London and Essex left Worcester on 19 October in an attempt to regain the strategic initiative by interposing his army between the Royalists and the capital. Both forces made slow progress, for they were immensely hampered by their baggage and artillery trains. The almost total lack of any system of intelligence-gathering meant that Essex and the King had only the faintest notion of the other's movements. On the evening of 22 October while the King made plans at Edgecote for resting his army on the following day, the Parliamentarian army, equally unsuspecting, was but 7 miles (11 kilometres) away at Kineton. The armies were only made aware of their proximity when the Royalist and Parliamentarian quartermasters encountered each other in the village of Wormleighton. Although Rupert urged an immediate attack, Charles decided to offer battle next day on the ridge of Edgehill which rises some 300 feet (91 metres) above the surrounding plain. The quarters of both armies were widely dispersed and the Royalists did not complete their concentration until early in the afternoon of the 23rd.

Prince Rupert commanded the cavalry on the Royalist right with perhaps 1700 men and Lord Wilmot the cavalry on the left with 1000 troopers. The five brigades of Royalist foot were deployed with three brigades forward and two in support. The brigades varied considerably in strength and they appear to have fielded equal numbers of musketeers and pikemen rather than the preferred ratio of 2 to 1. The brigade commanders were Colonels John Belasyse, Sir Nicolas Byron, Richard Fielding, Charles Gerard and Henry Wentworth, and they deployed in the region of 11,000 men. The three regiments of dragoons totalling approximately 1000 men were split between the wings, with two regiments on the left and one on the right. The lighter guns of the Royalist artillery were placed between or in front of the first line of infantry brigades,

while the heavier pieces were formed as a battery on the lower slopes of Edgehill.

The Earl of Essex had left garrisons at Northampton, Coventry, Warwick, Hereford, Worcester and Banbury, and he could match an almost equal number of men to the 14,000–15,000 of the Royalist army. Essex deployed his troops between the Kineton–Knowle End road and the Little Kineton–Lower Tysoe road with his front line approximately 1½ miles (2½ kilomtres) beyond the centre of Kineton. The left of the Parliamentarian army was formed by Sir James Ramsey with 24 troops of horse, 600 musketeers and 3 guns. Ramsey placed 300 musketeers between his first-line squadrons and 300 behind the hedges to his left. The Parliamentarian centre was deployed in two lines with the infantry brigades of Colonel Charles Essex and Sir John Meldrum in the first line, Colonel Thomas Ballard's Brigade in the second and Sir Philip Stapleton's and Sir William Balfour's Horse in support. The Parliamentarian right was formed by Lord Fielding's Horse supported by two regiments of dragoons. In all, the army mustered some 12,000 infantry, 2150 horse and 700 dragoons. Essex

ABOVE:
Sir John Hotham, the Governor of Hull.

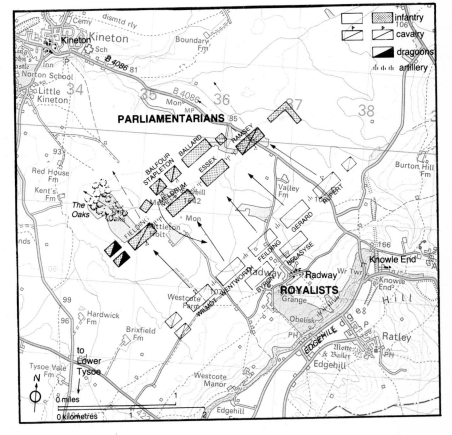

The battlefield of Edgehill.

had between 30 and 37 artillery pieces at Edgehill and there appears to have been a battery on the right of the army with perhaps the remainder of the guns distributed in pairs between the infantry.

There was little incentive for Essex to attack. The Royalists were deployed on a formidable defensive position and delay suited the Parliamentarian interest on both political and tactical grounds. The coming battle would be the first major engagement of a civil war and it would be as well for the King to be seen to be the aggressor. Also Essex could expect to be reinforced during the next twenty four hours by 11 troops of horse, 3 regiments of foot and 7 guns. Accordingly it soon became obvious that if there was to be a battle the Royalists would have to descend the slopes of Edgehill and attack Essex's position. The artillery of both armies had begun a rather speculative bombardment and a Royalist council of war sanctioned an advance. The first of many Royalist wrangles over who commanded whom had left Prince Rupert with an independent command and once the Royalist dragoons had cleared the musketeers on the Parliamentarian left Rupert launched his wing forward. The Royalist troopers hit Ramsey's stationary squadrons at the gallop and the Parliamen-

tarians turned and fled. Colonel Charles Essex's infantry joined the rout but Ballard's Brigade, though badly disordered by the retreating horse, managed to rally and keep the field. Prince Rupert succeeded in steadying a few troops of horse but the majority of the Royalist right joined the pursuit. On the left Lord Wilmot's Horse swept through Lord Fielding's Regiment and both Essex and the King witnessed the wings of their armies disappearing beyond Kineton. Only 200 Royalist troopers on the left had rallied under Sir Charles Lucas.

The Royalist foot had followed their cavalry in a general advance and the infantry quickly came to push of pike. Neither side gave ground but the surviving Parliamentarian cavalry under Balfour and Stapleton rode out from behind Meldrum's Brigade and charged the Royalist foot. Sir Nicolas Byron's Brigade halted Stapleton's charge but Balfour's troopers broke through Fielding's Brigade and attacked a Royalist battery of heavy guns. Parliamentarian attention now centred on Byron's men who were driven back with heavy loss. Sir Charles Lucas with the remaining 200 Royalist horse had attempted to cut his way into the rear of the Parliamentarian infantry but his men were deflected by the fugitives of Charles Essex's Brigade. Gradually

Edgehill, showing Radway Tower.

Rupert's troopers drifted back to the field on their own horses but although a body of them reformed, Rupert considered that their condition and the approach of night rendered any further cavalry action futile. The battle had petered out in a confusion of poor leadership, panic and exhaustion. Many of the infantry and cavalry of both sides left as darkness fell, and with 3000 dead and wounded to be added to the desertions of the day neither Essex nor Charles was anxious for a renewal of the fighting. Next day the Parliamentarian army fell back on Warwick while the Royalists prepared to take advantage of the open road to London.

The Royalists took Banbury with little difficulty on 27 October before marching to Oxford where the King was to establish his headquarters for the remainder of the First Civil War. By 4 November Charles had progressed with his army to Reading, all the time providing a breathing space in which Parliament could recover its nerve. On 8 November Essex's army reached London and four days later the Parliamentarian garrison of Brentford was overwhelmed by an attack led by Rupert. Far from sueing for peace at this demonstration of Royalist bellicosity, Parliament formed a new army of 24,000 men, including 6000 well-armed members of the London Trained Bands. On 13 November 1642 the rival armies watched each other across Turnham Green. The royal troops were overwhelmingly outnumbered and Charles withdrew during the night before a battle which he had little hope of winning could develop.

The Edgehill campaign had ended inconclusively with neither side possessing the strength or confidence to risk all in a decisive battle. Parliament had retained its hold on London, while the King had secured Oxford. As both sides hastened to dispose their troops in winter quarters men still talked of peace and negotiation, but for the realists the prime question now was how best to martial their resources for a long war.

*The general area of the battlefield lies between the B4086 Kineton to Warmington road and the A422 Stratford to Banbury road, and stretches from the slopes of Edgehill to the area known today as 'The Oaks'. Almost all of the battlefield is now Ministry of Defence property but a fine panoramic view is obtainable from Edgehill itself. Although the hill is now heavily wooded it should be remembered that in 1642 it bore only one clump of trees.*

# A STRATTON 16 May 1643
# B CHALGROVE 18 June 1643

## STRATTON

While the King and the Earl of Essex manoeuvred to win London, a smaller but in many ways more dramatic struggle was being fought for control of the West Country. Although driven out of Somerset, the Royalists secured their position in Cornwall at Braddock Down on 19 January 1643 and then twice invaded Devon under the leadership of Sir Ralph Hopton. Unable to persuade the Trained Bands of Cornwall to cross the Tamar into Devon, Hopton failed in his attempt to blockade Plymouth and was forced to fall back. A truce was agreed but upon its expiry on 22 April 1643 a Parliamentarian army under James Chudleigh advanced on Launceston. Hopton occupied

Beacon Hill and in a day-long battle defeated Chudleigh's forces, but the latter gained his revenge in a night attack on Hopton's army as it crossed Sourton Down. The Parliamentarians captured a number of letters amongst which were orders from the king for Hopton to advance into Somerset to co-ordinate his operations with an army under Prince Maurice. The Earl of Stamford was determined to prevent this juncture and on 15 May he advanced into Cornwall and deployed 200 horse, 5400 foot and 13 cannon on Stamford Hill at Stratton.

Hopton could assemble only 500 horse and 2400 foot for an assault on the Roundhead position. Stamford Hill rises for 200 feet (61 metres) and its east face was too

## CAVALRY IN THE CIVIL WAR

Two main types of mounted troops served during the Civil War: horse and dragoons. The horse was itself further divided into heavy cavalry as represented by cuirassiers and lighter cavalry as represented by harquebusiers and lancers. The cuirassier's three-quarter armour gave excellent protection but its weight and bulk imposed a tremendous strain on both man and horse during a mêlée, and very few regiments of cuirassiers served in the war. The most notable was that raised for Parliament by Sir Arthur Hesilrige which because of its heavy armour became known as Hesilrige's 'Lobsters'. The only lancers to be employed were those that accompanied the Scots army, and they were certainly in action at Marston Moor. The typical cavalryman of the Civil Wars was the harquebusier, armed, at least theoretically, with sword, carbine and a pair of pistols, and wearing for protection a buff-coat, back and breast plates and a pot helmet. Dragoons were primarily mounted in-

fantry who fought on foot after riding to the battlefield, and they were armed with sword and musket only and wore no protective armour.

At the time of the Civil Wars cavalry tactics were in a state of flux. Faced by infantry equipped with muskets and pikes the cavalry had adopted the tactic of the 'caracole', whereby each rank rode up to the enemy, fired its pistols, and then wheeled away to the rear, to be followed by each successive rank. This tactic seldom produced decisive results, for the cavalryman's wheellock pistol was only effective at a few yards' range. The Swedish king Gustavus Adolphus reintroduced the principle of shock action by deploying his cavalry in three ranks and ordering them to charge home with the sword, using their pistols only when in close contact with the enemy. Prince Rupert, who had served with Gustavus, employed these tactics at Edgehill and they were gradually adopted by both sides.

Part of the complex procedure for reloading on horseback. After John Cruso, *Militarie Instructions for the Cavallrie*, Cambridge 1632.

steep to allow an attack from that direction. Hopton therefore divided his small force into four columns each of 600 men, ordering two columns to attack from the west, one from the north, and the final column under Hopton from the south. The cavalry were held in reserve. Shortly after dawn on 16 May 1643 the Royalists attacked up the slopes of Stamford Hill in an attempt to gain the summit and force the Parliamentarians over the east face. By 3 pm the Royalists failed to achieve any decisive success and their ammunition was almost exhausted.

It was now that James Chudleigh launched a counter-attack with a stand of pikes. Though making some initial progress the attack faltered as the Royalists massed against it and Chudleigh himself was captured. Hopton's converging columns drove forwards to the top of the hill and began to roll up the enemy line. The Parliamentarian army disintegrated, losing 300 dead, 1700 taken prisoner and almost all its artillery and stores. Hopton's remarkable victory ensured that he was able to keep a rendezvous with Prince Maurice at Chard on 4 June.

---

*Stratton lies a mile (1½ kilometres) to the east of Bude in north Cornwall. The turning for Poughill from the A39 in Stratton leads to the summit of Stamford Hill. A plaque and obelisk commemorate the battle and the earthworks around which the action was fought are still visible.*

---

# CHALGROVE

At the start of the 1643 campaigning season the Royalists had three armies available for operations in the field. The King commanded an army based on Oxford, Sir Ralph Hopton an army based on Cornwall, and the Earl of Newcastle an army based in the north. Although no record of such a plan has survived the ultimate aim of the Royalist war effort was to co-ordinate the operations of these armies in an advance on London. The King at Oxford was only four days' march from the capital and it was vital that he should preserve this forward bastion. It was to be no easy task, for Charles was outnumbered and the Parliamentarian armies of the Earl of Essex and Sir William Waller threatened both Oxford and Royalist communication with Wales. Waller destroyed the Welsh army raised by Lord Herbert at Highnam on 24 March, but the King's forces struck back by occupying Stafford and briefly maintaining the defence of Lichfield. Though he lost his life in the process, the Earl of Northampton

halted a Parliamentarian advance on Stafford at Hopton Heath on 19 March, and Prince Rupert retook Lichfield on 21 April 1643. Prince Maurice added to the sequence of Royalist fortune by defeating a force under Waller at Ripple Field 3½ miles (5½ kilometres) north of Tewkesbury.

Further to the east the military situation gave cause for increasing concern, for Reading fell to the Parliament at the end of April. Fortunately for the King, Hopton's success at Stratton had distracted Waller, and the Earl of Essex halted his advance at Thame. Colonel John Urry, a Scots soldier of fortune and a man who almost made desertion to the enemy a profession, took the opportunity of Essex's proximity to Oxford to slip away and join the Royalists. He took with him details of the Parliamentary army's quarters and news of the expected arrival of a pay convoy with £21,000. For a man of Prince Rupert's adventurous temperament this was too good an opportunity to miss and he set out from Oxford on a mission of interception with 1000 horse, 500 foot and 350 dragoons. Rupert's force halted briefly at Chinnor and killed or captured the 170 Parliamentarian dragoons quartered there, but though the Royalists pressed on quickly, the pay convoy, warned of their advance, had taken cover in wooded country on the edge of the Chilterns.

Rupert reluctantly decided to retire on Oxford for the hue and cry had been raised and enemy forces were converging on his line of retreat. As the Royalists prepared to cross the River Thame at Chislehampton Bridge the pursuers were uncomfortably close and Rupert turned to fight. The Prince deployed his 1000 horse in Chalgrove Field and dispersed his dragoons along the lane leading to the bridge. The Parliamentarian dragoons spurred ahead of their column and opened fire on the Royalist line from the cover of a hedge. Rupert charged through the dragoons' position and after a short mêlée the Parliamentarian horse turned and fled. During the action Colonel John Hampden, a leading Parliamentarian, was mortally wounded. Rupert completed his retirement to Oxford and although he failed in his mission, the ease with which he cut through Essex's dispositions intensified the criticism of this long-suffering Parliamentarian commander.

---

*Chalgrove lies on the B480 in Oxfordshire between Cuxham and Stadhampton. The battlefield is to the west of the road from Chalgrove to Warpsgrove and Hampden's monument stands by the crossroads.*

---

# LANSDOWN 5 July 1643

In the summer of 1643 Royalist forces concentrated for a major assault on the Parliamentarian position in the West Country. A contingent of 3000 foot, 300 dragoons, and 500 horse under Lord Hopton was joined at Chard on 4 June by 1000 foot and 1500 horse under Prince Maurice and the Marquess of Hertford. The presence of three officers whose rank justified independent command raised the thorny question of who should actually control the operations of the army. The problem appears to have been solved by allowing Hertford to command in name, while Hopton commanded in the field and Maurice concentrated his attention on the horse. The Royalists were opposed by Sir William Waller whose army, of approximately equal numbers but stronger in cavalry, was deployed near Bath.

After some preliminary skirmishing the Royalists

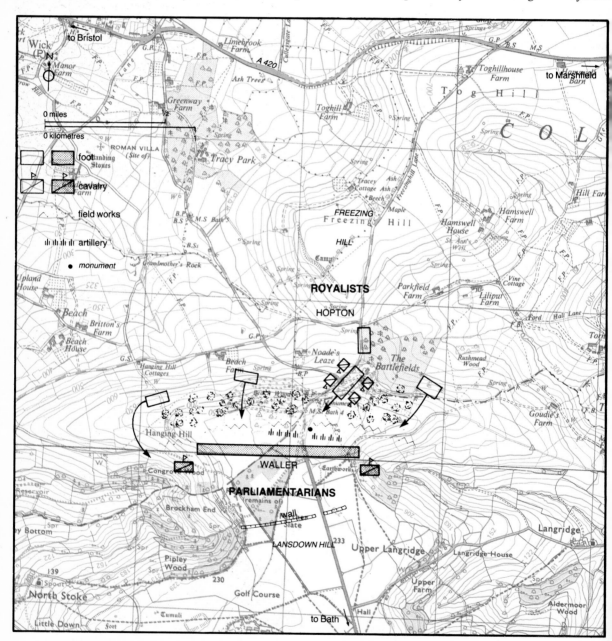

approached Lansdown Hill to the north of Bath on 4 July. Finding Waller's army firmly established on its summit, they temporarily withdrew to Marshfield. The Royalists again approached next day but Waller had constructed field fortifications on the northern end of the hill, thus strengthening the already formidable natural obstacle of a sharply falling hillside. After several clashes between the rival dragoons the Royalists again drew off and Waller dispatched 1000 cavalry to harry the enemy flank and rear in the valley between Lansdown and Freezing Hills. This cavalry assault was roughly handled and Hopton's Cornish infantry clamoured to be allowed to make what appeared a suicidal assault on the main Parliamentarian position.

Hopton ordered flanking attacks by parties of musketeers while the main assault was delivered in the centre along the road which wound its way to the summit. The Royalist horse were halted by a storm of fire poured down on them from above, but Sir Bevil Grenville's Cornish pikemen struggled to the crest, where they held their ground in the face of Waller's cavalry. The Parliamentarian troops abandoned their field works and retreated to the protection of a stone wall 400 yards (370 metres) along the summit. Parliamentarians and Royalists were by now near exhaustion, ammunition was short and a high proportion of Royalist officers had fallen in the assault. Both sides were anxious to maintain their position rather than undertake new attacks and the fighting petered out in an exchange of musketry. Shortly after midnight Waller withdrew to Bath and at dawn the Royalists retired to Marshfield.

---

*Lansdown Hill lies 4 miles (6 kilometres) to the north of Bath and can be reached from the A420 Chippenham to Bristol road. When approaching from Chippenham turn left on to a minor road 1300 yards (1190 metres) past the junction of the A420 and the A46. This road leads to Lansdown and as it ascends the summit of the hill the monument to Sir Bevil Grenville can be found on the left.*

---

RIGHT, ABOVE:
Sir Ralph Hopton, the King's Lieutenant-General of the West, painted *c.* 1637. An early opponent of the excesses of the Court, Hopton still felt duty-bound to support his king against rebellion, and proved to be a highly professional field commander. He died in exile in Bruges in 1651.

RIGHT, BELOW:
Sir William Waller. Etching published in 1643. Waller served with Hopton during the Thirty Years War and the two soldiers remained friends during the Civil War, although they fought on opposing sides.

# ROUNDWAY DOWN 13 July 1643

As night fell on Sunday 9 July 1643 the disheartened Royalist army commanded by Sir Ralph Hopton was bundled into the town of Devizes by the Parliamentarian cavalry of Sir William Waller. Only four days previously the Royalists had fought Waller's army to a standstill at Lansdown Hill, but on the day after the battle Hopton had been temporarily blinded and paralysed by the explosion of an ammunition wagon. Royalist morale plummeted and on 10 July they declined battle with the Parliamentarian army drawn up on Roundway Down to the north of Devizes. Instead, they prepared the town for a siege, withdrawing their artillery to Devizes Castle and erecting barricades across the approach roads. Before the town was fully encircled the Royalist cavalry under the Marquess of Hertford and Prince Maurice broke out and made for Oxford to raise a relieving force.

After a night march of 44 miles (70 kilometres) Maurice and Hertford reached Oxford on the morning of 11 July to find that steps had already been taken to aid Hopton. On both 9 and 10 July cavalry forces had been dispatched westwards as reinforcements, with the first under the Earl of Crawford also convoying an ammunition train. This was captured and Crawford's 600 troopers scattered by Waller's force, but although shaken the Royalist cavalry was able to rendezvous with Lord Wilmot and the rest of the relief force at Marlborough.

Wilmot, approaching Devizes on the morning of 13 July with 1800 cavalry but no infantry under his command, was faced with an interesting tactical problem. Between his cavalry and Hopton's 3000 besieged infantry lay a Parliamentarian force of 2000 horse and 2500 foot. If they fought in isolation both Royalist forces would be outnumbered and their only hope of victory seemed to rest on a combined attack upon the Parliamentarian army. Wilmot's essential problem was how to arrange for a concerted attack to strike the Parliamentarians at the same moment. The Royalists had brought two small cannon with them and Wilmot decided to fire these as signal guns to alert Hopton's infantry to the fact that he was attacking. A messenger sent to inform Hopton of the plan was captured and in the event, despite Wilmot's foresight, the two Royalist forces acted independently for the major part of the battle.

Waller withdrew most of his army from the siege to meet Wilmot's advance and he deployed his force in the shallow valley bounded in the north by King's Play Hill and Morgan's Hill and in the south by Roundway Hill. Hopton's beleaguered army had observed Waller's withdrawal and heard Wilmot's signal guns, which were fired from Roughbridge Hill, but the council of war summoned to analyse these developments suspected a Parliamentarian trap and refused to march out of Devizes. Hopton, still beset by his wounds, was unable to alter their opinion and the scene was set for one of the most dramatic battles of the Civil Wars. A cavalry force tired by a long approach march was about to attack an army of horse and foot which outnumbered it by nearly 3 to 1.

The Parliamentarian army deployed in conventional style with the infantry in the centre of the line and cavalry on both flanks. Wilmot's line consisted of his own brigade and that of Sir John Byron, with Crawford's Brigade in reserve. As Wilmot's troopers advanced, Sir Arthur Hesilrige on the right of the Parliamentarian line led his squadrons to meet them. During the ensuing mêlée of charge and countercharge his famous 'Lobsters' broke and fled. They were soon followed by Waller's Brigade, furiously pursued by Byron's troopers. The majority of the beaten cavalry took flight to the west covering nearly 1½ miles (2 kilometres) until to their horror they found that the ground before them fell abruptly for 300 feet (100 metres) in a treacherous slope. Unable to rein in, many of Waller's troopers plunged downwards out of control crashing into the 'Bloody Ditch' at the foot of the slope.

The Parliamentarian infantry were mere spectators of the catastrophe which befell their cavalry, for with no opposing infantry to fight there was little they could do. The musketeers could not intervene in the cavalry action for fear of hitting their own men and as their horse disappeared from the field the Parliamentarian infantry were left on a deserted battlefield to await events. They were not given long to speculate upon their fate, for the growing noise of battle had at last persuaded Hopton's infantry to march out of Devizes. Assailed from the north by Wilmot's victorious cavalry and from the south by 3000 fresh infantry, the Parliamentarian foot were soon overwhelmed and forced to surrender or flee. The Royalists claimed to have inflicted 600 casualties and taken 800 prisoners and they had certainly achieved their most decisive victory of the Civil Wars. To all intents and purposes, Waller's army had ceased to exist.

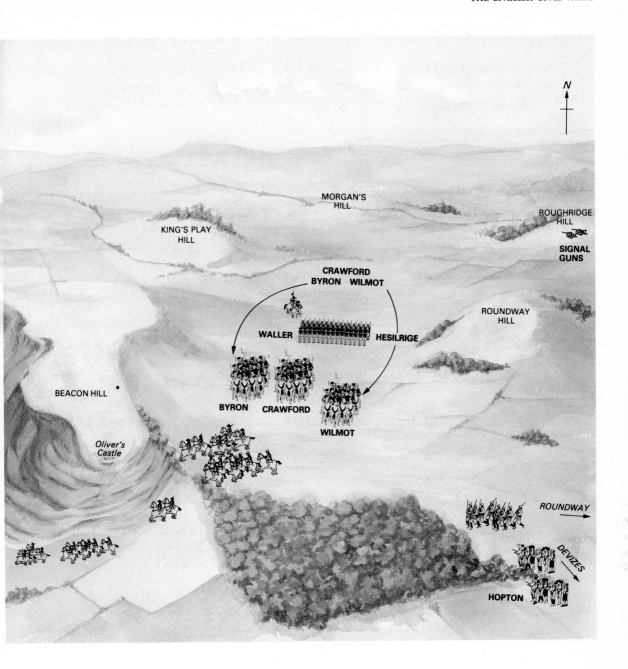

*The battlefield lies to the north of Devizes between A342, A4 and A361. It can be approached along the secondary road to Roundway which leaves the A361 about a mile (1½ kilometres) from the centre of Devizes, and King's Play Hill provides a convenient vantage point.*

# FIRST BATTLE OF NEWBURY 20 September 1643

On 10 August 1643 Charles and his Oxford army of over 10,000 men invested the city of Gloucester and its Parliamentarian garrison under Colonel Massey. In the first week of September a relief force of nearly 15,000 troops under the Earl of Essex reached Prestbury Hill, some 10 miles (16 kilometres) from Gloucester, and the King lifted the siege rather than risk encirclement. The opening move in Charles's campaign to safeguard Royalist communications with south Wales had failed but he was now in a position to intercept Essex's march back to London. If he could bring the Earl to battle and defeat him the war might be ended at a stroke. For Essex to make good his withdrawal he needed to reach Newbury before the Royalists and although the Parliamentarians maintained a lead of 8 to 10 miles (13 to 16 kilometres) for most of their retreat, an inexplicable dilatoriness as they neared the town allowed Prince Rupert and his cavalry to enter it before them. The King was now between Essex and London and there was little alternative but to fight.

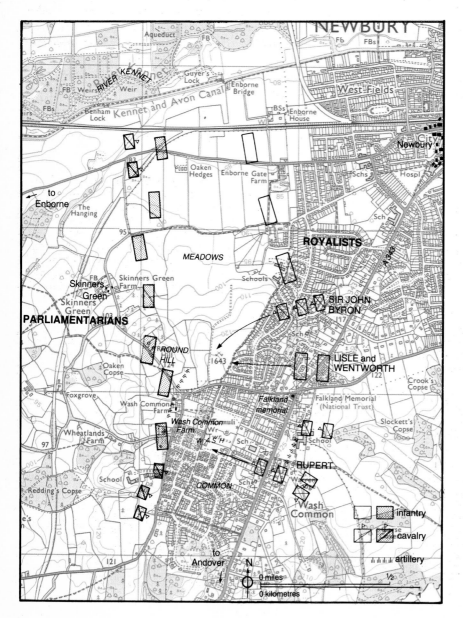

Robert Devereux, third Earl of Essex and Commander-in-Chief of the Parliamentarian forces until his resignation on the passage of the Self-Denying Ordinance.

Prince Rupert by Peter Lely (1618–80).

The Royalists had omitted to occupy the feature known as 'Round Hill' to the south-west of Newbury and between their own army and Essex's forces. The first indication that it had been taken by the enemy came when Parliamentarian cannon opened fire from the hill at first light on 20 September. The area was covered in enclosures and the hedges made it difficult country for both cavalry and infantry, but Charles realized that Round Hill must be captured if Essex was to be defeated. Colonels Lisle and Wentworth were ordered to advance their infantry but accurate musket fire halted both foot and supporting cavalry. Sir John Byron found that the way forward for his brigade of horse was blocked by a hedge with a gap sufficient for only one rider at a time. Observing this narrow passage Lord Falkland, serving in Byron's troops as a volunteer, spurred his horse through and was immediately shot down. A monument still stands to commemorate this heroic if foolhardy action.

The Royalist horse gradually drove the Parliamentarian infantry back to Skinner's Green Lane but failed to push the London Trained Bands from Round Hill. Prince Rupert had secured Wash Common, and a Royalist battery on the plateau became involved in a fierce duel with the enemy guns on Round Hill. Further attacks were ill-co-ordinated and neither side was able to gain a positive advantage before dark. During the night the Royalists withdrew to Oxford and the Parliamentarian forces resumed their march to London.

*The battlesite lies to the south of Newbury and some of it has been hidden by the growth of the town. From Newbury the A343 Andover road leads to the crossroads marked by the Falkland monument, which stands on roughly the centre of the Royalist line. Essex road and a footpath lead on the right to the summit of Round Hill and the centre of the battlefield.*

## CIVIL WAR COLOURS

During the Civil Wars the natural confusion of the battlefield was reinforced by the fact that both sides dressed in a similar manner and spoke the same language. Thus once the initial deployment of the armies had been disordered, it was often difficult to tell friend from foe, and to aid recognition, scarves or sashes were worn (red by Royalists, orange-tawny by Parliamentarians), field-signs such as pieces of paper were affixed to hats, and particular field-words were shouted by the opposing ranks. Even so, the most positive symbol of allegiance and also the most visible of the rallying points in battle remained the colours carried by every company of foot and every troop of horse. Infantry colours were $6\frac{1}{2}$ feet (2 metres) square, made of taffeta and usually designed to indicate each company's regiment and the rank of the officer in command. For ease of management, cavalry standards were only 2 feet (0.6 metres) square. They bore a fringe and favoured designs based upon heraldic devices from the arms of the troop commander or upon political slogans. The loss of a colour or standard to the enemy was the ultimate disgrace that could befall a unit, and in battle the fiercest fighting often took place in their immediate vicinity.

BELOW:
In addition to the company colours and troop standards of their regiments, senior officers also used personal standards derived from family arms or religious and political sentiments. These are Parliamentarian standards.

151

# CHERITON 29 March 1644

After failing to bring Sir William Waller to battle at Farnham in November 1643 Hopton dispersed his Royalist army to winter quarters in Winchester, Alresford, Alton and Petersfield. He rounded off the year by capturing Arundel, but Waller responded with a raid which decimated the garrison of Alton, and with the recapture of Arundel Castle in January 1644. Operations were brought to an end by a period of severe weather, but Hopton, who had been reinforced by troops under the Earl of Forth, was still anxious to bring Waller to battle. At the end of March, Waller moved on Winchester from the east, and Hopton and Forth after failing to catch the Parliamentarians at Warnford made contact near Cheriton.

Hopton's forces were deployed on a ridge to the north of Cheriton Wood with the Cheriton–Alresford road on their right. The Parliamentary camp was sited in the fields north of Hinton Ampner with cannon on the high ground close to the village itself. Although Waller had 10,000 men to Hopton's 6000, a council of war decided in favour of retreat and the Parliamentary transport had begun to move off before the order was countermanded by Waller. Deciding that the battlefield could be exploited in his favour, Waller moved his troops forward early on the morning of 29 March. On the right the City of London Brigade was ordered to occupy Cheriton Wood and on the left the Parliamentary line advanced to the ridge end close to Cheriton.

Hopton quickly realized the acute danger represented by the enemy presence in Cheriton Wood and he ordered Colonel Mathew Appleyard with 1000 musketeers to clear the left flank. After a ferocious musketry duel the wood changed hands and the length of the ridge was now commanded by Royalist troops. Hopton and Forth decided to stand on the defensive in the strong position they occupied to allow Waller's

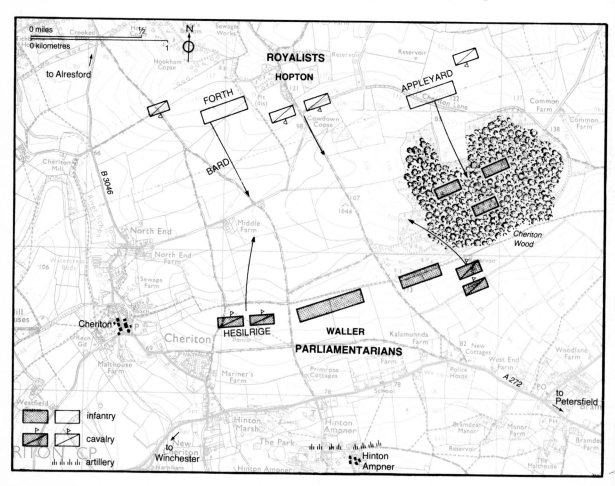

army to dissipate its strength in futile attacks. Their strategy was overturned by a Royalist officer, Sir Henry Bard, who on his own initiative led his regiment forward to attack the Parliamentary horse on the right. Sir Arthur Hesilrige took 300 horse against Bard's troops who were killed or captured to a man. The Royalist cavalry attempted to intervene but their access to the lower ground was via a single narrow lane and at the moment of deployment they were attacked by superior numbers of enemy horse. The fighting now became general and with their cavalry in disarray and their infantry under increasing pressure Hopton and Forth decided to fall back on Alresford before retreating to Basing House.

*Cheriton and Hinton Ampner lie either side of the A272 Petersfield to Winchester road in Hampshire. Cheriton is on the B3046 and the fighting took place east of this road in the valley between Cheriton Wood and the village.*

An Exact and full
# RELATION
OF THE LAST
# FIGHT,
Between the KINGS Forces
and Sir WILLIAM WALLER.

Sent in a Letter from an Officer
in the Army to his friend in *London*.

*Printed to prevent mif-information.*

LONDON
Printed for *Ben. Allen*, in Popes-Head-Alley.
*July* 5; 1 6 4 4.

Printed from a letter written by Thomas Ellis, an officer in Sir Arthur Hesilrige's cavalry regiment serving with Waller's army, this pamphlet presented a Parliamentarian account of the battle of Cropredy Bridge. The letter was circulated to 'prevent mis-information', an important consideration in a war which saw an intensive propaganda effort by both sides.

The battlefield of Cheriton.

153

# CROPREDY BRIDGE 29 June 1644

As the 1644 campaigning season opened the Royalist forces were widely dispersed, attempting to deal with Parliamentarian pressure against Oxford, Bristol, Reading, Lincoln, York and the West Country. Of immediate concern to the King was the safety of the Royalist capital of Oxford and at the beginning of June Charles, at the head of 7500 men, marched through the Cotswolds to Worcester to draw the armies of Sir William Waller and the Earl of Essex away from the city. Waller and Essex duly gave chase but the Royalists successfully evaded the pursuit, returning safely via Oxford to Buckingham. The Parliamentarian commanders divided their forces with Essex marching south to the relief of Lyme Regis while Waller continued operations against the King.

By the end of June Waller had reached Hanwell near Banbury and Charles, learning that his opponent was now advancing without support, decided to attack. Waller's position at Hanwell Castle to the west of the River Cherwell proved too strong for direct assault and on 29 June the Royalists turned northwards towards Daventry, following the east bank of the Cherwell. Waller conformed to this movement, heading north on the west bank along the Banbury–Southam road. Little more than a mile apart the armies were in full view of each other and Waller halted at Great Burton to survey the ground and the enemy.

Immediately to the north-east at the village of Cropredy the Cherwell could be crossed by a bridge carrying a road which linked the Banbury–Southam and Banbury–Daventry roads. A mile ($1\frac{1}{2}$ kilometres) to the south of the village and almost opposite Great Bourton a ford at Slat Mill offered another route across the river. At Cropredy itself the river turned to the north-east in the direction of Edgcote and the Banbury–Daventry road crossed it at Hay's Bridge. If the opportunity arose, there were thus a number of points at which Waller could cross the Cherwell to atttack the Royal army in flank. Mindful of this danger Charles detached a party of dragoons to hold the bridge at Cropredy until the army had passed.

Royalist cavalry scouting to the north reported the approach of 300 Parliamentarian horse on the west bank of the river. The strength of the opposing armies was finely balanced with approximately 5000 Parliamentarian horse and 4000 foot opposed to 5000 Royalist horse and 3500 foot. A reinforcement of even 300 horse could be of great help to Waller, and Charles decided that this late reinforcement must be intercepted and destroyed. The advance guard of Royalist horse was ordered forward to Hays Bridge, while the main body of the army increased speed to support the cavalry. Orders for the rearguard to accelerate its march were not given and a gap of over $1\frac{1}{2}$ miles ($2\frac{1}{2}$ kilometres) quickly opened between the centre and rear divisions of the army. Waller was quick to appreciate his opportunity and gave orders that the Royalist rearguard should be surrounded and destroyed.

Lieutenant-General John Middleton with two regiments of Horse (Hesilrige's and Vandruske's) and nine companies of Foot was sent to block the advance of the rearguard from Cropredy Bridge, while Waller with 1000 troops crossed the river at Slat Mill in the Royalist rear. Middleton took possession of the bridge and deployed on the west bank of the river, his cavalry pursuing the Royalist main body as far as Hays Bridge. Waller had meanwhile been attempting to drive in the

BELOW:
The seige of Oxford in June 1645 painted by Jan de Wyck.

Royalist rearguard, which was fighting back with considerable success. Waller was rapidly losing the initiative as his own forces fell back before mounting Royalist pressure. The Earl of Cleveland's Brigade charged Middleton's infantry and part of his horse driving them back in disorder, while the Earl of Northampton's Brigade pushed Waller's men back across the ford at Slat Mill. Charles had at last halted the Royalist body north of Hays Bridge and he now marched south to the aid of his rearguard. Supported by the King's lifeguards, Cleveland's troopers over-ran the Parliamentarian artillery which was just east of Cropredy Bridge and forced the enemy cavalry back over the river.

Waller's attack had been repulsed at both Cropredy and Slat Mill and leaving detachments of foot and dragoons to guard the river crossings, he withdrew most of his force to Bourton Hill. Charles reached Williamscot at about 3 pm, ordering attacks upon both the bridge and ford while his artillery pounded Waller's lines on Bourton Hill. The Royalists gained a small bridgehead across the ford but a spirited defence by the Tower Hamlets and Kentish regiments denied them the bridge at Cropredy. Both armies maintained their positions until the following day when the King, learning of the approach of 4500 Parliamentarian troops from London, marched west to Evesham. Royalist casualties were light but Waller lost some 700 men including deserters. The morale of his troops plummeted after Cropredy and by the middle of July his army had disintegrated in mutiny and chaos.

*Cropredy Bridge is still a rewarding battlefield to visit although an appreciation of the ground has been complicated by the presence of the Oxford Canal and the bridge which spans it. The Cherwell, for example, was probably much wider before the canal was constructed. The modern bridge stands on the same spot as the bridge of 1644 and a plaque commemorates the battle. A footbridge now spans the river on the site of the ford at Slat Mill and it can be approached along a public footpath to Pewet Farm.*

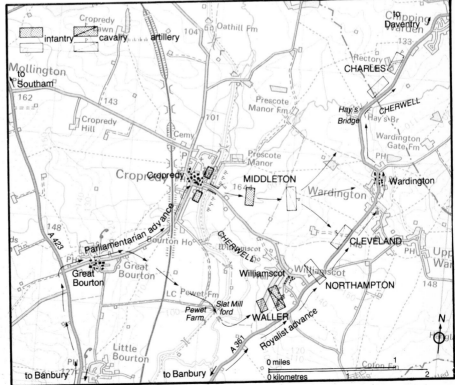

# THE WAR IN THE NORTH 1642–4

The war in the north of England had begun in earnest towards the end of 1642 and it was prosecuted for the King by the 1st Earl of Newcastle and for Parliament by Ferdinando, 2nd Baron Fairfax. Neither man was in the first flush of youth and Newcastle relied heavily upon the talents of a Scots soldier, James King (later Lord Eythin), and Fairfax upon those of his eldest son, Thomas. The strength of Parliament lay in the West Riding of Yorkshire and the fortress of Hull. Newcastle marched south to York with 6000 foot and 2000 horse to resuscitate the local Royalists, who had already suffered minor defeats at the hands of the Fairfaxes. By advancing to Tadcaster, Lord Fairfax over-reached his resources and was obliged to fall back after an inconclusive engagement with Newcastle on 6 December 1642. Newcastle was able to garrison Tadcaster, Pontefract Castle and Newark, thereby splitting the areas controlled by Parliament into isolated pockets, threatening Nottinghamshire and Lincolnshire, and securing a line of communication with the south. Sir Thomas Fairifax responded by capturing Leeds in January 1643, but a Parliamentarian assault on Newark in February was driven off and in March Sir Hugh Cholmley, who held the port of Scarborough for Parliament, changed allegiance to the King.

The Parliamentarian position in the north continued to deteriorate. Fairfax was routed at Seacroft Moor on 30 March and another Parliamentarian attempt on Newark had to be abandoned in May. Just as the Royalist supremacy seemed complete, Fairfax struck back by capturing Wakefield, but his army was broken at Adwalton Moor near Bradford on 30 June 1643 by a vastly superior force under Newcastle. Bradford and Leeds fell and Fairfax was obliged to take refuge in Hull where the Governor had been prevented from declaring for the King by the port's watchful citizens.

Newcastle marched south, taking Gainsborough and Lincoln before laying siege to Hull. Parliament's conduct of the war had reached a critical stage. Devon, Somerset and Dorset (with the exception of garrisons in Plymouth and Lyme) had been lost, Bristol had fallen, Gloucester was under siege, a peace party had formed in the House of Lords, and it was rumoured that the Earl of Ormonde was about to bring Irish troops to the support of the King. Although the Battle of Winceby probably destroyed any notions Newcastle possessed of invading the south, Parliament trembled at the prospect of a joint advance on London with the King. The solution to Parliament's problems in the north appeared to be an alliance with the Scots, and on 25 September 1643 the Solemn League and Covenant was concluded. In return for a monthly subsidy and the preservation of the reformed religion in England and Ireland, the Scots would invade the north in support of Parliament.

On 19 January 1644 a Scottish army of 18,000 foot, 3000 horse, and 500 dragoons crossed the River Tweed into England. The Royalists were now faced with a war on two fronts. While hurrying north to meet the Scots in Northumberland and Durham, the Earl of Newcastle had still to retain his hold on Yorkshire against Parliamentarian forces which could only be encouraged by this latest development. To aid him the Marquess of Montrose, the King's Lieutenant-General for Scotland, launched a small counter-invasion, and the Royalists strove to form a northern army under Lord Byron. Reinforced by five regiments of Irish foot, Byron made some progress in Cheshire but he was soundly beaten by Fairfax at Nantwich on 25 January. Prince Rupert was sent north to restore the situation and he began by relieving Newark in a hard-fought battle on 21 March. Newcastle had some success in holding the Scottish advance but in the middle of April had to fall back to York which was threatened by Fairfax. The Scots joined forces with the Yorkshire Parliamentarians and laid siege to York on 22 April.

# MARSTON MOOR 2 July 1644

Rupert set out to relieve York but marched from Shrewsbury by way of Lancashire in order to collect reinforcements. He received an inexpertly-phrased order from Charles dated 14 June and this he was to use as justification for an attack on the Parliamentarian and Scottish armies in Yorkshire, no matter what the circumstances. Rupert's army had increased to 14,000 men and Newcastle had perhaps 7000 in York, but the Allied army besieging the city totalled approximately 30,000. For a man of Rupert's nature there was now little question but that he must fight. The Prince's army reached Knaresborough 14 miles (22 kilometres) to the west of York on 30 June 1643 and the Parliamentarian forces moved to the north-west of Long Marston to cover their siege works against attack. The next day, however, Lord George Goring led a force of cavalry into

Marston Moor.

157

York and relieved the garrison. Rupert was determined to attack the Allied army but Newcastle and Eythin urged caution, arguing that the Royalists had everything to gain by delay. Sir Robert Clavering was on his way to join Newcastle with fresh troops and there was always the possibility that the enemy grouping of Scots under the Earl of Leven, Fairfax's troops, and the Earl of Manchester's forces, might break up if the Prince waited. The King's order to Rupert quoshed further argument and Marston Moor began to fill with troops as the rival armies assembled for battle.

The Allied army, with something approaching 28,000 men, was an enormous force to find on a Civil War battlefield but its troops were of varying quality. The Scottish army fielded approximately 13,000 infantry and 2000 cavalry, the latter of unproven ability. Fairfax deployed 3000 infantry and 2000 cavalry but his force was a far from homogeneous mix of experienced troops and raw levies from Lancashire. The army of the Eastern Association under the Earl of Manchester had marched north with 4000 infantry and an equal number of cavalry, and the horse under Cromwell were the pick of their troops. Rupert's army was composed of approximately 7000 infantry and 7000 cavalry, with his most experienced mounted troops, the Northern Horse under Goring, amounting to 4000 men. Newcastle's garrison in York consisted of 5000 infantry and perhaps 2000 horse, but not all of this force left the city for the battle.

The two armies deployed in the $1\frac{1}{2}$ miles ($2\frac{1}{2}$ kilometres) of ground between the villages of Tockwith in the west and Long Marston in the east. The Allied army was positioned on the forward slope of a ridge to the south of the Tockwith–Long Marston road, and the ground they occupied rose to a height of 125 feet (38 metres). From the ridge, the battlefield fell away northeastwards for almost a mile ($1\frac{1}{2}$ kilometres), dropping gradually after an initial sharp fall, to a height of 50 feet (15 metres). The Royalist army deployed to the north of the road on flat ground with a ditch line running intermittently along its front. As an obstacle to an Allied advance, the ditch was most formidable on the right between Moor and Atterwith Lanes where Fairfax had deployed his cavalry. Here the ditch encompassed a bank which dropped suddenly at least 6 feet ($1\frac{1}{2}$ metre) onto the moorland and this obstacle may have included a hedge. The ditch continued westwards for 150 yards (137 metres) beyond Moor Lane, again with a parallel but probably broken hedge line dividing the cultivated land running down the ridge from the moorland to the north. There was no natural barrier between the infantry on the left of the Allied centre and the enemy, but the ground by Cromwell's Horse had to be cleared of man-made rabbit warrens and a ditch again protected the enemy front.

The Allied army had begun the day by marching off the moor in the direction of Tadcaster and the Scots in the advance guard were within a mile of the town when they received an urgent order to return. The appearance of the Royalists in strength had prompted Leven to reverse the direction of the armies' march to rejoin the cavalry who were still covering the retirement from the moor. While their infantry were doubling back the Parliamentarian horse were disputing the possession of the tactically important features of the battlefield with the Royalist cavalry. The failure of the Royalist advance guard to gain any part of the ridge or the area on the left of the Allied position left the initiative firmly with the Parliamentarian commanders. Rupert was thrown onto the defensive and he sent musketeers forward to hold the bank–ditch–hedge line while he waited for the approach of Newcastle's troops from York. For the moment the Royalist foot in the centre of the line were deployed very thinly indeed. Newcastle arrived with his Lifeguard and a detachment of foot at some time after 10 am, but the bulk of his infantry had still not left York.

The Allied army deployed hastily as regiments arrived back on the moor with the Horse commanded by Cromwell and David Leslie taking the left flank and that under Fairfax the right. The infantry in the centre was composed of the foot of all three armies, deployed in 14 brigades, with 5 in the first line, 4 in the second and third lines and a single brigade in reserve. The front line of the cavalry on both flanks was stiffened by musketeers and Cromwell received the additional support of two artillery pieces. The Allied deployment was only completed between 2 pm and 3 pm and, perhaps to provide cover for the last anxious moments of assembly, the Parliamentarian artillery began a brief bombardment of the Royalist line at about 2 pm.

The long-awaited infantry from York arrived on the moor between 4 pm and 5 pm and began to deploy as a second line behind the Royalist centre. To their rear stood a body of cavalry under Sir William Blakiston with a further reserve under Rupert. The right of the Royalist line was taken by Lord Byron with 3000 horse and 500 foot under Colonel Thomas Napier, who used the ditch on this flank for much needed protection. Byron's wing faced the full might of the Eastern

Association's cavalry plus the Scots under Leslie, a total of over 5000 horse. Lord Goring commanded the Royalist left, which consisted predominantly of the Northern Horse, also supported by musketeers, and Sir Richard Dacre's cavalry brigade. With the completion of the Royalist deployment so late in the day Rupert appears to have concluded that there was insufficient time for further fighting before darkness fell. Preparations began for the issue of rations and a noticeable relaxation spread through the Royalist army.

At this moment the Allied army advanced down the slope at a running march as a rainstorm swept across the moor. This can hardly have helped the Royalist musketeers lining the ditch who were hurriedly preparing to receive a mass of charging infantry. The leading Parliamentarian troops in the centre were subjected to a brief burst of musketry before they crossed the ob-

stacles before them and attacked the Royalist foot. On the left the Parliamentarian dragoons cleared most of the ditch and hedges of enemy musketeers. Cromwell's horse moved forward with little difficulty to meet Byron's cavalry which had advanced and masked the fire of many of their own infantry. After a shot mêlée, during which Cromwell was wounded, Byron's first line of horse turned and fled. On the Parliamentarian right, Fairfax's troops had found the going extremely difficult and their attack was broken by Goring's horse and musketeers. Many of the Parliamentarian cavalry left the field and a good proportion of Goring's men followed in pursuit.

Rupert led his reserve against Cromwell in an attempt to stabilize the Royalist right, but after a hard struggle his troopers made off in the direction of York. In the centre the Royalist cavalry met with more success

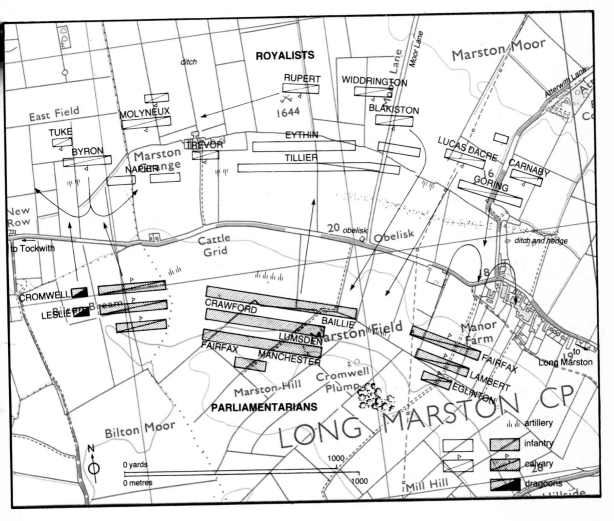

LEFT:
Marston Moor looking
south-east towards the
Parliamentarian position
and the clutch of trees
known as Cromwell's
Plump, reputedly the
spot on which the allied
commanders debated
their tactics before the
battle.

RIGHT:
A nineteenth-century
impression of the battle
of Marston Moor by
James Ward.

and a charge by Newcastle with a body of gentlemen volunteers, supported by Blakiston's cavalry, tore through the Allied infantry as far as the summit of the ridge. Sir Charles Lucas also charged the right flank of the Royalist infantry but his action was not co-ordinated with Newcastle's advance, and although many of the enemy regiments panicked, with a proportion of their men fleeing the field, the Royalist cavalry had ultimately to fall back. The ranks of both armies had by now been considerably reduced by desertion as well as casualties, and there were few Royalist horse left to meet the charge which Cromwell delivered against the enemy foot. The remainder of Goring's Horse were scattered and resistance now centred on Newcastle's infantry (amongst which was a regiment of the famous 'Whitecoats') and a brigade of 'Greencoats'. The musketeers and pikemen of the Whitecoats, protected to some extent by an enclosure they had occupied, held out against the Parliamentarian Horse and dragoons for almost an hour, until in the words of one contemporary, Colonel James Somerville, 'when all their ammunition was spent, having refused quarter, every man fell in the same order and rank wherein he had fought'. The battle was over and Rupert and Newcastle, pausing to draw breath in York, argued over the responsibility for the defeat. Rupert rode northwards with the remains of his cavalry to Richmond while Newcastle took ship to Germany and exile.

In the region of 6000 men were killed or mortally wounded during the battle and pursuit. The loss of life was particularly serious for the Royalists, since the death toll included a high proportion of their most experienced officers and soldiers. Newcastle's veteran infantry was finished as a fighting force and the Royalist grip on the north had been broken. York quickly surrendered and the Royalist threat in Northumberland, Durham and Yorkshire was reduced to a scattering of beleaguered garrisons.

*The battlefield is approximately 6 miles (10 kilometres) to the west of York alongside the B1224 and between the villages of Tockwith and Long Marston. One mile along the road from Long Marston to Tockwith an obelisk erected by the Cromwell Association commemorates the battlesite. Moor Lane, still little more than a rough track, leads from the monument along the route taken by Fairfax's Horse on the left flank.*

# LOSTWITHIEL 31 August 1644

In the early summer of 1644 the Earl of Essex marched into the West Country to relieve the Parliamentary garrison of Lyme. In so doing he eased the pressure on the King and his Oxford army, and by his own determination to advance into Cornwall placed the Parliamentary forces in the West in a potentially disastrous situation. On 10 June the King blunted Waller's enthusiasm at Cropredy Bridge and then marched west after Essex. The Parliamentarian advance met with some success; Weymouth and Melcombe Regis were occupied and the Royalist force under Sir Richard Grenville abandoned its siege of Plymouth. On entering Cornwall, however, Essex found himself in a county that was almost completely hostile. On 2 August Essex heard that Charles's army was within 20 miles (32 kilometres) of his own position at Bodmin. His only hope of reprovisioning depended upon the Parliamentarian fleet and he ordered his army to Losthwithiel to maintain his communications by means of the small port of Fowey. Detachments for garrison duty had reduced Essex's strength to about 10,000 men and the King was now closing from the east with 14,000 and Sir Richard Grenville from the west with 2400.

Essex deployed his troops in Fowey and on Beacon Hill to the east of Lostwithiel. The Royalist cordon closed inexorably on the Parliamentarian troops who were trapped with their backs to the sea. On 21 August a general Royalist advance swept over Beacon Hill and the approaches to Lostwithiel, penning Essex into a perimeter 5 miles (8 kilometres) deep and 2 miles (3 kilometres) wide. However, in the early hours of 31 August 2000 Parliamentarian Horse broke out and reached Plymouth with few casualties while the main body of Essex's force fell back on Fowey. Charles quickly followed up this withdrawal and a hectic struggle ranged from field to field as Essex's troops fought to stabilize their front. As night fell the Parliamentarians still held the earthworks of Castle Dore but their morale had taken a fatal beating during the day and men began to slip away from their regiments. The Earl of Essex took ship to Plymouth and Philip Skippon, upon whom the burden of the defence had rested for some days, accepted the decision of a council of war to surrender. On 2 September 1644, 6000 Parliamentarian troops marched off under escort to Portsmouth, suffering greatly from the plundering attacks of the local population. The invasion ended in signal defeat for Parliament's most experienced army.

Restormel Castle's *c.* 1100 wooden defences were replaced by stone fortifications *c.* 1200.

Lostwithiel lies on the A390 between Liskeard and St Austell. The B3269 leads south from Lostwithiel to Fowey and Castle Dore stands on this road. To the north of Lostwithiel, Restormel Castle, which was captured by Grenville is worthy of a visit, and Beacon Hill can be traversed by leaving the A390 approximately 1000 yards (914 metres) east of Lostwithiel.

# SECOND BATTLE OF NEWBURY 27 October 164

After his successful campaign in the West Country the King's plans centred upon the relief of the besieged garrisons of Banbury Castle, Basing House and Donnington Castle. Parliament, however, feared a grander design, believing that Charles was intent upon marching on London. The armies of the Earl of Manchester and Sir William Waller, and the remnants of Essex's army, were in the field to oppose the King but they were widely dispersed. Manchester was at Reading, Waller at Shaftesbury and Essex at Portsmouth. If London was to be secured and Parliament's armies avoid defeat in detail a rapid concentration was necessary. By 20 October all three armies were in touch around Basingstoke, and with a combined strength of 19,000 men they presented an apparently formidable challenge to the 10,000 strong royal army.

Charles was unable to relieve Basing House and therefore marched north to the aid of Donnington Castle, reaching Newbury on 22 October. By the 25th the patrols of the opposing armies were in contact between Newbury and Thatcham, and Charles, leaving a garrison in Newbury, took up a strong position just to the north of the town. The Royalist right flank was protected by the River Kennet and its left by the River Lambourn and Donnington Castle. The Royalist centre rested upon the strongpoints of Speen village and Shaw House. Although weak in numbers, Charles's army was a veteran one, having detachments of both horse and foot from Prince Maurice's Western Army to support the Oxford troops. Lord Goring commanded the horse, Lord Astley the foot, and Lord Hopton a formidable artillery train of twenty-nine guns.

The numerical strength of the Parliamentarian armies was undermined by a command structure which fostered strategic confusion and poor battlefield control. Although the three armies had joined forces, no single commander had been appointed and authority was vested in a council composed of Manchester, Essex, Waller, other officers and a sprinkling of civilians. The effectiveness of the council was further reduced by the early departure of Essex to a sick bed in Reading. After a day of patrol activity and a desultory artillery duel, the council decided that the Royalist position was too strong to be taken by a direct assault from the east. Orders were issued for a divided attack to be launched simultaneously from the west and east, striking the Royalists in front and rear. Waller was detailed to take a force of 12,000 men on a flank march of some 13 miles (20 kilometres) via Hermitage, Chievely, North Heath, Winterbourne, Boxford and Wickham Heath. Manchester, who had been assigned the task of occupying the Royalist's attention from Round Hill, would attack with 7000 men when he heard Waller's guns open fire on Speen. If the enemy learned of this strategem while Waller was still on the march, Manchester could face some very hard fighting indeed.

The cuirassiers were fully armoured with the exception of the leg below the knee and the rear of the thigh.

Donnington Castle, a Royalist stronghold throughout the War, stands to the north of the battlefield.

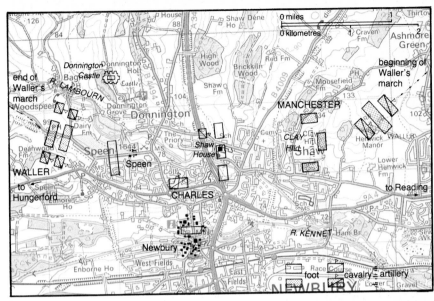

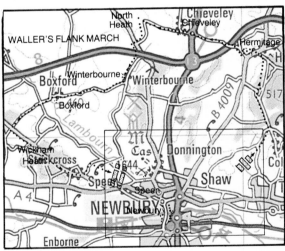

Late in the evening of 26 October the outflanking force, which included Waller's and Cromwell's Horse, Essex's army and a brigade of the London Trained Bands, set out northwards, bivouacking briefly at North Heath before resuming its march in the early hours of 27 October. The Parliamentarians clashed with a Royalist force at Boxford and were spotted by the garrison of Donnington Castle, but word of their progress does not seem to have reached Charles. This may have been due to the diversionary attacks launched by Manchester whose troops, perhaps overawed by the implications of failing in their task, became heavily embroiled in an assault across the Lambourn. Waller mounted his attack on Speen at about 3 pm with Skippon's infantry in the centre, Balfour's Horse on the right and Cromwell's Horse on the left. The Royalists were taken by surprise and though they defeated the initial attack a second assault drove them out of Speen village. The situation on the left was now critical and a charge by Balfour's troopers dispersed Maurice's supporting cavalry. Prompt action by Goring and the Queen's Regiment halted Balfour, and when Cromwell belatedly attempted to intervene he was driven back in disorder.

With dusk rapidly approaching it was essential for Manchester's troops to act quickly but they only appear to have realized that Waller had launched his attack at about 4 pm. Two columns then advanced down Clay Hill against Shaw House and Shaw village but were repulsed in hard fighting. Night fell with both Royalist and Parliamentarian believing that the day had gone against them. The latter had failed to take advantage of their overwhelming superiority in numbers, and Charles, realizing that his own troops would be hard pressed to hold their positions next day, ordered a retreat to Oxford.

*Although the battlefield is to a large extent obscured by the buildings of Speen and Newbury, the ruins of Donnington Castle still stand and Shaw House is now a school. The castle can be reached via the A34 Oxford road and it provides by far the best viewpoint for the battlefield.*

# A NASEBY 14 June 1645
# B LANGPORT 10 July 1645

## NASEBY

In the third week of May 1645 the New Model Army commanded by Sir Thomas Fairfax arrived before Oxford and proceeded to invest the city. It was a duty that was not to Sir Thomas's liking, for it tied his army to a static role and to a siege which he believed held out little hope of success. The Royalists, however, were far from certain that Oxford was sufficiently well provisioned to maintain a prolonged defence and they decided to draw Fairfax away by threatening cities held for Parliament. Accordingly on 30 May a Royalist force stormed and sacked Leicester, which was garrisoned by Parliamentarian troops under Sir Robert Pye. Ordered to recover Leicester, Fairfax raised the siege of Oxford on 5 June and marched to Newport Pagnell. The King, unwilling to begin a campaign in the north of England until Oxford was secure, kept his army around Daventry, and Fairfax now moved rapidly against him. By 12 June the New Model had reached Kislingbury 8 miles (13 kilometres) to the east of Daventry, and its cavalry patrols drove in the unsuspecting royal outposts. The confusion caused by Fairfax's sudden appearance did not prevent the royal army from standing to arms in a strong position on Burrow Hill, but the King decided upon a retreat towards Market Harborough and the Royalist garrison of Newark. Fairfax lost little time in resuming his pursuit. By the evening of 13 June his main force was at Gainsborough and his scouts had already entered Naseby, much to the discomfort of a Royalist patrol taking refreshment at the village inn. Awakened with this alarming news, the King called a council of war in the early hours of 14 June and the decision was taken to stand and fight on the high ground 2 miles (3 kilometres) to the south of Market Harborough.

Both armies were on the move early and Prince Rupert had deployed the Royal army along the East Farndon–Oxendon ridge well before 8 am. He was now in a position to block any Parliamentarian advance towards Market Harborough. The New Model had concentrated on Naseby by 5 am but Fairfax, unwilling to risk blundering into the royal army in the early morning mist, had halted to await firm news of the enemy's movements. Fairfax and Cromwell went forward to reconnoitre the ground towards Clipston at about the same time that Prince Rupert, disbelieving the report of his Scoutmaster-General that there were no Parliamentarian troops within 4 miles (6 kilometres) of

the Royalist position, rode towards Naseby to find the enemy for himself. Fairfax contemplated deploying one mile (1½ kilometres) to the south of Clipston where his front would be protected by a stream and boggy ground, but Cromwell argued that Rupert would realize that an attack in this direction could place his cavalry at a disadvantage, and would therefore refuse action or swing round the Parliamentarian flank onto firmer ground. Fairfax agreed to fall back to the Naseby ridge, where Rupert's cavalry would have to charge uphill to reach the Parliamentary line. During his reconnaissance Rupert observed Fairfax and Cromwell withdraw towards Naseby with their escort and he ordered his army to swing right towards Dust Hill from where he hoped to flank Fairfax's position. Seeing this movement, the New Model began moving to its left and by 9 am the armies were marching westwards on a parallel course. As they drew abreast of the open valley now known as Broadmoor they halted and deployed.

Fairfax, now preparing the New Model for its first major battle, had approximately 13,500 men composed of 6000 infantry, 6500 cavalry and 1000 dragoons. The infantry were deployed in two lines with a 'forlorn hope' of musketeers in front of the first line and a reserve from Harley's Regiment behind the second. From left to right the first line of foot consisted of Skippon's, Hardress Waller's, Pickering's, Montague's and Fairfax's Regiments, and the second line of Hartley's (commanded by Lieutenant-Colonel Thomas Pride), Hammond's and Rainsborough's Regiments. The cavalry were drawn up on either flank, Ireton commanding the left wing composed of 11 squadrons, and Cromwell the slightly stronger right with about 3500 troopers in 13 squadrons. The first line of the left wing was formed by the regiments of Butler, Vermuyden, and Ireton, and the second line by the regiments of Rich and Fleetwood and the Eastern Association Horse. On the right the first line of cavalry consisted of Whalley's, part of Pye's and Cromwell's own regiment, the second line of Sheffield's, the remainder of Pye's, and part of Fiennes's Regiment, and the third of the Associated Horse and the remainder of Fiennes's. Rossiter's Regiment, 400 strong, which arrived on the field as the battle was starting, deployed to the right rear of the first line and on the right of the third line. At the last moment Colonel Okey's dragoons were ordered to line part of Sulby Hedges from where they would be able to enfilade the right of the Royalist line. Fairfax's artillery

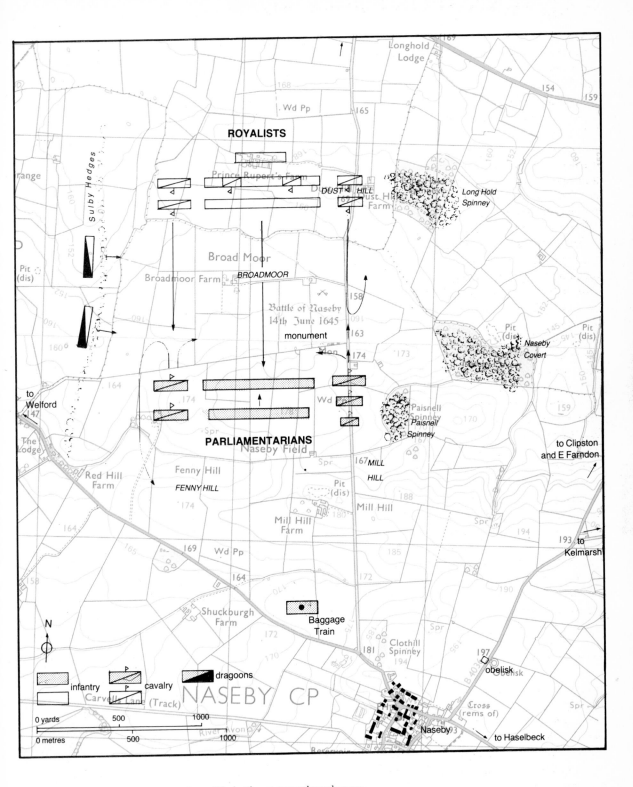

The battle of Naseby. Contemporary versions of the battle appear on the endpapers.

commanded by Lieutenant-General Hammond was positioned between the infantry regiments of the first and second lines with a total, as depicted in contemporary engravings, of eleven guns on the battlefield and three in the baggage park.

A contemporary line engraving of the battle of Naseby.

Across the moor the Royal army numbered around 9000 men with approximately 4500 infantry and an almost equal number of cavalry. The foot, commanded by Lord Astley, were deployed in three brigades under, from left to right, Sir George Lisle, Sir Henry Bard and Sir Bernard Astley. They were supported by the 900 troopers of Colonel Howard's Horse and a reserve of 1300 men formed by the King's Lifeguard and Prince Rupert's Regiment. The main body of the cavalry was deployed on the flanks with 2000 horse under Rupert on the right wing and 1600 under Sir Marmaduke Langdale on the left. The Royalist artillery comprised twelve cannon deployed in pairs between the regiments and two mortars. The army was an experienced one

with a high proportion of officers and the King himself at its head, but it was seriously outnumbered.

At the final stage of his deployment Fairfax withdrew his line one hundred paces with the result that most of his troops were hidden from view by the crest of the ridge. Apart from broken ground to the right of the Parliamentarian position and some marshy ground on the left the battlefield was favourable for cavalry and perhaps for this reason the outnumbered Royalists took the initiative. At 10 am the royal army began a general attack, advancing slowly across the half mile of moorland which separated them from the New Model. As they approached Fairfax moved his line forwards over the crest of the ridge but both Ireton's and Rupert's squadrons halted for a few moments within a short distance of each other. Rupert obviously succeeded in keeping his cavalry in check for Astley's infantry appear to have been the first Royalist troops to join action.

As Rupert's cavalry charged home on the left, Ireton's squadrons were already in confusion for while some advanced to meet the Royalist horse others stood fast. When Rupert's second line joined the mêlée the Roundhead cavalry on the extreme left broke and were swept from the field. The Royalists pursued them until they came upon the Parliamentarian baggage train to the west of Naseby. A vain attempt was made to overcome the baggage guard and nearly an hour passed before Rupert was able to rally his troopers and lead them back to the battle. In the meantime Ireton had led his remaining squadrons against the right flank of the Royalist foot in an attempt to aid Skippon's infantry who were being steadily pushed back. The Roundhead charge did little to ease this pressure, for Ireton was wounded and taken prisoner and his squadrons repulsed. It was only after Fairfax and Skippon had brought the reserve to the support of the Parliamentarian centre that greatly superior numbers began to tell against the Royalist pikes and muskets.

On the Parliamentarian right Cromwell had calmly watched the advance of Langdale's Northern Horse before leading his squadrons in a spirited but controlled charge which broke the outnumbered Royalist horse. As they streamed to the rear pursued by Cromwell's foremost squadrons, the remaining Parliamentarian cavalry – both Cromwell on the right and Okey's dragoons on the left – charged the flanks of the Royalist foot. It was too much even for such veteran infantry who now abandoned by their own cavalry and by their King were ridden down and forced to surrender. The

Parliamentarian victory was complete and Rupert's return at last with his blown squadrons could not retrieve the position.

Parliament lost less than 200 men on the field at Naseby, whereas Royalist losses totalled nearly 1000 killed and 4500 captured. It was a battle with a most definite result. King Charles had lost his infantry, his baggage train, his artillery, his private papers and effectively his throne.

*Naseby is a rewarding battlefield to visit for in its essentials it has changed little since the seventeenth century. A good view is obtained by following the Naseby–Sibbertoft road (which runs almost parallel with the B4036) and the monument erected by the Cromwell Association marks the approximate position of Cromwell's squadrons at the start of the battle. The Naseby obelisk, placed in 1825, is a good mile (1½ kilometres) from the scene of the action.*

## LANGPORT

At Naseby the New Model had served notice that Parliament at last had an army which could win the war. If the King was to avoid defeat he must concentrate his forces against the New Model and destroy it. Charles arrived at Hereford on 19 June and was able to muster 4000 cavalry and approximately 3000 infantry, the latter of indifferent quality. To the north of the King, Royalist troops under Lord Byron were attempting to hold their own at Chester, while to the south-west Lord Goring was trying to fight his way into Taunton. If Charles could combine with Goring he would have an army of a size, if not quality, superior to that he had lost at Naseby.

Taunton was held for Parliament by Colonel Robert Blake and Fairfax was ordered to march to his relief. As Royalist garrisons at Bristol, Bath and Devizes blocked Fairfax's most direct route from the Midlands, he advanced southwards using south-coast ports for re-provisioning. By 4 July the New Model were nearing Crewkerne, and Goring withdrew his forces from Taunton and fell back to the line of the River Yeo between Yeovil and Langport. Fairfax, now reinforced by Weldon's Brigade from Taunton and by the 4000 men under General Massey, turned Goring's line by capturing Yeovil. The Royalists regrouped at Langport and Goring dispatched three brigades of cavalry under George Porter south-westwards, in the hope of convincing Fairfax that Taunton was again threatened. Goring calculated that Fairfax would split his forces, thereby reducing the numerical disparity between the two armies to manageable proportions. Fairfax despatched 5500 Horse in pursuit of Porter who was intercepted and defeated near Ilminster. On 10 July Goring began to withdraw in the direction of Bridgwater. To allow his baggage and artillery trains to cover the 12 miles (19 kilometres) to Bridgwater, Goring prepared to fight a delaying action from high ground to the east of Langport. He could oppose roughly 7000 men to Fairfax's 10,000.

Goring's position was fronted by a brook known as the Wagg Rhyne and by a good deal of marshy ground. The Langport–Somerton road crossed the brook at a ford before ascending the hill in the centre of the Royalist line. The road and surrounding fields were bordered by hedges which Goring lined with his musketeers, and he sited two guns to cover the ford, with cavalry in support. It was an apparently strong position and the nature of the ground offered Fairfax little alternative but a frontal attack along the road. After a Parliamentarian battery had silenced the Royalist guns, 1500 musketeers were sent forward to clear the hedges surrounding the ford. As the Royalist infantry fell back, three troops of Cromwell's Horse commanded by Major Bethell charged across the ford and up the slopes beyond. The first two ranks of Royalist horse broke before this charge but Goring's remaining cavalry massed against Bethell and began to push him back. At this critical moment three troops from Fairfax's Regiment struck Goring's cavalry in flank and the Parliamentarian foot began to arrive on the hill. Goring's army brok and fled, and although only 300 Royalists were killed many more were captured or deserted. After garrisoning Bridgwater, Goring retreated into Devon with the remnants of the Western Army.

*Langport stands at the junction of the A372 and the A378 between Taunton and Somerton. The battlefield lies approximately 1000 yards (914 metres) to the east of the town on the B3153 to Somerton.*

# THE SECOND CIVIL WAR:

# PRESTON 17/18 August 1648

After the collapse of Goring's army at Langport, the Royalist strongholds in the West Country, including Bristol, fell to the assaults of Fairfax's and Cromwell's troops. The majority of Royalist commanders realised that the war could not be continued, and Rupert urged the King to secure what he could by making peace with Parliament. Charles still believed that it was his duty to fight on and he planned to march to Scotland to join forces with Montrose. The defeat of the latter at Philiphaugh and the rout of Charles's cavalry near Chester overthrew this strategy. Amid increasing acrimony with Rupert, the King returned via Newark to Oxford. On 12 March 1646 the remains of Hopton's troops in the west surrendered to Fairfax, and nine days later Charles's last field force was scattered at Stow-on-the-Wold. On 5 May Charles surrendered himself to the Scots army besieging Newark and his remaining garrisons capitulated under assault; the last being Harlech, which fell on 13 March 1647. Though the King was now a captive, his son and many of his principal supporters had escaped to Europe.

Charles had hoped to be able to exploit the differences between the Scots and Parliament to the extent of gaining military support from the former. The cost of such support was the adoption of Presbyterianism in England and to this Charles would not at first agree. Parliament secured the person of the king by paying off the Scots for their participation in the war, and opened negotiations with Charles for the restoration of his throne. Encouraged by dissension within the Parliamentary cause, as Presbyterians clashed with Independents and the New Model Army refused to disband or serve in Ireland until its arrears of pay were forwarded, the King prevaricated and re-opened negotiations with the Scots. In November 1647 Charles escaped to Carisbrooke Castle on the Isle of Wight and from there he signed an 'Engagement' with the Scots on 26 December. In return for a three-year trial period of Presbyterianism in England the Scots agreed to help Charles regain his kingdom. The prospect of the King once more in arms reunited the factious elements of the Parliamentarian camp and the New Model returned to duty.

During April and May 1648 the military situation facing Parliament gave considerable cause for concern. Revolts on behalf of the King had occurred in South Wales, Kent and Essex, and ships of the navy had mutinied. Luckily, Fairfax was able to deal with these threats in turn and he was supported by a strong framework of Parliamentarian garrisons in north Wales, the Midlands and the north of England. While Cromwell supervised the campaign in Wales, Fairfax fought his way into Maidstone and besieged Colchester. On 8 July a Scottish army of 6000 infantry and 3000 cavalry under the command of the Duke of Hamilton crossed the border. Three days later Cromwell was able to switch his army from Wales to the north to support the 3500 troops under John Lambert who had been charged with delaying the Scottish advance. This was a timely move, for although Lambert had been joined by 2700 Lancashire troops under Ralph Assheton, Hamilton too had been reinforced by 7000 more Scots and the 3500 men of Sir Marmaduke Langdale.

Lambert evacuated Penrith on 14 July, falling back into Yorkshire in the expectation that the Scots would advance down the eastern side of the Pennines. Hamilton chose instead to march via the western route through Lancashire, and Lambert lost touch with the enemy. Cromwell and Lambert met at Wetherby on 12 August before marching on Preston, in the hope of cutting across the Scottish line of advance or of taking it in flank. Because of the heavy rain and the daily need to forage, Hamilton's column of march became overextended as the Scots pushed southwards. When Cromwell's troops made contact with Langdale's rearguard on 16 August, the Scottish infantry had barely reached Preston, while their horse were 16 miles (26 kilometres) further south at Wigan and their artillery was still far to the north.

Langdale warned Hamilton of the danger threatening the army's eastern flank, but the Duke dismissed the Parliamentarian presence as a mere reconnaissance in force. On 17 August Langdale's Regiments stood to arms at dawn and fell back to within 2 miles (3 kilometres) of Preston on the lane from Longridge. Sir Marmaduke posted his musketeers and pikemen in the enclosures on the west of Ribbleton Moor where the hedges and soft boggy ground made it difficult for the opposition to manoeuvre. It was not until 4 pm that the Parliamentarian regiments were finally deployed. When attacked the Royalists stood their ground well, and a fierce struggle ensued from hedge to hedge. As Langdale's troops were gradually pushed clear of the enclosures, Cromwell's Horse cut into the flanks and the withdrawal developed into a rout. While Langdale's men fell or were captured the Scottish foot continued south-

The battle of Preston painted by Charles Cattermole (1800–68).

wards over Preston Bridge, putting the Ribble between themselves and the pursuing Parliamentarians. Once Cromwell had cleared Preston of Royalists his men stormed the Bridge, driving in the defending Scottish brigades. The next bridge to fall was that crossing the Darwen, but by then it was already dark and fighting petered out.

Hamilton's army had escaped, though 5000 Royalists had been killed or captured in the process. During the night the Scottish infantry attempted to link up with their cavalry which was now returning to Preston, but as the two bodies were moving southwards and northwards respectively on different roads, the first troops encountered by the horse were Cromwell's victorious Parliamentarians. After a running fight along the Standish road, the Scottish cavalry were at last reunited with their infantry on Wigan Moor. With his army disintegrating around him, Hamilton rode off with the horse leaving the foot to surrender at Warrington. The fragments of the Scottish army still at large were hunted down by Lambert and the local Parliamentarian commanders, and Hamilton was captured at Uttoxeter. Cromwell carried the pursuit into Scotland and with the Royalist surrender at Colchester on 28 August the Second Civil War was over.

*The site of the fighting on Ribbleton Moor is now within Ministry of Defence property and thus is a prohibited area to the public. The original Walton bridge no longer stands and the new bridge is approximately 50 yards (46 metres) upstream. The Darwen bridge has also been replaced although the present bridge stands more or less exactly on the site of the old structure.*

# THE THIRD CIVIL WAR:
# DUNBAR 4 September 1650

With the execution of Charles I on 30 January 1649, monarchy in England was abolished. The Scots, however, were willing to accept Prince Charles as Charles II on condition that he accepted the Solemn League and Covenant. Charles landed in Scotland at the end of June 1650 and was proclaimed King in July. To Parliament it now seemed only a question of time before a Scottish army once again invaded England and it was decided that the New Model should mount its own invasion of Scotland to preempt Charles. A proportion of the New Model was still serving in Ireland, and the demands of garrisoning England against Royalist risings meant that some new regiments had to be raised. In July 1650

Cromwell marched north with 5000 horse and 10,000 foot, the vast majority of them veterans.

After re-provisioning at Dunbar Cromwell made contact with a Scottish army in excess of 20,000 men under David Leslie on 29 July. The Scots were deployed in an exceptionally strong position between Edinburgh and Leith, and in appalling weather conditions the New Model retreated to Musselburgh and then to Dunbar. It was a fighting withdrawal, for the Scots harried the rearguard and attacked the army's quarters at Musselburgh. Already between 4000 and 5000 of Cromwell's troops were sick, and it was imperative that he bring about a battle before his army wasted away. Cromwell

The battle of Dunbar.

again advanced and attempted to turn the right flank of the Scots position but Leslie was equal to this manoeuvre and the New Model returned to Dunbar on 1 September. The Scottish army now advanced and deployed on a strong position on Doon Hill, effectively cutting the land route to England. Cromwell would have to evacuate his army by the sea or fight his way out of encirclement. Equally, Leslie would have to attack if he was not to see his prey slip away on board the English fleet.

The Scots' deployment extended inland from the coast for over 3000 yards (2,740 metres) with the majority of their troops positioned on the forward slope of Doon Hill, between the summit and the Brox burn. After reconnoitring the Scots position, Cromwell and Lambert judged it to be vulnerable, and a council of war held on the night of 2/3 September approved orders for

an assault early the next morning. Between 5 am and 6 am Lambert with six regiments of horse and Monck with just over three regiments of foot charged and surprised the Scottish right. The Scots nevertheless defended fiercely until the arrival of Cromwell with a reserve of horse and foot, which cut through the enemy right and began to roll up their line. The centre and left of Leslie's army disintegrated in surrender or flight and the Horse of the New Model set off in pursuit. With 3000 Scots killed and over 10,000 captured Leslie's army had been almost wiped out.

*The battlefield lies just to the south of Dunbar and can be approached via the A1 road, which cuts along the Lammermuir Hills as they run down to the coast.*

ABOVE:
General George Monck, later Duke of Albemarle. A professional soldier, Monck fought for Charles during the First Civil War, then served Parliament until 1660, and in that year was instrumental in the restoration of the Stuart monarchy.

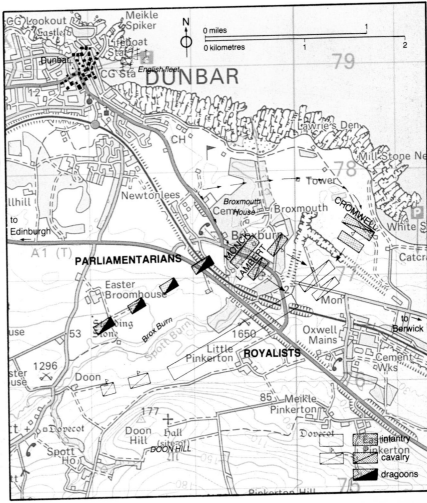

# WORCESTER 3 September 1651

After the battle of Dunbar Cromwell pursued Leslie and the remains of his army to Stirling, but the Parliamentarian forces were not strong enough to risk an assault on the town's fortifications. Cromwell withdrew to Edinburgh and for the next eight months the Scots and the English, both too weak to risk a decisive battle, skirmished with each other and the weather. By June 1651 both sides had been reinforced, and Charles II's army was now an irascible blend of his Scots and English supporters. Cromwell's attempts to force David Leslie, whose army now numbered 21,000, to accept battle failed and the Parliamentarian commander proceeded to cut the Scots supply line north of Stirling. Leslie now had little alternative but to fight or march south into England, and in the first week of August 1651 the Royalist army crossed the border. Charles was intent on an advance by the western route, with

London as his ultimate goal. After completing the capture of Perth Cromwell set off in pursuit, sending Lambert ahead with five regiments of Horse to join the troops of Colonel Rich and Major-General Harrison in the border country.

Although Charles pushed steadily southwards the counties failed to rise in his support as he had hoped and his army was constantly harried by Lambert and Harrison. By the time he reached Worcester on 22 August his dispirited and exhausted army of 16,000 men was facing a combination of 28,000 Parliamentarian troops under Cromwell. On 28 August Lambert seized Upton Bridge, enabling Cromwell to advance on both banks of the River Severn. The Parliamentarian forces proceeded to invest Worcester and Charles withdrew behind the River Teme. Cromwell planned to force a crossing of the Teme and launch an attack on the

Huych Allaerdt Exc.

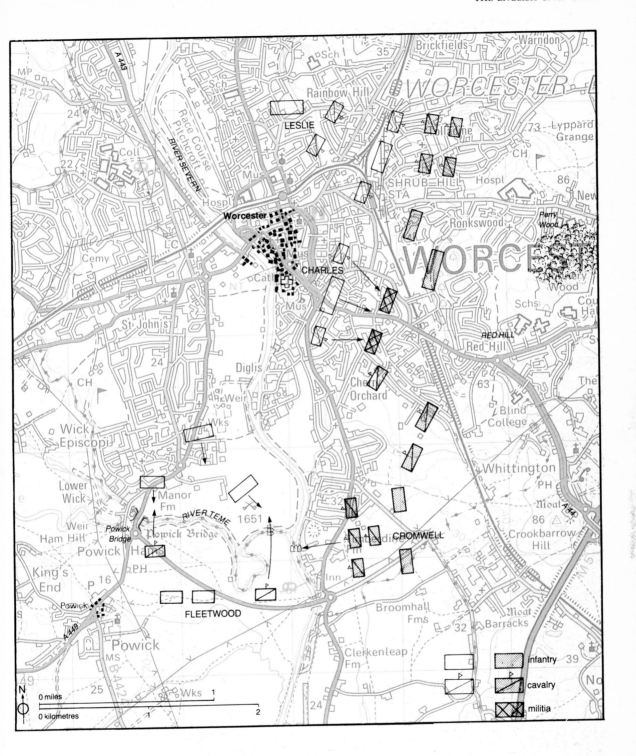

LEFT:
Charles II (rear right) is crowned by the Marquess of Argyll at Scone
in 1651. On the left the King is prepared for battle, with Scotland
presenting a pistol, and Ireland adjusting his armour.

The battle of Worcester 1651. A mezzotint by W. Giller after T. Woodward, published by E. T. Boys in 1844.

city from the west, while a force under his own command attacked from the east. Communication between the two was to be maintained via a bridge of boats constructed acrosss the Severn below its junction with the Teme and across the Teme itself jut to the west.

On 3 September Charles Fleetwood led a Parliamentarian force across the Teme by the bridge of boats and by the ford near the destroyed Powick Bridge. His men met considerable resistance and Cromwell brought four regiments of horse and two of foot from the east bank to Fleetwood's support. While Cromwell was thus occupied, Charles led an attack against the Parliamentarian deployment on the east bank. After some initial success against the Cheshire and Essex militia, the Royalist horse was broken by Cromwell's regulars. Abandoned by their cavalry the Royal infantry surrendered and Charles fled, making his way eventually to France. The process of attrition which had begun at Marston Moor and Naseby and been continued at Preston and Dunbar was over. Stuart military power in Britain had been unequivocally crushed.

*A great deal of the area of the battle is now obscured by subsequent building but a good general view can be obtained from the tower of Worcester Cathedral. A visit to Powick Church is also worthwhile, for marks of musket balls can still be seen on its tower.*

The city of Worcester and the River Severn.

# WARFARE IN
# THE AGE OF REASON
## 1660–1746

The settlement of 1660 which restored Charles II to the throne fell short of providing a durable framework for either the English Constitution or the Church. Both the King and his subjects believed that a return to the position before the outbreak of the Civil Wars would restore the nation to an orderly style of life and government. These hopes were to prove a delusion, for the constitutional questions which had given rise to the Civil Wars could not be erased from the nation's history or conveniently ignored by the generation that had lived through them. The armed struggle of Cavalier and Roundhead became the factional struggle of Tory and Whig in Parliament.

While Charles II possessed the skill to manipulate the chaos of sectional politics to his own advantage, his brother, who succeeded as James II in 1685, contrived through his obdurate support of Catholicism to manoeuvre himself into political isolation and exile within the space of three years. His short reign witnessed a 'Protestant' rebellion by the Duke of Monmouth, Charles II's illegitimate son, and in 1688 the 'Glorious Revolution', which dispensed with the Stuart Dynasty in favour of the Dutch king, William of Orange. A flurry of military activity by James's supporters in Scotland, who took the name Jacobites from *Jacobus*, the Latin form of his name, failed to disturb this new settlement; but the ground had been prepared for a series of rebellions against the throne which were to extend into the middle of the eighteenth century. Although Britain at last found a solution to her dynastic problems in the House of Hanover and George I, the Hanoverian settlement was to be challenged on three occasions by Jacobite armies.

The army which defended the throne in the late seventeenth and early eighteenth centuries was insignificant in terms of numbers but of great significance in terms of the Constitutional settlement. During the Civil War Parliament had defeated the Crown using a regular, disciplined army, and during the Commonwealth the nation witnessed the threat it could pose to the liberty of the individual. At the Restoration this army had been disbanded and although Parliament had not declared a standing army in time of peace illegal, equally it had not provided for its maintenance. But, assuming that the necessary question of finance could be solved, Charles II and James II could raise troops as and when required and employ them without Parliament's consent. For Charles the question of finance was always decisive, and upon his accession James found an English army numbering 8865 men, of whom 7472 were available as marching regiments and 1393 as permanent garrisons. Separate military establishments were maintained in Ireland and Scotland until the Act of Union in 1707 but they were equally under the authority of the King, and James could add 7500 troops from Ireland and 2199 from Scotland to the total of his armed strength. The Monmouth rebellion provided James with an opportunity to expand the army, and by December 1685 there were 19,778 regular troops under arms in England. By the time James was preparing to defend his kingdom against Dutch invasion in 1688 the army in England could deploy nearly 40,000 men. Such strength was a rare phenomenon in peacetime and when George I was called upon to protect his newly-won throne he disposed of slightly less than 22,000 men of whom nearly two-thirds were in the Colonies or Flanders. In 1746 George II's army fought the battle of Culloden with troops hastily recalled from a European war. By Continental standards forces such as these were pathetically small and the very inadequacy of the Crown's military resources encouraged disaffected elements to risk rebellion.

Toryism included a Jacobite following amongst its ranks, but the ideology of Jacobitism embraced a

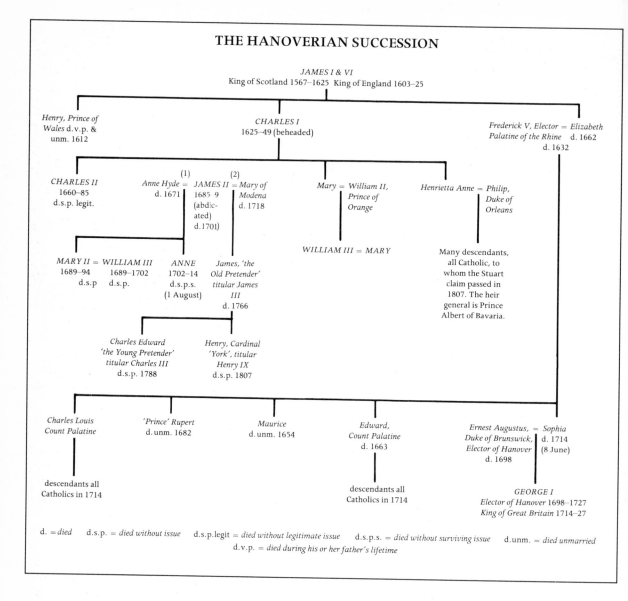

# THE HANOVERIAN SUCCESSION

*JAMES I & VI*
King of Scotland 1567–1625  King of England 1603–25

*Henry, Prince of Wales* d.v.p. & *unm.* 1612

*CHARLES I*
1625–49 (beheaded)

*Frederick V, Elector* = *Elizabeth Palatine of the Rhine* d. 1662
d. 1632

*CHARLES II*
1660–85
*d.s.p. legit.*

(1)
*Anne Hyde* = *JAMES II* = *Mary of Modena*
d. 1671  1685–9  d. 1718
(abdic-ated)
d.1701)
(2)

*Mary* = *William II, Prince of Orange*

*Henrietta Anne* = *Philip, Duke of Orleans*

*MARY II* = *WILLIAM III*
1689–94  1689–1702
*d.s.p*  *d.s.p.*

*ANNE*
1702–14
*d.s.p.s.*
(1 August)

*James, 'the Old Pretender' titular James III*
d. 1766

*WILLIAM III* = *MARY*

Many descendants, all Catholic, to whom the Stuart claim passed in 1807. The heir general is Prince Albert of Bavaria.

*Charles Edward 'the Young Pretender' titular Charles III*
*d.s.p.* 1788

*Henry, Cardinal 'York', titular Henry IX*
*d.s.p.* 1807

*Charles Louis Count Palatine*

descendants all Catholics in 1714

*'Prince' Rupert*
d. *unm.* 1682

*Maurice*
d. *unm.* 1654

*Edward, Count Palatine*
d. 1663

descendants all Catholics in 1714

*Ernest Augustus,* = *Sophia*
*Duke of Brunswick,*  d. 1714
*Elector of Hanover*  (8 June)
d. 1698

*GEORGE I*
*Elector of Hanover 1698–1727*
*King of Great Britain 1714–27*

d. = *died*   d.s.p. = *died without issue*   d.s.p.legit = *died without legitimate issue*   d.s.p.s. = *died without surviving issue*   d.unm. = *died unmarried*
d.v.p. = *died during his or her father's lifetime*

shifting mass of people and interests drawn in many cases by the opportunism apparent in an alternative monarch and his court. The exiled Stuarts were convenient figureheads to which many of the alienated elements of British society could attach themselves to work out their grievances, but armed support for Jacobite rebellion in England was always more prospective than real. Tory and Jacobite mobs took to the streets in 1714 and 1715, but the faltering steps of Stuart military strategy did nothing to encourage them to translate rioting into armed rebellion. For its military wing Jacobitism had perforce to look to the Highlands of Scotland. Between Dundee's victory at Killiecrankie

in July 1689 and the final defeat of armed Jacobitism at Culloden in April 1746 lay nearly sixty years of Highland support for the exiled Stuarts. The readiness of certain clan chiefs to risk the lives and fortunes of their clansmen in armed struggle against the established monarch and government was one of the few constant features of Jacobitism.

The Highlands were regarded by most Englishmen, and indeed by many Lowland Scots, as a remote and uncivilized region inhabited by men who posed a considerable threat to the peace of Scotland. Although this was a generalization born of ignorance and prejudice, there was sufficient eccentricity in the lifestyle of

ABOVE LEFT:
James Francis Edward Stuart, the Old Pretender *c.* 1712. Studio of
Alexis Simon Belle.

ABOVE RIGHT:
British troops prepare for battle against the Jacobites in an
engraving by Luke Sullivan after William Hogarth, entitled
*A representation of the March of the Guards towards Scotland in the
Year 1745*. Published in 1761.

the Highlander to explain the antipathy towards him
among those south of the Forth and Tay. The
Highlander's overriding loyalty was to his clan chief
and the feudal order which the clan system imposed.
Clansmen were trained to war, for violence, whether in
single combat, inter-clan battles, or cattle raids, was a
natural and honoured part of Highland life. John Hume,
who had been captured by the Jacobites at Falkirk in
1746, recorded that the Highlanders 'always appeared
like warriors; as if their arms had been limbs and
members of their bodies they were never seen without
them; they travelled, they attended fairs and markets,
nay they went to church with their broadswords and
dirks; and in latter times with their muskets and
pistols'. The fighting strength of the clans in the
eighteenth century has been variously estimated at
between 25,000 and 35,000 warriors and the House of
Hanover could thus count itself fortunate that not all
the clans made common cause with the Stuarts.

The clans who joined the rebellions did so for a
variety of reasons, ranging from political resentment at
the union of England and Scotland under one parlia-

ment to the defence of religion. Only a minority of the
clans supported militant Jacobitism as a matter of
course, although many professed a Romantic attach-
ment to the history of Stuart kingship, and the reason
why a chief brought out his clan could be as prosaic as
the need to save his followers from starvation. The
pattern of support also changed from rebellion to
rebellion, and some clans who were Jacobite in 1715
and 1719, such as the Mackenzies and the Macleods,
refused to come out in 1745. In 1689 John Graham of
Claverhouse found little support in the Lowland and
urban areas of Scotland or amongst the principal and
largest clans. The chiefs who supported him seem to
have done so from a genuine sense of loyalty to James II
and VII, but Claverhouse failed to attract sufficient
military and political strength to restore the Stuarts. In
1715 support for the Earl of Mar was initially widespread, with Jacobitism strong in the Lowlands north of
the River Tay, in the north-east of Scotland, and in the
Grampian Highlands. In 1745 the Lowlands and major
towns of Scotland were openly hostile or, at best,
unenthusiastic towards the Jacobite cause, and
although twenty-two clans took up arms for the Stuarts,
as against ten supporting the government, few of them
ranked as either military or economic heavyweights.
Although Charles Edward knew that the Whig clans –
the Campbells, Grants, Munros, Mackays and Suther-
lands – would be openly hostile to his cause, the '45 was
remarkable for the ambivalent support afforded him by
even his traditional followers. Several of the chiefs who

ABOVE:
A soldier of the 25th Foot depicted in the 1742 Clothing Book which had been issued in an attempt to regulate the dress of the Army.

RIGHT:
The grenadiers of Barrell's Regiment prepared to meet the Highland charge at Culloden. From the painting by David Morier entitled *An Incident in the Rebellion of 1745.*

sent their clansmen to fight contrived to keep a foot in both camps by delegating command of the clan regiment to their sons while they themselves stayed at home.

A Jacobite army in the field comprised two main groups: the clan regiments, such as the Appin Stewarts, and those tenants whose land tenure obliged them to serve their lord, such as the men of the Atholl Brigade. On occasion, the Jacobite ranks also included contingents detached from the Stuart army in Ireland, or from the armies of Spain and France. Additionally, regiments or companies were formed from volunteers who felt their interests lay sufficiently with the Jacobite cause to warrant taking up arms in its support. In 1745 barely half the Jacobite army consisted of men from the Highland clans and many of these later claimed that they had been 'forced out' by threats to their property

and persons. It is probably true that for the typical clansman the main factor in his willingness to fight was clan loyalty rather than any determination to see a Stuart king on the throne again. This bond of loyalty to the clan and its chief gave the Highland army a remarkable resilience and discipline in a tight corner and Hanoverian troops broke far more quickly and completely under pressure.

The clan regiments deployed for battle in a strict hierarchy; the chiefs leading with the most important

men of the clan in the front rank and the impoverished clansmen in the rearmost rank. This ensured that those with the most modern and effective weapons were always to the fore. The chief and his immediate tenants would normally be armed with the full array of Highland weapons: a musket, a pair of pistols, a broadsword, a long dirk and a circular wooden shield covered in leather known as a 'targe' or 'target'. Progressing through the ranks of the regiment towards the rear, the selection of weapons per man would be more restricted and the clansmen in the rear rank might possess only a dirk, a Lochaber axe, or just a pitch-fork. The firearms brought by the clans were often of indeterminate antiquity and the supply of muskets from France and Spain was an important addition to the Jacobite armoury.

The clans' invariable battle tactic against government troops was the Highland Charge. It was a simple manoeuvre, as befitted an army for which complicated drills were inappropriate, and it was described by

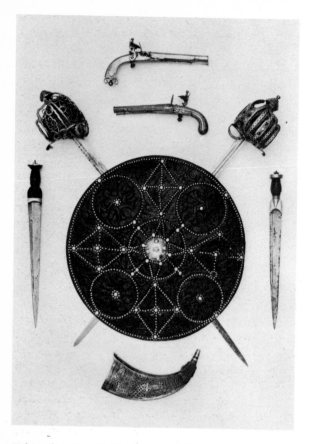

Eighteenth-century Highland weapons: dirks, broadswords, pistols, powder horn and targe.

sustain the psychological impact of several thousand clansmen charging full tilt towards them, but having fired their initial volley as the Highlanders approached they seldom had time to reload before the charge struck home. With an empty musket the only weapon available to them was the bayonet and in the era of the plug bayonet, which fitted into the end of the musket barrel like a cork in a bottle, they were effectively prevented from using the musket again until the battle was over. With the general introduction of the socket bayonet towards the end of the seventeenth century the musketeer was freed from this predicament, but even so the contest between bayonet and broadsword could be fatally one-sided.

The balance was redressed to a large extent by the introduction before Culloden of a new bayonet drill, but the key to defeating the Highland Charge lay in the development of seasoned, regular troops who could keep their heads and deliver their volleys at the best possible moment. Ironically, Hawley had successfully identified the requirements of a successful defence before his defeat at Falkirk:

> The sure way to demolish them is at 3 deep to fire by ranks diagonaly to the Centre where they come, the rear rank first, and even that rank not to fire till they are within 10 or 12 paces but If the fire is given at a distance you probably will be broke for you never get time to load a second Cartridge, & if you give way you may give your foot for dead, for they being without a firelock or any load, no man with his arms, accoutrements &c. can escape them, and they give no Quarters, but if you will but observe the above directions, they are the most despicable Enimy that are.

General Hawley in orders issued to his troops in January 1746:

> They Commonly form their Front rank of what they call their best men, or True Highlanders, the number of which being allways but few, when they form in Battallions they commonly form four deep, & these Highlanders form the front of the four, the rest being lowlanders & arrant scum.
>
> When these Battallions come within a large Musket shot, or three score yards, this front Rank gives their fire, & Immediately thro' down their firelocks & Come down in a Cluster with their Swords & Targets making a Noise & Endeavouring to pearce the Body, or Battallions before them becoming 12 or 14 deep by the time they come up to the people they attack.

In view of what was to happen four days later at Falkirk, Hawley's contempt for the clans was somewhat premature. The Highland Charge was particularly effective against raw troops, for not only must they

That the Highland Charge could still be a potent weapon even when met by these tactics was shown at Culloden where a charge, badly timed and disorganised, still succeeded in penetrating Cumberland's front line.

The components of government armies continued to be horse, foot, dragoons and artillery, although there were gradual changes in the balance between the various arms and in the weapons with which they were issued. Regiments of horse played little part in the Jacobite Rebellions and when they did participate they were usually an acute embarrassment on both sides. Rebel cavalry tended to be even less operationally adequate than their opposite numbers, for they were usually vastly understrength and invariably improvised from the rebellious gentry and their servants. In the 45 the best of the Jacobite cavalry were probably

Elcho's Lifeguards, but during the campaign the strength of the squadron, which at its maximum was only 160, fell on occasions by as much as 50 per cent.

Dragoons were still the maids of all work amongst the government forces and their capacity to undertake a variety of roles as flank, rear, and advance guards, mounted pioneers and infantry or reconnaissance and escorts, led to a considerable increase in their strength and in the frequency with which they were used in a traditional cavalry role. Thirteen new dragoon regiments were raised in response to the '15, each usually with a strength of 200 men formidably armed with swords, carbines or musketoons, bayonets and an issue of axes and hatchets. Although the dragoon regiments seldom distinguished themselves in battle against the Jacobites, their mobility and resourcefulness made them of great value during the search for and pursuit of the enemy, particularly in the Highlands.

The infantry was composed of Guards and line regiments each of the latter, with the exception of the Royal Regiment which had two, consisting of one battalion identified by its colonel's name. Each battalion should have contained roughly 820 all ranks divided between headquarters and up to twelve companies. In the field, and particularly during an extended campaign, battalion strengths seldom rose much above 500 men, although exceptionally Mackay's battalions at Killiecrankie averaged over 700 men each. From the late 1670s one of the thirteen companies was formed by grenadiers; men chosen as a regimental elite because of their courage, discipline and physique. In addition to the normal infantry weapons of musket bayonet and sword, the grenadier was issued with hand grenades for siege operations and, until the early eighteenth century, a hatchet.

The period 1660–1746 witnessed two major changes in the weapons used by the infantryman, with consequent improvements in his tactical effectiveness. The replacement of the cumbersome and unreliable matchlock musket by the flintlock brought a greater rate and consistency of fire without materially improving range and accuracy. With the introduction of the pre-packed cartridge containing both powder and ball, infantry using flintlocks could double the rate of fire they had been able to achieve with matchlocks. This improvement in offensive power reduced the need for pikemen in support, and the introduction of the bayonet further increased the musketeer's independence. By the 1680s the ratio of pikes to musketeers had been reduced to 1 to 5 and by the turn of the century the pike had

disappeared altogether. As a result, the infantry company became a more mobile and in some respects a more flexible tactical unit.

Royal troops were placed at a disadvantage in their attempt to counter the Highland Charge by the failure of their artillery to play a significant part in any battle before Culloden. The effective range of the brass three-pounders used at Culloden was only some 450 yards but, together with the five available howitzers (range approximately 1300 yards), they not only inflicted heavy casualties but also further reduced the sagging morale of the Jacobite army. Inadequate as the government artillery often was, it could not compete with the sheer incompetence of the rebel attempts to employ cannon and mortars in support of their own troops. The Jacobite artillery was an impediment on the march, often late on the field, and invariably incapable of contributing more than one or two shots to the outcome of the battle.

Jacobite armies were bedevilled by a lack of experienced officers, and the talents of the foreign adventurers who flirted with the Stuart cause fell far short of remedying this deficiency. The French and Irish officers who joined the '45 with the Marquis d'Eguilles were almost without exception mediocraties, and the Prince's promotion of the worst of them infuriated the Scots. The English Jacobites who failed to take up arms frequently used the excuse that their untrained followers would be mere cannon fodder in the absence of effective officers. The foremost tactician in the Stuart camp was undoubtedly Lord George Murray who had considerable experience of Jacobite campaigning, having turned out in 1715, 1719 and 1745. In the '45 Murray was fully capable of outmanoeuvring the Duke of Cumberland and he possessed a genuine concern for the welfare of his troops, doing his utmost to arrange for their adequate provisioning. His tragedy was that a high-handed manner and an apparent lack of respect for the Prince's person had early alienated Charles Edward, thereby providing ample opportunity for the intriguers who wished to bring Murray down.

One of the remarkable features of the battle of Culloden was the youth of the opposing commanders, Charles Edward being but twenty-six years old and the Duke of Cumberland only twenty-five. Cumberland's experience of command in the field was still in its infancy but he had been wounded at the battle of Dettingen and he did lead British troops into action at Fontenoy. He was undoubtedly successful in restoring

Charles Edward, the Young Pretender, steps ashore on Eriskay in the Outer Hebrides in July 1745 to begin his quest for the English throne. A late eighteenth-century painting of the French School.

the morale of the Hanoverian troops after Falkirk and the rank and file seemed to have respected his soldierly abilities. Cumberland's youth and self-confidence were by this stage greatly needed, for the elder statesmen of the Hanoverian army, Generals Wade, Cope and Hawley, had all failed to crush the Rebellion.

The '45 was the end of armed Jacobite attempts to oust the Hanoverians from the British throne. Whether they had ever possessed the military potential to achieve their object is open to doubt, but the outcome could have been so different had they succeeded in bringing a French, Spanish or Swedish army with them across the Channel.

# A DRUMCLOG 1 June 1679
# B BOTHWELL BRIDGE 22 June 1679

The struggle for control of the Church of Scotland between Episcopalians and Presbyterians flared once more into violence in the early summer of 1679. The increasing severity of government measures against non-conformists, including the death penalty for anyone preaching at a field conventicle, heavy fines for absence from church on Sundays, and the free quartering of 9000 troops on the Covenanter south-west, brought the west of Scotland to the brink of revolt. The actual recourse to arms was precipitated by the murder of Archbishop Sharp of St Andrews on 3 May 1679, rather than by a planned rising. The assassins rode west to Clydesdale where their pursuit was taken up by a small force of horse and dragoons under John Graham of Claverhouse (later Viscount Dundee).

Claverhouse planned a descent upon the armed conventicle to be held at Loudoun Hill on 1st June but the Covenanters, warned of his approach, deployed three squadrons of horse and four battalions of infantry at Drumclog. They probably outnumbered Claverhouse's 150 troopers and dragoons by nearly 10 to 1, although the Covenanters were armed with a motley collection of weapons and encumbered with several thousand non-combatants. They had, however, selected a strong position and their front was covered by marshy ground which was impassible to a mounted force. Undismayed, Claverhouse dismounted his dragoons and advanced them within pistol shot of the enemy. Incensed by their accurate fire, the Covenanters charged across the marsh and struck Claverhouse's centre and left flank with considerable force. Unable to stand against sword, pike and pitchfork at close quarters the Government troopers, seeing Claverhouse carried away by his wounded and uncontrollable horse, followed suit and fled from the field. Over forty of Claverhouse's men fell during the battle or in the pursuit, and emboldened by their success the Covenanters next day unsuccessfully attacked Glasgow.

A thoroughly alarmed government sent the Duke of Monmouth north to take command of the Royal forces in Scotland. With both militia and regular troops under his command, Monmouth was able to field about 5000 men against the unprepared and largely leaderless rebels he encountered at Bothwell Bridge. Using Colonel Oglethorpe's dragoons, Monmouth forced the defences of the bridge on the morning of 22 June. Deploying his army on the enemy bank he routed the Covenanters, inflicting losses of between 600 and 700 killed and 1200 taken prisoner. The brief rebellion against the government was over.

---

*Drumclog and Loudoun Hill lie approximately 16 miles (25 kilometres) to the south of Glasgow on the A71 and Bothwell 7 miles (11 kilometres) south-east on the A724.*

---

The battle of Drumclog. Mezzotint by C. E. Wagstaff after George Harvey. Published by Hodgson and Graves in 1838.

# SEDGEMOOR 6 July 1685

James Scott, Duke of Monmouth, landed at Lyme Regis in Dorset on 11 June 1685 to raise the standard of rebellion against his uncle, James II. Monmouth's invading force, conveyed from Holland in three vessels, amounted to eighty-two men, a quantity of arms, and an empty exchequer. His arrival was not unexpected, for the government was well supplied with information regarding 'His Majesty's rebellious subjects in the Low Countries' by its agent in Amsterdam, Bevil Skelton. They were also accustomed to the prospect of rebellion, since the rumour and substance of treason were perennial features of English politics while a Catholic monarch reigned. In England the centres of potential rebellion were London and the West Country where Dissenting and Republican sympathies ran strong and where the Duke of Monmouth enjoyed considerable popularity. While a landing in the West seemed most probable, there was a possibility that Monmouth might make for Ireland or Scotland. Indeed the Earl of Argyll, the head of the powerful Clan Campbell, had already landed in Scotland to raise rebellion amongst the Highlanders and Covenanters.

With a national army of under 9000 men, James could ill-afford to disperse his troops by garrisoning all the possible landing areas, and he concentrated his main forces in London at the centre of the nation's road system. The inevitable delay between Monmouth's landing and his confrontation by regular forces had to be accepted and there was the possibility, however remote it might seem to many, that the militia could crush the rebellion at its inception. To stiffen the militia James dispatched five companies of foot, four troops of horse and two of dragoons under John, Lord Churchill towards the West. But James was not yet prepared to weaken the defence of London and reinforcements were ordered to the capital from Surrey and Essex.

The West Country men who joined Monmouth came predominantly from the urban and industrial classes of Somerset, West Dorset and East Devon. Although Monmouth's recruits included farmers and agricultural labourers, the majority earned their living from the traditional occupations of the Nonconformist, as tailors, shopkeepers, clothworkers and carpenters. Most were mature men in their thirties or forties who were driven to rebellion by a belief that they must defend themselves and the Protestant religion against an autocratic, papist king. To them Monmouth was a convenient and popular figurehead whose military experience offered

the chance of victory against James's regulars. Ironically, Monmouth's greatest feat of arms had been at Bothwell Bridge in 1679 against a rebel army not dissimilar to the one he now commanded.

Although over 7000 men joined Monmouth within a week of his landing, he had arms for only 1500 and the remainder had to depend upon whatever weapons they could bring from home or secure on the march. Some were armed with little more than a hatchet, a knife, or a scythe tied to the end of a pole to form a crude halberd. Monmouth had engaged the services of a professional Dutch gunner but his artillery train consisted of only four cannon, and many of his 800 cavalry matched their commander, Lord Grey of Warke, in his lack of either appropriate training or equipment. Monmouth formed his infantry in five regiments designated as Red (Nathaniel Wade), White (Colonel Foukes), Yellow (Colonel Matthews), Green (Colonel Holmes) and Blue (Colonel Basset).

For Monmouth to sustain the momentum and credibility of the rebellion it was essential for him to capture a town of political and economic importance. Bristol, then the second city of the land, and only 48 miles (77 kilometres) to the north-east was an obvious target and it became the key to his strategy. Brushing aside the Devon and Somerset militia at Axminster, the rebels reached Taunton and an enthusiastic welcome on 18 June. After an ill-judged delay of three days, during which Monmouth was proclaimed King, the advance upon Bristol by way of Bridgwater and Keynsham was resumed. But the government forces had been granted valuable time in which to reinforce the city and establish a *cordon sanitaire* of regular and militia units around the periphery of the rebellion.

Dismayed by a brief cavalry assault upon his army at Keynsham (on 26 June) and by the false news that the entire royal army was at hand, Monmouth ordered a retreat. After a fierce and successful action against the royal forces at Norton St Phillips, Monmouth reached Bridgwater again on 3 July. Here he learned that the royal army, commanded since 19 June by the Earl of Feversham, had made camp at Westonzoyland, only three miles away across the moor.

Although the government troops had pitched their tents behind the protection of the Bussex Rhine, a drainage ditch running from the moor to the River Parrett, they had not entrenched their camp. Monmouth saw an opportunity for a last desperate gamble –

a night attack upon an unsuspecting enemy. From the first, Monmouth had been far from confident of his army's ability to withstand regular troops in pitched battle, but the confusion of a mêlée in the dark against men suffering from the effects of the local cider seemed to offer a chance of success, providing surprise could be achieved. But on the night of Sunday 5 July, Feversham ordered precautions against just such an attack, including the deployment of 150 troopers in Chedzoy, infantry picquets in front of the Bussex Rhine, and the dispatch of the King's Horse Guards under Colonel Ogelthorpe to Bawdrip. These outposts forced Monmouth to adopt a circuitous route involving a march of 6 miles (10 kilometres) and the crossing of the Black Ditch, the Langmoor Rhine and the final barrier of the Bussex Rhine.

At 11 pm 4000 rebels marched out of Monmouth's camp at Castle Field under the most savage discipline against unnecessary noise. Any man disturbing the army's silent progress was to be immediately killed by his neighbour. Following the Bristol road the rebels reached Peasey Farm, where they left their baggage train, and continued their advance until they reached the Langmoor Rhine. Here their guide, a local man named Godfrey, could not immediately locate the crossing and as he beat round in the darkness the rebels were discovered by an alert government trooper. Firing his pistol to warn the patrol at Chedzoy, he galloped to the bank of the Bussex Rhine to raise the camp, calling repeatedly, 'Beat the drums, the enemy is come, for the Lord's sake, beat the drums'.

Feversham's men seized their weapons and deployed between the tents and the Bussex Rhine in good order. The right of the Royal line was taken by Dumbarton's Regiment (Colonel Douglas), with on its left two battalions of the 1st Foot Guards (the Duke of Grafton), the 2nd Foot Guards (Colonel Sackville), Trelawney's Regiment (Colonel Charles Churchill), and on the extreme left Kirke's Regiment. The Royal artillery train was 500 yards away down the Bridgewater Road and the main body of the cavalry – the King's Horse Guards, the King's Regiment of Horse, and the Royal Dragoons – were billetted in Westonzoyland itself. Altogether Feversham commanded about 2600 men and although they were outnumbered, they were all regular troops whose discipline enabled them to respond effectively and quickly to the sudden emergency of Monmouth's attack.

When the alarm was raised the rebel infantry was still a mile from the Royal camp, but the cavalry

James Scott, Duke of Monmouth at Sedgemoor. Engraving after Jan Wyck.

galloped hard for the crossing over the Bussex Rhine known as the 'upper plungeon'. En route they clashed with Compton's mounted picquet which was falling back on the camp, and although the rebel horsemen outnumbered the picquet 3 to 1 the fire of the regulars drove them back. Compton was able to secure the vital crossing-point, forcing Grey and his troops to turn along the front of the Royal position in the hope of finding another passage across the Rhine. As they passed the Guards, a devastating volley of musketry poured into their flank and what little order and control remained amongst the cavalry disappeared as terrified horses and riders thought only of escape. Monmouth's cavalry turned and fled in all directions, some even riding down their own infantry which was now approaching out of the darkness of the moor.

The infantry had covered the last mile of their march at a very fast pace and as they neared the Bussex Rhine their ranks were in some confusion. Indeed a considerable gap had opened between the regiments of Wade, Matthews and Holmes and the rest of the rebel column. The men at the rear failed to arrive in time for the battle and some companies were still marching up as the foremost regiments fled the field. When still forty yards from the Rhine, Wade deployed his regiment from column to line and halted to order its ranks. Although Wade believed that he was opposite the left of the Royal line, he was in fact abreast of Dumbarton's Regiment and the first battalion of the Guards. Thus as Matthew's and Holmes's Regiments came up on Wade's left, the rebel line began to outflank Feversham's right. To meet this extension Churchill ordered the regiments of Kirke

James II by an unknown artist, *c.* 1690.

James Scott, Duke of Monmouth by Sir Peter Lely (1618–80).

and Trelawney to march across the rear and deploy on the right fronting the regiments of Matthews and Holmes.

The delay caused by the need to order the rebel line was fatal for in those few moments the impetus of the attack evaporated and Monmouth's infantry refused to cross the Rhine. Holding their ground, they began to fire furiously towards the Royal regiments who for the most part lay still in the darkness waiting for the arrival of dawn before returning fire. For over an hour the rebels wasted ammunition in this futile exercise and only their artillery inflicted any serious measure of casualties in the Royal line. Feversham was content to wait for the light of day before he attacked, but he used the final hour of darkness to prepare his assault. The Royal cannon were at last dragged into a position from

which they could bring their fire to bear and gradually the rebel artillery was silenced. Feversham led his cavalry across the upper and lower plungeons with orders to take the rebel army in flank.

As dawn broke and the strengthening light revealed the disciplined Royal infantry to their front and the enemy cavalry on their flanks, it can have taken little imagination for the rebels to realise that defeat was only minutes away. Monmouth, for one, could see all too clearly the inevitable outcome, and he spurred from the field with Lord Grey at his side. As the Royal infantry dashed across the Rhine in a general assault and Feversham's cavalry charged in on the flanks the rebels wavered and broke. Only Wade managed to preserve any order among the retreating regiments and many of the rebels were cut down by the pursuing cavalry as

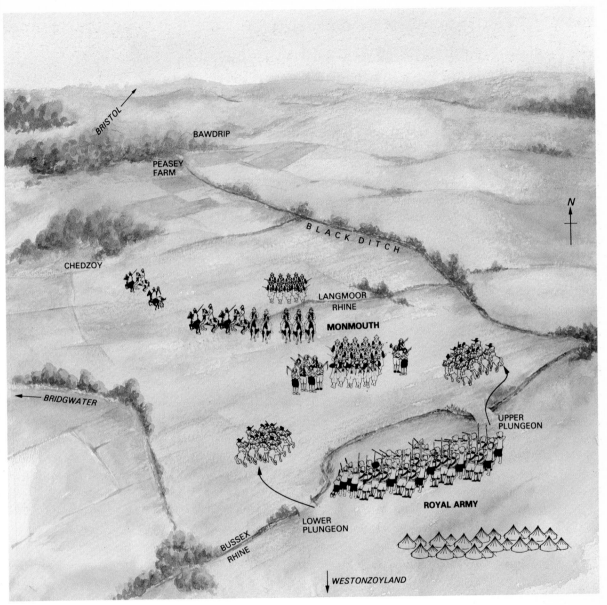

they struggled to cross the Langmoor Rhine and the cornfields beyond. Probably between 200 and 400 rebels fell during the battle itself and perhaps 1000 during the pursuit. With a government determined to crush rebellion in the west once and for all, the weeks following Sedgemoor saw the execution of 250 rebels and the transportation of 850 more. Monmouth was captured two days after the battle and on 15 July 1685 he met death bravely at the hands of the executioner, Jack Ketch, on Tower Hill.

*The battlefield lies just over 3 miles (5 kilometres) south-east of Bridgwater along the A372, and a signposted track leads from the outskirts of Westonzoyland to the probable position of the Royal camp. Many of the landmarks which influenced the course of the battle are no longer to be seen. The Bussex and Langmoor Rhines were filled in long ago and the King's Sedgemoor Drain, constructed in the eighteenth century, absorbed the Black Ditch. The features of the seventeenth-century moor have been altered by farming and by time and the visitor will need to take his imagination with him.*

# A KILLIECRANKIE 27 July 1689

# B DUNKELD 21 August 1689

At the beginning of October 1688 the small standing army of Scotland marched south to join the forces assembling near London against the anticipated invasion by William of Orange. Its departure deprived James II's Scottish administration of its main authority and in the wake of the King's own flight from England his supporters north of the border were ousted from government. A Convention Parliament meeting in Edinburgh in the spring of 1689 offered the Scottish throne to William and Mary and declared the commander of James's remaining forces in Scotland, John Graham of Claverhouse, Viscount Dundee, a fugitive and a rebel. Dundee responded by raising the standard of King James on Dundee Law in April 1689, thereby initiating the first Jacobite Rebellion.

Alarmed by this development, the Convention dispatched a force under General Hugh Mackay of Scourie to apprehend Dundee, believing that his capture would quell the revolt before the Highland clans could rise to join it and before James II could send reinforcements from his army in Ireland. Unexpectedly Dundee took the offensive, leading his small band on a raid of the Lowlands where he impounded treasure, remounts and arms in King James's name. The funds Dundee secured were quickly disbursed to cement the loyalty of the clans and by 18 May 1689 the Highland chiefs had assembled in Glenroy, the home of Cameron of Lochiel.

It was vital for the wider campaign envisaged by Dundee that Blair Atholl in Perthshire, controlling the strategically important route between the Highlands

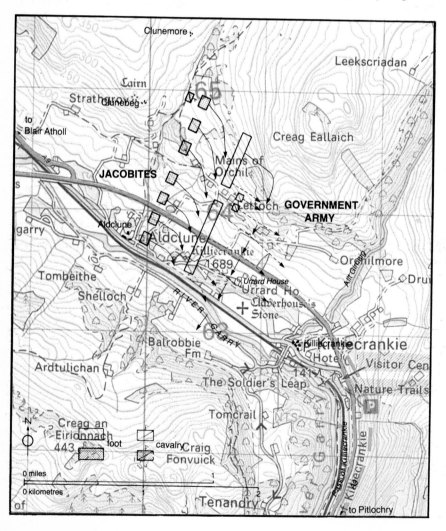

John Graham of Claverhouse, Viscount Dundee. Portrait by W. H. Geissler after an unknown artist. Although Killiecrankie was a Jacobite victory 'Bonnie Dundee's' death during the battle spelt the end of the 1689 Rebellion.

General Hugh Mackay of Scourie c.1692. After Sir Godfrey Kneller. Mackay was to be killed in another defeat, at Steenkirk, three years after Killiecrankie.

and the Lowlands, should be held for the Jacobites. Equally it was in General Mackay's interest to forestall Dundee and both men set their forces in motion towards Blair Castle in July 1689. Approaching by way of Dunkeld and Pitlochry the government troops negotiated the Pass of Killiecrankie on the afternoon of 27 July. As Mackay waited near Urrard House for his army to close up, his advance guard reported that Dundee's force was moving towards Aldclune. Dundee had decided to fight, despite the numerical inferiority of his force which mustered only 2500 foot and a troop of horse. The strength of the Highland army had been falling for some days as clansmen slipped home with their booty, but a late reinforcement had arrived from the Jacobite army in Ireland in the form of Colonel Alexander Cannon with 300 infantry, 74 officers and 35 barrels of powder.

As the main body of Dundee's force came into sight marching down into the valley between Clunemore and Clunebeg, Mackay realised that his army must climb the steep bank to its front to deny the Highlanders the advantage of high ground. Executing a turn to the right, Mackay's troops forced their way up the slope, which was densely planted with trees and shrubs, only to find another ridge rising above them, only a 'short musket shot' away. Dundee's Highlanders were already drawn up long its crest. The initiative now lay with Dundee for, as Mackay noted in his *Memoirs*, his own position was on 'a ground fair enough to receive the ennemy, but not to attack them'.

Mackay's force had deployed in the order in which the regiments emerged from the Pass of Killiecrankie. From left to right the line consisted of 200 fusiliers commanded by Lieutenant-Colonel Lawder, Balfour's and Ramsey's regiments of the Scots Brigade, and Kenmure's, Leven's, Mackay's, and Hastings' infantry regiments. Finding that his deployment was not sufficient to hold the available ground, and fearing that he might be outflanked by Dundee, Mackay gave what proved to be a disastrous order. Dividing his infantry

The battlefield of Killicrankie with, centre right, the slope down which the Highlanders charged.

into half-battalions, he advanced the three rearmost ranks of each battalion into the line in order to extend his position to the right. He lengthened his line further by leaving a considerable space between Kenmure's and Leven's Regiments in the centre, relying upon his two troops of horse, Belhaven's and Annandale's, to plug the gap. Mackay's extended line, now only three ranks deep, formed the perfect target for a Highland charge.

Dundee countered the extension of Mackay's line simply by increasing the distance between each clan regiment, thereby preserving their cohesion and solidity in the charge. Each clan grouping was instructed to attack a particular regiment in the enemy line, although Dundee, equally sensitive regarding his flanks, allowed a gap to remain in his own line where it fronted Leven's Regiment. On the extreme right, opposite Balfour's Regiment, Dundee placed the Macleans, then Cannon's Irish contingent, the Clanranald Macdonalds, Glengarry's clan, the Camerons under Lochiel, a mixed clan battalion under Sir Alexander Maclean, and finally on the extreme left of his line the Macdonalds of Sleat. Dundee took position with his troop of horse on the left.

The armies remained inactive for over two hours while Dundee waited for the sun, which was directly in the Highlanders' eyes, to lose its power. The clans were eager to attack and the waiting was enlivened by some ineffective musketry and an abortive sortie by the Cameron marksmen. A desultory artillery bombardment of the Highland position ended abruptly when the carriages of Mackay's three light guns disintegrated.

As the sun set, Dundee gave the signal to attack and the clans swept down the slope before them. Since the ground fell away to their right, the charging clansmen naturally inclined in that direction and their assault swept across the front of the troops on the right of Mackay's line leaving Hastings' regiment and half of Leven's unscathed. As the Highlanders closed the government line, both sides appear to have delivered a volley of musketry, although that of Mackay's troops, fired from a static position, would have had the greater effect and must have accounted for the bulk of the 600 casualties suffered by Dundee's force. The impetus of the Highland charge, however, carried it into the opposing line before Mackay's infantry had time either to reload or to prepare to receive the Highlanders with the bayonet. Despite their superior numbers, the government troops were no match in close-quarter fighting for Highlanders armed with dirk and broadsword. The left of Mackay's line disintegrated as Lawder's, Balfour's and most of Ramsey's Regiments

took to their heels. In a desperate attempt to salvage something from the battle, Mackay, now on the right of the line with the intact portion of Leven's Regiment and the whole of Hastings's, ordered his cavalry to take the Highlanders in flank. Belhaven's troop advanced a short distance before recoiling into Kenmure's Regiment which it carried away in the rapidly spreading stampede from the field. In the moment of victory Dundee, charging at the head of his troop of horse, fell mortally wounded by a musket ball fired from the ranks of Mackay's own regiment. The clans harried the enemy as far as the government baggage train, where the attraction of loot proved stronger than that of killing. As night fell, Mackay forded the River Garry and made good his retreat to Stirling, which he reached with little more than a quarter of his force thirty-six hours after the battle.

With Dundee's death, Colonel Cannon assumed command but he possessed neither Dundee's powers of leadership not his subtlety of diplomacy. As the Highlanders advanced down the valley of the Tay, clan interests, never far below the surface, began to take precedence over the cause for which they were fighting. At the town of Dunkeld to the north of Perth, the Jacobite army was approaching a test of its cohesion and endurance greater than that posed at Killiecrankie.

Dunkeld was held by 1200 men of the newly-raised Earl of Angus's Regiment who had begun fortifying the area between the church and the Marquess of Atholl's house as soon as they had arrived in the town. Cannon attacked with 5000 Highlanders early on the morning of 21 August and close-quarter fighting with musket, sword and pike raged around the church and Atholl's house. After four hours of bitter struggle and with a good deal of the town ablaze, the Highlanders fell back dispirited and exhausted. Refusing to attack again they marched away towards Blair Castle, leaving behind 300 casualties to the 45 suffered by the defenders. After Dunkeld most of the Highlanders drifted back to their homes while Cannon and his Irish troops returned to Lochaber to winter. Desultory fighting resumed the following year but the Jacobites were defeated at Cromdale on 1 May 1690 and their last forces scattered.

---

*The A9 goes through the Pass of Killiecrankie and the battlefield lies at one side of the road with a National Trust for Scotland car park and visitor centre on the other.*

*Dunkeld lies approximately 12 miles (19 kilometres) to the south of Killiecrankie along the A9.*

---

# A PRESTON 12 November 1715

# B SHERIFFMUIR 13 November 1715

A planned Jacobite rising in the south-west of England in 1715 was prevented by the arrest of the ring-leaders and the deployment of regular troops in Oxford, Bath and Bristol. It was to be left to north-east England and the Highlands of Scotland to provide the most tangible support for a Stuart restoration. Paradoxically, the man who was to raise the Jacobite standard in Scotland had earlier worked to secure the accession of George I. John Erskine, Earl of Mar, had entered politics in 1696 as a supporter of William III and in 1713 he had been appointed as Secretary of State for Scotland. His tenure of office, however, did not survive the collapse of the Tory party and George I lost little time in making it plain that Mar could not expect the King's favour. In desperation, Mar sought to restore his prestige and influence through rebellion and he calculatingly adopted the Stuart cause in the knowledge that men would fight to restore the Pretender. It is doubtful if James Francis specifically authorised the rebellion and the news that Mar had raised the Jacobite standard at Braemar on 6 September 1715 certainly came as a surprise to the Stuart court in France. Yet Mar quickly

John, 2nd Duke of Argyll by Thomas Bardwell dated 1740.

gathered recruits and by October his army numbered 6000 men with further clan reinforcements marching to his support.

It was fortunate for the Hanoverian cause that the garrison of Scotland was commanded by John, 2nd Duke of Argyll, the head of the Clan Campbell and a soldier of considerable ability. Argyll had served with the Duke of Marlborough and his military skill went some way to redress the alarming disparity in numbers between the opposing forces. For while Mar commanded an army of more than 7000, Argyll, even after he had been reinforced, could deploy a field army of less than half that number. Argyll occupied Stirling in the hope that he could block the Jacobite route to the south, but there can be little doubt that had Mar moved rapidly the whole of Scotland would have fallen to the Jacobite cause. Instead Mar spent most of September

and the beginning of October idly in Perth. On 9 October he stirred briefly to dispatch 2000 Highlanders under Macintosh of Borlum in search of Jacobite forces in the Lowlands and the north of England. A rendezvous was achieved at Kelso, where Macintosh joined forces with the Jacobite gentry of Northumberland and a Lowland rising under Lord Kenmure. With Thomas Forster, the Tory Member of Parliament for Northumberland, in command, the united force, now numbering nearly 3000 men, marched south to raise Lancashire and the north-west of England. Its progress via Penrith, Kendal and Lancaster, was dogged by an almost total lack of recruits to the Jacobite cause and news of the approach of a Hanoverian force from Newcastle under General Carpenter.

By 10 November the rebels had reached Preston, where they found themselves menaced by a second

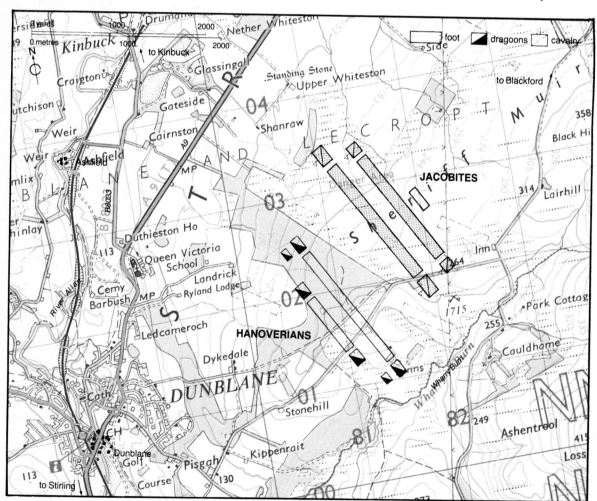

The battle of Sheriffmuir.

Hanoverian force under General Wills comprising one regiment of infantry (Preston's), five newly-raised regiments of dragoons (Wynn's, Honeywood's, Munden's, Dormer's and Stanhope's) and one of horse (Pitt's). Faced by this double threat, Forster ordered the fortification of Preston and then retired to his bed, leaving Mackintosh to supervise the defence of the town. Barricades were set up astride the four main approaches while houses commanding the narrow lanes were turned into strong-points. The work was done in a soldierly manner and when Wills attacked on 12 November his troops made little progress and suffered casualties. But effective as the Jacobite defence had been it did not prevent the juncture of Wills's and Carpenter's forces and the subsequent encirclement of the town. On 14 November the defenders surrendered though they had suffered only 40 casualties to the 200 of the government troops. The Jacobites had achieved tactical success but in the absence of a coherent strategy and forthright leadership they dissipated their resources and squandered precious time in argument and confusion. The battle of Preston was the end of the 1715 rising in England. By 14 November the rebellion in Scotland had also reached a climax.

Mar had marched southwards from Perth on 10 November, convinced at last that he must advance if he was ever to link up with the Jacobite force in Northern England. The rebels planned to detach 3000 troops at Dunblane to occupy Argyll's attention while the main Jacobite army crossed the River Forth above Stirling. Forewarned of this plan, Argyll concentrated his forces and moved north to occupy Dunblane before the enemy arrived. On the bitterly cold morning of 13 November 1715 the armies drew up two miles apart on the bleak, undulating ground of Sheriffmuir. The moor was named from its use as a training ground by the Menteith Militia, and the terrain favoured the government troops with their more effective cavalry. Argyll deployed his infantry in two lines, the first comprising six battalions (Forfar's, Wightman's, Shannon's, Morrison's, Montagu's and Clayton's) and the second two (Egerton's and Orrey's). Portmore's and Evans' dragons were on the right of the first line, supported by a squadron of gentlemen volunteers to their rear, while Kerr's and Carpenter's dragoons held the left flank. Two squadrons of Stair's dragoons supported the second line of infantry bringing Argyll's total strength to 960 dragoons and 2200 infantry. Mar took the field with 807 horse and 6290 foot deployed in two lines with, initially at least, horse on either flank.

John Erskine, 6th Earl of Mar by Sir Godfrey Kneller. Mar's political allegiance changed with the prevailing wind of power and he was aptly nicknamed 'Bobbing John'.

The morale of the clansmen had soared at the prospect of battle, but their impetuous advance towards the enemy threw their left wing into confusion. Both armies found that their right wings outflanked the left wing of the enemy, and Mar's attempt to extend his left to cover Argyll's right only served to increase the muddle into which his first and second ranks had fallen. When the left wing was launched precipitously into the attack, 2000 Highlanders advanced as a mob and although their musketry discomforted Argyll's right, the clansmen were forced to retreat when Portmore's dragoons took them in flank. Argyll advanced with the whole of his right wing and troops from the centre, but the Jacobite left continued to resist stubbornly as it gradually retreated. For nearly two miles the Highlanders were driven back in a half circle until they crossed the River Allen under fire near Kinbuck. However, while Argyll had been busy pursuing the Jacobite left his own left wing had fled before an attack from the Highland right. Thus both commanders, although victorious on the right of their line, had suffered defeat on the left. Argyll with his intact wing was now to the north of his original position, and Mar with his victorious right was moving south towards Stirling. The battlefield itself was almost deserted. Upon hearing of the fate which had befallen the remainder of their command, both men marched back

to the battlefield, but the final hours of daylight were spent in watchful inactivity, despite the fact that Mar's surviving troops still outnumbered Argyll. As dusk fell both armies finally withdrew, Argyll to Dunblane and Mar to Ardoch.

Probably 600 men died in the battle with the proportion of casualties heaviest on the government side. Since Argyll reoccupied Sheriffmuir on the following morning, victory was technically his. Although Mar claimed the field, anything short of a decisive Jacobite victory was in fact a defeat. Not even the arrival of James himself, at the end of December 1715, could breath life into the Jacobite cause after Sheriffmuir. Mar with a force of Highlanders outnumbering the enemy by nearly 3 to 1 should have annihilated Argyll's tiny force. But as at Preston the absence of strong leadership had fostered indecision and recrimination, robbing the Jacobites of success.

The battle of Sheriffmuir by John Wootton (1686?–1764).

The battlefield of Sheriffmuir, 6 miles (10 kilometres) to the north of Stirling, has changed little since 1715, and though it is difficult to identify the precise location of the opposing armies, it seems probable that the present Dunblane to Blackford road runs through the positions of the rival forces at the start of the battle.

The Jacobite headquarters during the occupation of Preston was situated in Market Square in a building which stood on the present site of the Harris Museum and Art Gallery.

# GLENSHIEL 10 June 1719

With the outbreak of hostilities between Spain and Britain in 1718, a dual strategy of a Spanish landing in England and a Highland rising in Scotland was agreed between the Jacobite James Butler, Duke of Ormonde, and Philip V's chief minister, Cardinal Alberoni. Spain would provide 29 ships, 30,000 stands or arms and 5000 troops under Ormonde's command for the venture against England, while a smaller force under George Keith, the Earl of Marischal, sailed for Scotland. The main Spanish fleet left Cadiz in March 1719 but it was shattered by a storm before it could join Ormonde at Corunna. Unaware of the fate which had befallen the main expedition, Marischal's force made landfall on the west coast of Scotland in April.

The invading force, comprising 307 Spanish troops and a party of exiled Jacobites, disembarked at the head of Loch Alsh amidst a bitter dispute as to who should command in Scotland. A fateful compromise was reached whereby Marischal commanded the fleet and the Marquess of Tullibardine the land force. Unsure of whether they could expect further help from Spain, their escape blocked by the Royal Navy, and faced by an alert Scottish garrison, the two Jacobite leaders had to make what they could of a botched strategy and a ramshackle force.

By May their position was desperate, for General Wightman and a force of government troops were preparing to move against them from Inverness, and as yet little more than token assistance had been provided by the clans. The failure of Ormonde's expedition had convinced many Highland chiefs that the rising was already lost, and only Rob Roy Macgregor, Lord George Murray, Cameron of Lochiel and Lord Seaforth brought in any significant number of clansmen.

To avoid encirclement, the Jacobites had to halt Wightman's advance and by the beginning of June they had established a blocking position at Glenshiel. The natural strength of the Jacobite deployment, which was protected by the River Shiel on the right and a ravine on the left, was further strengthened by entrenchments thrown up across the rugged ground of their centre. A barricade had been erected on the drove road to the north of the river and had the 1000 Highlanders and 250 Spaniards of Tullibardine's force possessed the will to fight, it should have proved an impregnable position.

Wightman attacked on 10 June 1719 with 850 infantry, 120 dragoons, 130 Highlanders from loyal Whig clans, and four Coehorn mortars. After a short bombardment by the mortars which obliged the Highland right to withdraw and a turning movement against their left, the entire Jacobite line took to its heels. Although Jacobite casualties had been few their army disintegrated, the clansmen returning to their homes, and the Spaniards, deserted and conspicuous in a harsh environment, surrendering to General Wightman.

*The A87 road from Invergarry to the Kyle of Lochalsh runs through Glenshiel between Loch Cluanie and the head of Loch Duich. The battle took place at the narrow pass slightly to the east of the road bridge across the Shiel.*

LEFT:
James Butler, 2nd Duke of Ormonde. Attributed to Michael Dahl, 1714.

FAR LEFT:
George Keith, 10th Earl Marischal painted by Pierre Parrocel.

# PRESTONPANS 21 September 1745

Two years of Jacobite intrigue came to fruition on 25 July 1745 when a twenty-five-year-old Stuart prince, Charles Edward, the Young Pretender, set foot on Scottish soil. The Highland response to his arrival was muted and it was only the young man's evident determination to proceed with an armed rising which persuaded the clans to come out. Yet many of the most powerful Highland chiefs refused to risk another Jacobite venture, and had it not been for the support of Clan Cameron led by Lochiel the Younger, the raising of the standard at Glenfinnan on 19 August would have been to little avail.

That the insurrection prospered during its early months was due more to external factors than to any degree of skill or energy applied by the Jacobites to their task of seizing a nation. The war against France had drained Britain of government troops and despite early intelligence of Jacobite plans Scotland's garrison numbered only 3000 men in the summer of 1745. That garrison was commanded by Lieutenant-General Sir John Cope and it says much for his sense of duty that, far from adopting a policy of careful surveillance, he followed the politically desirable strategy of confronting the Highland army with whatever force could be assembled. As the Jacobites began their march south to the Lowlands, Cope moved north towards Fort Augustus, but he failed to intercept the Highland army or prevent it from occupying the city of Edinburgh. With the enemy now to his rear Cope embarked his force at Aberdeen and took ship southwards to Dunbar. Learning of Cope's arrival, the Jacobites marched out of Edinburgh to meet the Hanoverian advance. The opposing armies sighted each other on 20 September 1745 as they approached the village of Tranent. Cope found the ground to his liking and halted to await the arrival of the enemy.

As the Highlanders marched down from the hills above Tranent, Cope deployed his line facing south, confident that the natural strength of his position, with marsh and ditch to the front, Preston and Seaton House on the flanks, and the sea to the rear, gave him every advantage. In fact the intervening ground made it almost impossible for either army to assault the other and as evening fell the Highlanders marched east through Tranent seeking a more exposed flank. The armies passed the night in the open and by 3 am the Highlanders were again on the move eastwards. To conform to this movement Cope manoeuvred his line to

A Jacobite broadsheet published after Prestonpans comparing remarks made by 'Charles Prince Regent' with those of Sir John Cope, 'General of the Usurper's Army', shortly before the battle. Charles appealed for the 'Assistance of God'; Cope promised his men 'eight full hours . . . pillage' in Edinburgh after they had defeated the Highlanders. The caricature (RIGHT) of 'Sir J.C.' (almost certainly Sir John Cope) is by George Townshend, 4th Viscount, 1st Marquess Townshend (1724–1807).

face east and his 2300 troops prepared for battle. From left to right Cope's line was now formed as follows: two squadrons of Hamilton's Dragoons, nine companies of Murray's Regiment, eight companies of Lascelle's, two of Guise's, five companies of Lee's Regiment, two squadrons of Gardiner's Dragoons, six one-and-a-half-pounder guns and six Coehorn mortars protected by an artillery guard. The third squadron of the dragoon regiments took position in reserve.

The Highlanders negotiated the bog along a convenient track but in endeavouring to ensure that the rear of the army had cleared the morass the Duke of Perth, leading the advance, marched too far to the north before turning left to face the enemy. As a result a gap opened in the centre of the Jacobite line, and both armies found that their left wings were outflanked by the enemy right. The Highland reserve, still fifty yards to the rear, struggled to catch up to fill the gap but no sooner had the Jacobite line halted than its left wing began to advance. It was quickly followed by the right wing and 2500 Highlanders in dense columns began to move towards Cope's line. The columns formed by the Highlanders generally coalesced as clan regiments, the advance being led from left to right by Cameron of Lochiel, Stewart of Appin, MacGregor of Glencarnock, the Duke of Perth's Regiment, the MacDonalds of

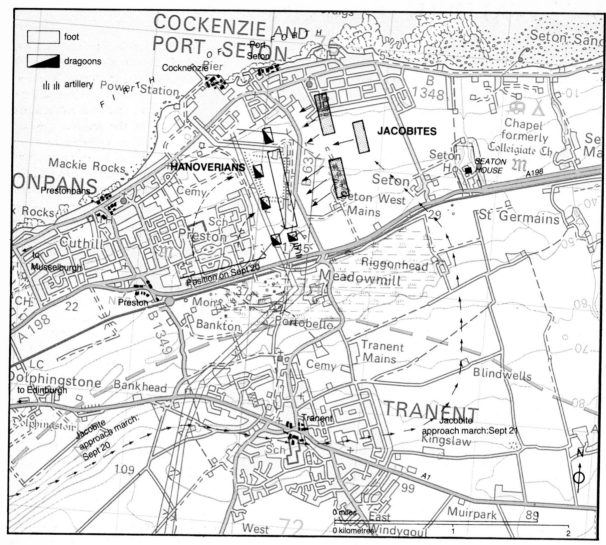

Keppoch and Glencoe, Grant of Glenmoriston, MacDonald of Glengarry, and MacDonald of Clanranald. The reserve was formed by the Athollmen, Menzies of Shian's followers and the MacLachlans.

As the sun rose the government troops beheld the spectacle of the 1400 Highlanders of the front columns bearing down upon them. The 'hideous shout' given by the Highlanders as they charged proved too much for Cope's artillerymen, who promptly disappeared leaving Lieutenant-Colonel Whitefoord and Mr Griffith, the Master-Gunner of Edinburgh Castle, with sufficient time to fire only one round from each piece. When ordered to take the first Highland column in flank, Gordon's Dragoons recoiled scattering the artillery guard who fired an ineffective volley and fled. Most of Cope's infantry managed to fire one disorganised volley, but having done so they immediately made off. Within minutes the entire Hanoverian army was in flight. Such indeed was the speed of the débâcle that the Highland reserve never really caught up with the battle. Most of the Hanoverian casualties fell during the pursuit, and 80 officers and more than 1000 men were captured. Jacobite casualties were probably no higher than 50 and the battle was an enormous boost to their morale. In never once attempting to seize the initiative Sir John Cope had condemned his men to fighting on the Highlanders' terms, a course of action which a commander of un-blooded troops took at his peril.

*The battlefield lies just to the north of Tranent on the A1 in Lothian.*

# A CLIFTON 18 December 1745

# B FALKIRK 17 January 1746

After the Jacobite success at Prestonpans, with morale high, new recruits coming forward, and renewed promises of aid from the French, Charles Edward argued that an advance via Newcastle to London was not only desirable but possible. The rout of Cope's army in a mere ten minutes of battle had convinced the Prince that his Highlanders were invincible. The panic caused by their victorious charge had indeed spread far beyond the battlefield itself, and an anxious government in London began a massive transfer of troops from Flanders. Three Guards battalions, eighteen line regiments, nine squadrons of cavalry, four artillery companies and 6000 Dutch troops together with George II's younger son, the Duke of Cumberland, embarked for Britain.

The Prince was dissuaded from advancing to the east of the Pennines via Newcastle by Lord George Murray who argued that a westerly route was a sounder strategy. A Highland army marching through eastern England could only be making for London and the Hanoverian armies would be able to concentrate to oppose it. A western route, however, opened a number of possibilities, since this line of advance could signify a descent upon London, a rendezvous with a French landing on the west coast, or a combination with a rising in the south-west. Whatever course was finally adopted, the Hanoverian forces assembling in Newcastle under General Wade, in the west Midlands under Sir John Ligonier and along the south-east coast, might be kept guessing until the last moment. Accordingly a Highland army of something over 5000 men left Edinburgh on 3 November 1745 and began a march into north-west England.

Starved of transport and impeded by deep snow General Wade abandoned his attempt to reach Carlisle and the town fell to the Jacobites on 15 November. Leaving behind a garrison of 100 men, Charles Edward advanced by way of Penrith, Lancaster and Preston, reaching Manchester and an enthusiastic welcome from the townspeople on 29 November. Despite these outward shows of success, the Jacobite position was steadily worsening, for the support expected in England had not materialised. Only some 200 members of the Manchester unemployed volunteered to join the Prince and they frankly proclaimed that they had been prepared to enlist in whichever army had reached Manchester first. Since leaving Edinburgh the Jacobites had lost nearly 1000 men through desertion and the

advance had reached a critical point. As the enemy had yet to be encountered, the decision was taken to advance as far as Derby, decoying the Duke of Cumberland, who had assumed Ligonier's command, westwards in the process. At Derby, which was reached on 4 December, the seriousness of the Jacobite position could no longer be ignored. With Cumberland waiting at Stone, Wade marching slowly southwards, and a third army assembling to defend London, the Highlanders would eventually be facing 30,000 government troops. While they might conceivably defeat one of these armies, it was unlikely that the Highlanders would prove equal to the task of routing two or possibly three armies in quick succession. Dismayed at what he believed to be the abandonment of his certain restoration, Charles nevertheless accepted the decision to retreat to Scotland. On 6 December the Jacobite army left Derby and retraced its steps northwards.

The Duke of Cumberland took up pursuit on 9 December with a force of cavalry, dragoons and 1000 mounted infantry. Although slowed by deep snowdrifts and orders from London countermanding his advance, Cumberland eventually caught up with the Highland rearguards to the north of Shap. On 18 December fierce skirmishes took place between government dragoons and the Highland horse in the lanes around the village of Clifton. At 5 pm Cumberland ordered three regiments of dismounted dragoons (Bland's, Cobham's, and Kerr's) across Clifton Moor to attack Lord George Murray's reinforced rearguard of Cluny MacPherson's Regiment, the Appin Stewarts, Roy Stewart's Regiment, and the Glengarrys. Deployed amongst a series of hedged enclosures, the Highlanders returned the musket fire of the advancing dragoons as darkness fell. The most determined attack fell upon the MacPhersons, and after receiving one particularly heavy volley the Highlanders, led by Murray and Cluny, drew their Claymores and charged a party of dragoons lining a ditch about 100 yards away. The dragoons held their position and met the charge in hand-to-hand fighting during which the Highlanders broke several swords on the dragoons' iron skull-caps. Outnumbered, the government troops were forced to retire on their main body across the moor and Murray, well pleased with the evening's work, ordered a general withdrawal towards Penrith. There had been few casualties, probably no more than forty dead and wounded on the government side and twelve on the

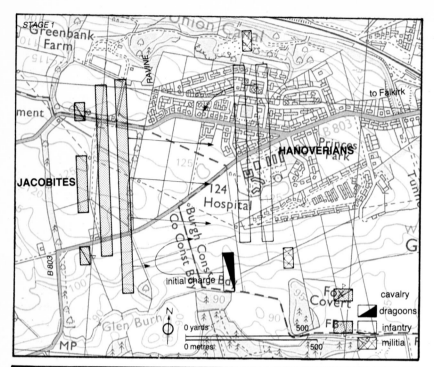

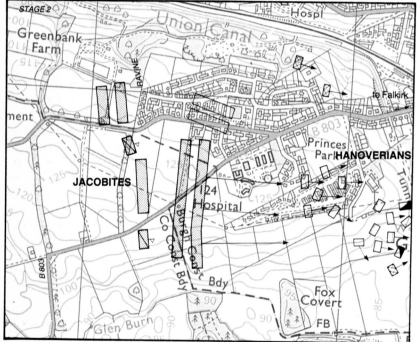

Field Marshal George Wade by Johann Van Diest. Appointed Commander-in-Chief in Scotland in 1725, Wade was responsible for the completion of the chain of forts along the line of the present Caledonian Canal and for the road network which linked the English outposts to the Lowlands.

Lord George Murray armed with the Highlander's traditional weapons in a contemporary portrait. After Culloden, Lord George spent eight months as a fugitive in the Highlands before escaping abroad, first to Holland, then Rome and finally to exile in Germany.

LEFT:
The battle of Falkirk.

*The village of Clifton stands on the A6 six miles (ten kilometres) south of Penrith.*

*The city of Falkirk lies between the M9 and the A803 and the battle was fought on the high ground to the south-west. Follow the B803 south towards Slamannan to see what is still a comparatively unspoilt battlefield. A monument stands at the head of the ravine which protected the Hanoverian right flank.*

Jacobite, but this brief encounter effectively brought Cumberland to a halt. The wintry weather, the exhaustion of his men after a series of forced marches, and the difficulty of the country that lay ahead argued against any immediate pursuit. The Jacobite army crossed safely into Scotland on 20 December with only a forlorn garrison of 400 men left in Carlisle to mark the passage of the last campaign fought on English soil.

Once in Scotland Charles was able to double the strength of his army, for clan reinforcements under Lord Strathallan, and a contingent of 750 Irish troops from France commanded by Lord John Drummond, were waiting at Perth. With fears of a French invasion still paramount in the government's mind, Cumberland was recalled to supervise the defence of London and the south-east. General Wade was rightly considered to be too old to deal with the Jacobites in Scotland and he was replaced by Lieutenant-General Henry Hawley, a soldier renowned for his love of discipline rather than adept leadership. While Hawley was assembling his army in Edinburgh the Prince was busy attempting to reduce Stirling Castle with a train of heavy artillery landed from France.

Hawley's force of 8000 men advanced towards Stirling on 13 January 1746 and Charles, leaving 1000 Highlanders to screen the Castle, concentrated his army on Plean Muir. For the Jacobites the key position was a ridge of moorland rising steeply to the south-west of Falkirk about a mile from Hawley's camp. The forward slope of this ridge would provide an ideal springboard for a Highland charge, and on 17 January Murray advanced to occupy the ridge south-westwards and crossed the River Carron at Dunipace. Meanwhile a deception force under Drummond marched towards Falkirk on the main road from Bannockburn.

As Murray's Highlanders wound their way up the ridge from the west, Hawley at last realised the seriousness of his position and dispatched his three regiments of dragoons (Ligonier's, Hamilton's and Cobham's) up the eastern face. Both armies reached the crest in the midst of a rain storm and immediately deployed for battle. The Jacobites formed two lines with the first company, from left to right, the Appin Stewarts, Camerons, Frasers, MacPhersons, Mackintoshes, Mackenzies, Farquarsons, and Macdonalds, and the second two battalions of Gordon's and Ogilvy's and the three battalions of the Atholl Brigade. Drummond's deception force, coming late to the battlefield, took up position as a reserve behind the second line with the Irish regulars flanked by the Jacobite cavalry. Hawley

had pushed his infantry forward in two lines of six regiments. In the first line were Wolfe's, Cholmondeley's, Pulteney's, the Royal, Price's and Ligonier's Regiments of Foot, and in the second Blakeney's, Munro's, Fleming's, Barrel's, Battereau's and Howard's Foot. The 600 men of the Glasgow Volunteer Regiment took station behind the dragoons while the 1000 Argyllshire Militia drew up on the extreme right near the bottom of the slope.

Before his infantry had time to order its ranks, Hawley launched the dragoons on the left of the Hanoverian line in a charge against the Jacobite right. A shattering volley of musketry delivered when the dragoons were within ten yards of the Highland line brought down eighty horsemen and most of the survivors turned and fled. Careering from the field pursued by the Macdonalds, the dragoons crashed into the Hanoverian left wing and the Glasgow Volunteers, scattering men in every direction. Having already discharged their muskets and being unable to reload because of the lashing rain, the Highland centre drew swords and charged. Equally hampered by damp powder, the Hanoverian centre fired a desultory volley at the approaching clansmen and then ran for their lives. Only on the right, where the infantry were protected from a charge by the ravine, did any regiments hold their position. Here Ligionier's, Price's, and Barrel's Regiments joined forces and advanced up the hill to enfilade the advancing Highland line. So effective was this fire that the pursuit stopped and the Highland ranks began to waver, with many clansmen leaving the field convinced they had been defeated. The situation was restored by the arrival of the Irish picquets who obliged the three Hanoverian regiments to follow the rest of their army along the road to Linlithgow.

Night was falling and Murray, with his own regiments dispersed over the countryside, was content to occupy Falkirk and the enemy camp where quantities of arms, provisions and wines quickly found new owners. The Jacobite loss had been small with no more than 50 dead and 80 wounded, but Hanoverian casualties were substantial with perhaps 350 dead and over 300 taken prisoner. The battle had lasted little more than twenty minutes.

# CULLODEN 16 April 1746

The Jacobite cause gained little from the victory at Falkirk, for the Highland army progressively surrendered the initiative to the government forces. Instead of pursuing Hawley as he retreated to Edinburgh, Charles returned to the siege of Stirling Castle, a task to which his Highlanders were not suited either by inclination or by experience. While Cumberland, who had arrived in Edinburgh on 30 January 1746, was breathing new purpose and confidence into the Hanoverian troops a Jacobite council of war could only suggest retreat. By 21 February the Highland army had fallen back to Inverness there to await the Hanoverian advance. The Jacobites occupied themselves with an attempt to consolidate their hold on the north of Scotland. A remarkable series of sieges, assaults and expeditions was launched with an energy and skill which belied the vulnerability of the rebels. At the end of February Brigadier Walter Stapelton led his Irish picquets, later reinforced by two clan regiments, against Fort Augustus whose garrison (Guise's Regiment) surrendered on 1 March. Stapleton next turned to Fort William, but this proved a tougher proposition and the siege had to be abandoned on 4 April. A raid against government positions in Atholl was successful and Lord George Murray was on the point of capturing Blair Castle when he was recalled. As Cumberland's advance drew closer all the outlying detachments were ordered to rejoin the main force, even though the Prince's comissariat could not provide for their subsistence.

With the arrival of better weather and the concentration of his army at Aberdeen, the Duke of Cumberland was ready to begin operations in the first week of April 1746. On the 12th he crossed the River Spey unopposed by a Highland force which was still widely dispersed. By the 14th Cumberland was approaching Inverness and the Jacobite army drew up on Culloden Moor (known to contemporaries as Drummossie Muir) ready to give battle. The choice of ground was the cause of bitter dispute between John William O'Sullivan, the Prince's Quatermaster and Adjutant-General, and Lord George Murray. O'Sullivan had rejected Murray's choice of a rough, broken ground with strong defensive possibilities near Dalcross Castle in favour of the open moorland at Culloden. Murray rightly argued that to meet a Hanoverian army well equipped in cavalry and artillery on such a ground would be inviting defeat. It was probably his disquiet at the prospect of fighting on

the moor which persuaded Murray to agree to the Prince's scheme for a night march against Cumberland's camp eight miles away at Nairn. Although at least a third of the Highland army were out foraging and only 4500 men could be assembled for this enterprise, the rebels marched off in two columns as night fell on the evening of 15 September. From the start things went awry, and even though the advance guard could barely make two miles an hour its progress was too rapid for the remainder of the force. The heavily encumbered Irish picquets at the rear of the column were falling further and further behind and many of the Highlanders dropped out through hunger and exhaustion. With some distance still to go, Lord George realised the futility of proceeding and despite the Prince's objections and cries of betrayal he ordered a retreat.

It was dawn on 16 April before the famished and worn out Jacobite army returned to Culloden and already their opponents were on the march. Cumberland was determined not to allow the Highlanders time to recover from their nocturnal activity and the news of his approach stunned the Jacobite camp. Officers roused their sleeping men only with the greatest of difficulty, many Highlanders were still out searching

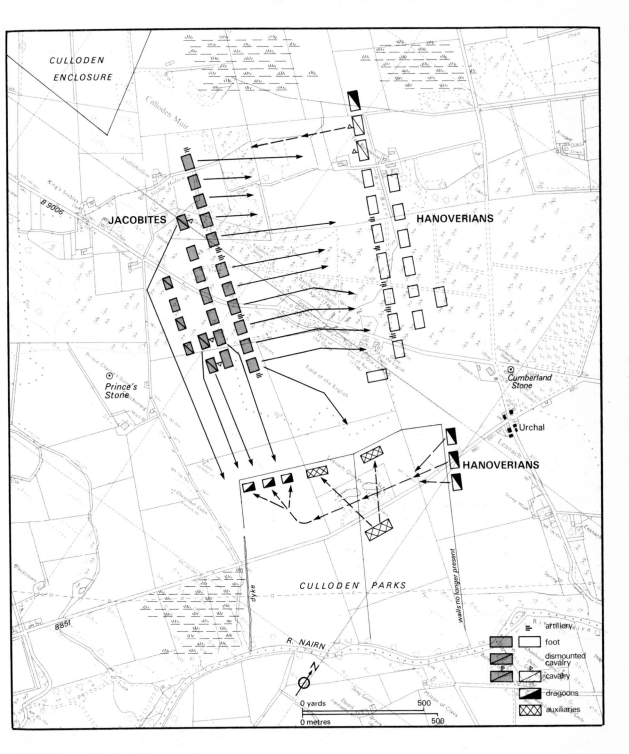

CULLODEN ENCLOSURE

JACOBITES

HANOVERIANS

Prince's Stone

Cumberland Stone

Urchal

HANOVERIANS

CULLODEN PARKS

R. NAIRN

artillery

foot

dismounted cavalry

cavalry

dragoons

auxiliaries

0 yards 500

0 metres 500

OPPOSITE:
A silver tankard made by Gabriel Sleath for William Augustus, Duke of Cumberland, to commemorate his victory at Culloden. The engraved decoration derives from an engraving published six weeks after the battle.

207

Fort Augustus. Pen and grey wash by Thomas Sandby. The fort was constructed in 1726 at the south-west tip of Loch Ness as part of the attempt to pacify the Highlands. The camp of the royal army can be seen on the left and in the foreground a game of nine-holes is in progress as a gun and team pass along the road.

for food, and there was apparently no time to issue fresh orders. The deployment of the army was based on those of 14 and 15 April, including the incomprehensible decision to place the Macdonalds, who claimed it as their right to fight on the right wing, on the left of the line. Charles Edward had perhaps 7000 men in the vicinity of Culloden, but when Cumberland's advance was reported little more than 1000 could be mustered for battle. A wiser commander would perhaps have fallen back to Inverness to allow time for stragglers to be collected, for the Highlanders to be rested and fed, and for the reinforcements who were hurrying south to arrive. Charles, however, was determined to fight, still believing that he could match the enemy in numbers and firepower. In the event, his 5000 Highlanders would face 9000 government troops and a vastly superior train of artillery.

By 11 am the two armies had sighted each other at some 2 miles (3 kilometres) distance and Cumberland halted to deploy his troops. The fifteen regular battalions of Hanoverian infantry drew up in three lines of six, six and three battalions. In the first line, commanded by the Earl of Albermarle and Brigadier Sempill, were the Royal, Cholmondeley's, Price's, Campbell's, Munro's and Barrel's Regiments. In the second, under Major-General Huske, were Howard's, Fleming's, Bligh's, Sempill's, Ligonier's and Wolfe's Regiments. The reserve, commanded by Brigadier Mordaunt, com-

prised Pulteney's, Battereau's, and Blakeney's Regiments. Before the battle began, Pulteney's was ordered up to join the first line and Battereau's the second, while Wolfe's Regiment was moved forwards to flank the Hanoverian left and enfilade any attack on Barrel's Regiment. The Hanoverian horse, commanded by Lieutenant-General Hawley and Major-General Bland, were deployed on either flank, with Kerr's on the left, Kingston's on the right and Cobham's split between both. Loudoun's Independent Company and the Argyllshire Militia fronted the left flank of the army using some convenient stone walls for protection.

The Jacobite front line was composed mainly of Highland regiments, with on the right, under Lord George Murray, the Atholl Brigade, the Camerons, and the Stewarts of Appin. In the centre, under Lord John Drummond, were the Frasers, the Clan Chattan Regiment, the Farquarsons, the Maclachlan-MacLean Regiment, the Chisholms, and the Edinburgh Regiment of John Roy Stewart. The left of the line was held by the MacDonald regiments under the Duke of Perth. Seventy yards to the rear stood the Jacobite second line made up, from right to left, of the regiments of Lord Ogilvy, Lord Gordon, Gordon of Glenbucket, the Duke of Perth, the *Royal Ecossais* and the Irish picquets. Behind the second line were the remnants of the Jacobite horse, of whom many fought dismounted as infantry.

The Jacobite artillery possessed twelve guns of varying calibre, served by indifferent gunners, with which to oppose the Hanoverian three-pounders distributed in five pairs between the regiments of the first line. Shortly after 1 pm, with the sky darkening and rain squalls driving into their faces, the Highland artillery opened the battle. Their fire was slow and largely ineffective but one of their early shots is reported to have narrowly missed the Duke of Cumberland. Weighing nearly 18 stone (114 kilos) and mounted on a large grey horse, the Duke must have been a stimulating target for any gunner. The Hanoverian artillery quickly replied and its superior accuracy and rate of fire at a range of little over 500 yards (455 metres) began to cause mounting casualties in the Jacobite line. For perhaps twenty to twenty-five minutes the Highlanders endured this bombardment with increasing anger and impatience. The roundshot were tearing bloody gaps through the ranks of the Highland regiments and already men were beginning to waver. The order to advance had not been given and it appears that Charles was too far to the rear to appreciate the extent of the casualties his troops were suffering. When the enemy artillery began firing grapeshot the position of the foremost Highland ranks became untenable and Lord George Murray urged the Prince to allow him to advance. No sooner was the order given than the whole of the Jacobite centre surged forward, followed a minute or two later by the right. Only on the left was there futher delay, for here the Macdonalds, still bitterly resentful of their position in the line, refused to charge.

Already driven to breaking point by the enemy artillery, the Highlanders charged in the wildest confusion. Clan Chattan took the lead and as the clans neared the Hanoverian front line they were swept by a storm of grapeshot and musketry. Because this fire was probably heaviest on their left some of the centre clans swerved to the right. As a result the Stewarts, Camerons and Atholl men were pressed into a dense mass and pushed towards the right and the flanking fire of Wolfe's Regiment. Although great gaps were torn in this mass of clansmen, the momentum of the charge carried them into the midst of Barrel's and Munro's Regiments. While Highlander and Hanoverian were locked in bloody hand-to-hand combat, Cumberland ordered Major-General Huske to advance Bligh's and Sempill's Regiments to support the front line. The Highlanders who succeeded in breaking through Munro's and Barrel's were brought to a halt by the fire of these supporting regiments. Trapped between the Hanoverian first and second lines, the clansmen who stood to fight were systematically shot or cut down.

On the Jacobite left the Macdonalds had by now advanced to within 100 yards of Cumberland's line, but with their right flank uncovered by the collapse of the Highland centre, and with their left and rear menaced by Kingston's Horse, the majority of the Clan chose flight before death in a lost cause. As the Highland left fell back, Cobham's dragoons and Kingston's troopers attacked the centre of the Jacobite second line where the Irish Picquets and the *Royal Ecossais* held their ground and then retreated in good order. For some time the cavalry on the left of the Hanoverian line had been moving to outflank the Jacobite right which was protected to some extent by the stone walls of Culloden Parks. The Campbell Militia had been scouting in advance of Hawley's cavalry and they demolished sections of the wall to allow the dragoons through. The latter were able to ride through the Parks and deploy on the moor in the rear of the Jacobite right. The Highland army was now almost encircled and the little cohesion it still retained evaporated in a retreat which quickly became a rout.

As many as 1200 Jacobites died on Culloden Moor and the next day Prince Charles dismissed his remaining followers. With a reward of £30,000 on his head he wandered in the Highlands and Islands for five months before escaping to France and a cheerless exile which still had forty-two years to run. The Duke of Cumberland, who had lost only 50 killed and 260 wounded on the battlefield, returned to London in triumph to have the flower 'Sweet William' named after him. In the Highlands the compliment was reciprocated by the renaming of a particularly unpleasant weed as 'Stinking Willie'.

*The battlefield, which lies a little to the east of Inverness, is now in the care of the National Trust for Scotland and the B9006 running east from the A9 to Nairn leads to the Trust's battlefield information centre and car park.*

# THE BATTLE OF BRITAIN

## THE ROYAL AIR FORCE
### 1918–1940

The Royal Flying Corps was formed on 13 May 1912 with both a military and a naval component. The Naval Wing was officially designated the Royal Naval Air Service on 1 July 1914 and the Royal Flying Corps became an exclusively military formation. The division of Britain's air arm into two almost rival organizations created a number of problems during the First World War and it was in an attempt to solve them that the Royal Air Force (RAF) was established on 1 April 1918. After the war the RAF contracted dramatically and by 1920 its establishment had been reduced to 28,280 personnel and 33 squadrons of which only 12 were based in the United Kingdom.

The deterioration in Anglo-French relations, following France's occupation of the Ruhr in 1923, led to the formation of a Committee under Lord Salisbury whose terms of reference included 'the standard to be aimed at for defining the strength of the Air Force for purposes of Home and Imperial Defence'. The government agreed with the committee's findings that the RAF should achieve parity with the French Air Force by raising its establishment to 52 home squadrons and a first-line strength of 550 aircraft. This expansion was to be completed within five years, but economic and political factors so delayed the programme that even by 1934 only 42 squadrons were in service.

The turning point came when the growing international anxiety over the apparent invincibility of air attack convinced the government that Britain's air defences should be urgently expanded and modernized. The horrific prediction by military experts that hundreds of thousands of civilian casualties could be expected in the first weeks of an air war created a public concern which the politicians could not ignore. The renaissance of the German Air Force, whose modernity and professionalism was amply demonstrated during the Spanish Civil War, strengthened the case of those British politicians who had urged rearmament. The effect on the RAF was dramatic. In the early 1930s the majority of squadrons were flying aircraft types that dated from the First World War; by 1939 they were operating metal monoplane fighters and heavy long-range bombers. In 1934 the RAF had 564 aircraft based in the United Kingdom and 168 overseas. In September 1939 the figures were 1476 and 435 respectively. During the same period the regular strength of the service grew from 30,000 to 118,000 and the reserve from 11,000 to 68,000.

The manufacturing capacity to increase the aircraft strength of the RAF was provided gradually until, by the autumn of 1939, 800 new aircraft a month were being produced. A large proportion of these were used to expand the reserves supporting the front-line units rather than simply to increase the number of squadrons. When war came, the operational squadrons were supported by 2000 reserve aircraft, and the number of airfields had also grown, from 52 in 1934 to 138 in 1939. From 1938 the RAF's rearmament was based on a programme known as 'Scheme M' which envisaged a United Kingdom strength of 163 squadrons and an overseas deployment of 49 squadrons. The home force would include 50 fighter squadrons with 800 first-line aircraft, and 85 heavy bomber squadrons with 1360 aircraft. The scheme was not, however, due for completion before March 1942 and when the war began Bomber Command mobilized 33 squadrons, Fighter Command 39 and Coastal Command 19. A total of $34\frac{1}{2}$ squadrons were based on stations in the Middle East, India, Singapore and Malaya. At the outbreak of war the RAF's functional Commands were divided into Bomber, Fighter, Coastal, Balloon, Training, Maintenance and Reserve Commands, plus the Advanced Air Striking Force and the British Expeditionary Force Air Component.

Hurricanes (foreground) and Spitfires in close formation. Both aircraft were powered by liquid-cooled Rolls-Royce Merlin engines of 1030 hp, but whereas the Hurricane had a maximum speed of 328 mph (525 kph) at 20,000 feet (6096 metres) the Spitfire could reach 362 mph (579 kph) at 19,000 feet (5791 metres).

The Hawker Hurricane, one of the RAF's new generation of aircraft, became operational with Fighter Command at the end of 1937, shortly before the Luftwaffe accepted the Messerschmitt Bf 109E, the fighter which was to represent the Hurricane's main opponent. Although technically outclassed by the Bf 109, the Hurricane achieved remarkable success during the Battle of Britain and 1715 Hurricanes took part in the fighting between July and October 1940. The contribution the Hurricane made is often overlooked in the light of the subsequent performance of its more dashing colleague, the Supermarine Spitfire, but during the Battle the operational ratio of Hurricanes to Spitfires was 5 to 3. The Hurricane and Spitfire were supported in fighter operations by the Boulton Paul Defiant, the Gloster Gladiator and the Bristol Blenheim.

While the new fighters were being developed research was also proceeding into a radio direction finding (RDF) technique which was ultimately to make a vital contribution to their success. The work of a team of scientists on the principles of radar provided a means of locating approaching aircraft up to a height of 10,000 feet (3048 metres) and a distance of 100 miles (160 kilometres). The construction along the south and east coasts of twenty radar stations, known as Chain Home (CH), operating on a 10 metre waveband provided a defence against aircraft operating at normal heights but not against low-flying intruders. This potentially serious gap in the system was filled by the Chain Home

Low (CHL) stations which operated on a 1.5 metre waveband. Although of short range these stations were effective in tracking low-flying targets. The CH and CHL stations were supported by a number of mobile stations capable of providing temporary cover in the event of damage to the fixed radar. During the Battle, information from the radar stations was passed to the filter room at Fighter Command HQ (RAF Bentley Priory) which also received details of visual sightings of aircraft from the Observer Corps. After evaluation, the main control centre at Fighter Command passed the relevant information to Group control centres, which authorized Sector controllers to scramble fighter squadrons against the approaching target. As a result the slender resources of aircraft and men in Fighter Command could be employed in the most tactically effective manner amidst a sequence of developing attacks.

Enemy aircraft which evaded the fighter screen had to run the gauntlet of the ground defences manned by Anti-Aircraft Command and Balloon Command. The seven divisions comprising Anti-Aircraft Command were part of the British Army but came under the operational direction of Fighter Command. They deployed nearly 4000 searchlights and 2000 guns, of which two major types were the heavy 4.5 inch (11.4 centimetres) and the mobile 3.7 inch (9.4 centimetres). The latter fired a shell weighing 28 pounds (12.7 kilograms) to an altitude of 25,000 feet (7620 metres). During the Battle of Britain 500,000 men and women served in Anti-Aircraft Command and they claimed 164 enemy aircraft destroyed. The role of Balloon Command was to prevent low-level precision bombing and by the end of July 1940, 1466 balloons were deployed around key targets.

# THE BATTLE OF BRITAIN
## 10 JULY–31 OCTOBER 1940

The move of the British Expeditionary Force (BEF) to Europe in 1939 was accompanied by two RAF formations, the Advanced Air Striking Force of Bomber Command and the Air Component BEF. When the German assault upon the Low Countries began, the Air Component was progressively reinforced and after 23 May the fighters of No 11 Group were sent into action across the Channel. In the months of May and June 1940, 931 RAF aircraft were destroyed and 1526 personnel became casualties or prisoners of war. After the BEF's evacuation from France the RAF's task was primarily a defensive one of maintaining air superiority over Britain. In the early summer of 1940 its ability to carry out this role was by no means certain since it was short of pilots, planes and anti-aircraft guns. In the first week of July, Fighter Command, on whom the brunt of the battle would fall, could muster only 58 squadrons against an estimated requirement of 120. Existing squadrons still needed 197 pilots to bring them to full strength, while Anti-Aircraft Command possessed only 55 per cent of its establishment in heavy and 30 per cent of its establishment in light weapons.

Hitler believed that with the defeat of France Britain would seek an armistice. When Winston Churchill expressed the nation's determination to fight on, Hitler decided to launch Operation Sealion, the seaborne invasion of Britain. The High Command of the German Army and Navy regarded the operation with considerable misgivings and only Reichsmarschall Hermann Goering, Air Minister and Commander-in-Chief of the Luftwaffe, viewed the campaign with enthusiasm. The destruction of the RAF was a vital prerequisite of a successful invasion and Goering was eager to prove that the Luftwaffe unaided could bring Britain to her knees. The Luftwaffe was, however, a short-range airforce designed primarily for tactial operations in support of the army, and it was ill-prepared for a long strategic battle in enemy skies. Goering's chance of success lay in a sharp, decisive onslaught which would overwhelm the RAF's defences and destroy its airfields and support services.

During July 1940 Goering assembled over 2800 aircraft organized in three Luftflotten (air fleets), each of which was a self-contained airforce allocated to a specific area of operations. Luftflotte 2, under General-oberst Kesselring operated from north-eastern France and the Low Countries; Luftflotte 3 under Hugo Sperrle was based in the remainder of occupied France; and Luftflotte 5 under Hans-Jurgen Stumpff operated from Norway. Such a dispersion of force required finely-tuned co-operation between the Luftflotten for an effective campaign against the RAF. The Luftflotten flew three types of twin-engined bombers, the Heinkel 111 H-2, the Dornier 172 and the Ju 88A-1, and all suffered from a relatively-low flying speed and poor defensive armament. A single-engined bomber, the Ju 87 Stuka also took part in the early attacks on Britain, but heavy losses necessitated its withdrawal from the Battle in mid-August. The Luftflotten deployed an excellent single-seat fighter, the Messerschmitt Bf 109, and a twin-engined long-range fighter, the Bf 110C, which although heavily armed lacked the manoeuvrability of the Hurricane and Spitfire.

To meet the onslaught the RAF possessed 591 serviceable aircraft and 1200 pilots at the start of July 1940. The available squadrons were deployed in four Groups: No 10 (south-west England), No 11 (south-east England), No 12 (eastern counties and Midlands) and No 13 (N. England, Scotland and N. Ireland). At the end of the year they were joined by two newly-formed Groups, Nos 9 and 14. The fighter squadrons were supported by the Observer Corps, Anti-Aircraft Command, Balloon Command and No 60 Group controlling the chain of radar stations. The number of squadrons in each Fighter Group varied with tactical requirements. On 9 July, for example, 10 Group held four operational squadrons while 11 Group in the vulnerable south-east deployed twenty-two. Each Group contained sector stations which controlled a number of squadrons ranging, depending upon the overall size of the Group, from one to four. No 11 Group was divided into seven sectors – Middle Wallop, Tangmere, Kenley, Biggin Hill, Hornchurch, Northolt and North Weald – each of which directed its squadrons on to enemy formations once the aircraft had been scrambled by Group. The normal fighter complement of each squadron was twelve aircraft and during the Battle single-seater squadrons averaged a strength of nineteen pilots. The eight available night-fighter squadrons (six Blenheim and two Defiant) were dispersed around Britain, with the Blenheims allocated between 10, 11, 12, and 13 Groups in the ratio 1:2:2:1, and with the Defiant squadrons deployed between 11, 12 and 13 Groups.

Although German bombers mounted night raids against land targets in Britain from the end of the first week of June 1940, the Battle of Britain only began

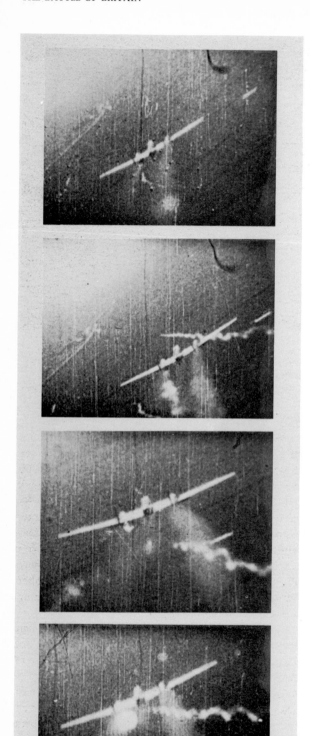

officially on 10 July with the commencement of daylight raids against south-coast ports and merchant shipping. Many attacks took place in the Channel where the defending fighters were operating close to their own maximum range and that of the defensive system which supported them. It was impossible to maintain permanent figher cover over the convoys and the need to fly nearly 600 sorties a day in defence of shipping produced a testing period for the aircraft and pilots of Fighter Command. Even so, 217 German aircraft were lost between 10 July and 10 August against 96 by the RAF. The coastal attacks were merely the forerunner to the decisive battle for air superiority over Britain which the Luftwaffe had to fight and win if Operation Sealion was to succeed.

By 11 August the RAF could put 749 fighters into the air against a total of 2550 German aircraft, of which 1029 were fighters. In ensuring that Fighter Command was able to cope with such odds its commander, Air Chief Marshal Sir Hugh Dowding, and his Group commanders faced a task which required great judgement and daring. The endurance of Dowding's fighter aircraft was little more than sixty minutes, and if they were scrambled too early or launched against a raid which was only a feint, they might be unable to stay in the air to meet the enemy's main attack. Against this, the fighters had to be given adequate time (about fifteen minutes) to climb to a height from which they could intercept enemy aircraft. The radar stations played a vital role in this deadly equation, for the information they supplied of the number, strength and direction of raids allowed Fighter Command to commit its aircraft to battle in the most efficient way and at the most effective moment. On 12 August the Luftwaffe mounted a large raid against the radar stations on the south coast of Britain. Five were damaged and one, at Ventnor on the Isle of Wight, destroyed. A gap had been torn in the radar defence and German bombers poured through to attack Fighter Command's airfields. Fortunately, aircraft from 11 Group were able to attack all the major raids and only the airfields at Lympne, Hawkinge and Manston were badly damaged.

LEFT:
The destruction of a Messerschmitt Bf 110C recorded by the camera gun of an RAF fighter. The Bf 110, which was flown by the elite of the Luftwaffe's pilots, was fast (maximum speed 349 mph/558 kph at 22,960 feet/6998 metres) and its nose armament packed a powerful punch ($4 \times 7.9$ mm machine guns and $2 \times 20$ mm cannon). Its wide turning circle limited its effectiveness as a pure fighter aircraft, but it was to achieve considerable success as a fighter/bomber.

Air Chief Marshal Lord Dowding of Bentley Priory, C-in-C, Fighter Command, July 1936 to November 1940. Dowding's vision, determination and keen awareness of the complexities of aerial warfare, produced a quality and strength of leadership which enabled Fighter Command first to survive and then to defeat the Luftwaffe's offensive.

The Operations Room at HQ Fighter Command. The state of the battle at any moment could be seen on the plotting table in the well of the operations room. Members of the Women's Auxiliary Air Force (WAAFs) maintained the plot which gave details of the height, strength, position and direction of raids on Britain.

The Luftwaffe's major assault on the RAF was planned as 'Eagle Day' (*Adlertag*), and it was launched on 13 August 1940 when 1485 sorties were flown; repeated on 15 August with 1786 sorties; and then continued in mounting desperation into September. The German planners had allowed four days for the destruction of Fighter Command's resources in southern England, and four weeks for the defeat of the entire RAF. Yet four weeks after *Adlertag* the RAF's fighters were still rising to meet the Luftwaffe's major raids. Despite the fact that the Luftwaffe was putting over 1000 planes into the air every day, Fighter Command was in fact losing aircraft at a rate which, with the number of new planes being produced, it could maintain for some time. Where it was being dangerously weakened was in the number of pilots available for operations. Between 8 and 18 August 154 fighter pilots were lost and only 63 replacements arrived from the training schools. If pilot losses continued at this rate Fighter Command, no matter how many aircraft it possessed, would be swept from the skies over Britain.

The Luftwaffe, however, had also suffered serious losses and with 'Sealion' scheduled for 15 September the air attack was running out of time. The invasion date was postponed until 21 September but for even this date to be feasible the RAF had to be eliminated by the 11th. In an attempt to achieve a final breakthrough the Luftwaffe turned its attention to London. By attacking the British capital the Germans hoped to draw Fighter Command into a final battle of annihilation, while at the same time breaking civilian morale and paralysing the machinery of government. The bombing of London was also in revenge for RAF Bomber Command's raids on Berlin, an attack which Goering had said could never take place.

In the late afternoon of 7 September 900 German aircraft crossed the English coast bound for London. The fighter defences, expecting the customary raids on the sector stations, were unprepared for this change of target and the German bombers were able to deliver their load of high explosives and incendiaries against little opposition. That night a further 250 bombers arrived over the capital and Londoners experienced their first taste of the terror which was to become known as 'The Blitz'. During the day Britain's anti-invasion forces had been ordered to Alert 1: 'Invasion imminent, and probable within twelve hours', and as London burned through the night the code-word

Two Dornier 17s bombing the Royal Docks in the East End of London on 7 September 1940.

'Cromwell' was flashed to the Home Forces bringing them to immediate readiness. At sea the Royal Navy waited to intercept the invasion fleet while Bomber Command attacked the French and Belgian ports from which that fleet might sail. Over the next days the Luftwaffe launched repeated raids on London, but by day Fighter Command was waiting and its aircraft harried the German bombers to and from their target. Only at night was the Luftwaffe able to achieve significant results. On Sunday 15 September nearly 1000 aircraft were dispatched against London, in a day of combat which was to prove the climax of the Battle of Britain. Squadron after squadron of British fighters were sent into the air to meet this attack and when Winston Churchill, who was visiting 11 Group's Operation Room at Uxbridge, questioned Air Vice-Marshal Park on the state of Fighter Command's reserves, he received the reply 'there are none'. The battle, however, went decisively in the RAF's favour and for the loss of twenty-six aircraft they shot down sixty.

On 17 September Hitler postponed 'Sealion' indefinitely, but the Luftwaffe's attack continued with day and night raids on London and other important cites. In the two months between 7 September and 13 November there was only one night on which London escaped bombing, and each raid consisted of up to 300 aircraft. The Blitz continued until May 1941 and nearly 90,000 civilians were killed or injured by the Luftwaffe. During the Battle of Britain, Fighter Command lost 507 aircrew killed (of 14 different nationalities) and 500 wounded, but for the loss of 915 aircraft they destroyed 1733 German planes. In all the praise given to the Allied pilots who preserved Britain and the free world from Nazi conquest, there has been no more eloquent tribute than that paid by Winston Churchill . . ., 'Never in the field of human conflict was so much owed by so many to so few.'

---

*The Battle of Britain Museum at Hendon, to the north of London, houses the world's most comprehensive collection of aircraft and equipment used in the Battle. Both German and British aircraft are displayed, and a Spitfire and Hurricane can be seen in a re-creation of the 'E' Pens used on Fighter Command airfields to protect aircraft from blast.*

*The Battle of Britain Memorial Flight stationed at RAF Coningsby in Lincolnshire preserves aircraft of the period in flying condition, and they can often be seen in flight over the many airshows held in Britain.*

---

# REGIMENTAL TABLE

*In order that the reader may identify the later service of regiments which fought in Britain between 1660 and 1746, a selective listing of their subsequent regimental titles is given below. The dates in brackets are those after which each title came into use. Regiments which were disbanded at the conclusion of a campaign have not been included.*

## SEDGEMOOR 1685

**The King's Regiment of Horse Guards:** (1819) The Royal Horse Guards (The Blues), (1969) The Blues and Royals (Royal Horse Guards and 1st Dragoons) (on amalgamation with the Royal Dragoons)

**The King's Regiment of Horse:** (1746) 1st King's Dragoon Guards, (1959) 1st The Queen's Dragoon Guards (on amalgamation with the Queen's Bays)

**The King's Own Royal Regiment of Dragoons:** (1751) 1st (Royal) Dragoons, (1969) The Blues and Royals (Royal Horse Guards and 1st Dragoons)

**The First Regiment of Foot Guards:** (1815) 1st, or Grenadier Regiment of Foot Guards

**The Second Regiment of Foot Guards:** (1817) The Coldstream Guards

**Dumbarton's Regiment:** (1751) 1st or The Royal Regiment of Foot, (1920) The Royal Scots (The Royal Regiment)

**Kirke's Regiment:** (1727) The Queen's Own Royal Regiment of Foot, (1881) The Queens (Royal West Surrey Regiment), (1959) The Queen's Royal Surrey Regiment (on amalgamation with the East Surrey Regiment), (1966) 1st Battalion, The Queen's Regiment

**Trelawney's Regiment:** (1751) 4th, or The King's Own Regiment, (1881) The King's Own Royal Regiment (Lancaster), (1959) The King's Own Royal Border Regiment (on amalgamation with the Border Regiment)

## KILLIECRANKIE AND DUNKELD 1689

**Hasting's Regiment:** (1751) 13th Foot, (1881) The Somerset Light Infantry (Prince Albert's), (1959) The Somerset and Cornwall Light Infantry, (1968) 1st Battalion, The Light Infantry

**Leven's Regiment:** (1751) 25th (Edinburgh) Foot, (1805) 25th (The King's Own Borderers) Foot, (1887) The King's Own Scottish Borderers

**Earl of Angus's Regiment:** (1751) 26th Foot (The Cameronians), (1881) The Cameronians (Scottish Rifles), (1968) Disbanded

## PRESTON AND SHERIFFMUIR 1715

**Pitt's Regiment of Horse:** (1746) 2nd Queen's Dragoon Guards, (1921) The Queen's Bays (2nd Dragoon Guards), (1959) 1st The Queen's Dragoon Guards (on amalgamation with 1st King's Dragoon Guards)

**Portmore's Regiment of Dragoons:** (1751) 2nd Royal North British Dragoons, (1921) The Royal Scots Greys (2nd Dragoons), (1971) The Royal Scots Dragoon Guards (Carabiniers and Greys) (on amalgamation with 3rd Carabiniers)

**Carpenter's Regiment of Dragoons:** (1751) 3rd (King's Own) Dragoons, (1861) 3rd (King's Own) Hussars, (1958) The Queen's Own Hussars (on amalgamation with 7th Queen's Own Hussars)

**Evans's Regiment of Dragoons:** (1751) 4th Dragoons, (1861) 4th (The Queen's Own) Hussars, (1958) The Queen's Royal Irish Hussars (on amalgamation with 8th King's Royal Irish Hussars)

**Stair's Regiment of Dragoons:** (1751) 6th (Inniskilling) Dragoons, (1922) 5th/6th Dragoons (on amalgamation with 5th Dragoon Guards), (1935) 5th Royal Inniskilling Dragoon Guards

**Kerr's Regiment of Dragoons:** (1751) 7th, or Queen's Own Dragoons, (1805) 7th (Queen's Own) Hussars, (1958) The Queen's Own Hussars

**Wynn's Regiment of Dragoons:** (1751) 9th Dragoons, (1816) 9th Lancers, (1921) 9th Queen's Royal Lancers, (1960) 9th/12th Royal Lancers (Prince of Wales's) (on amalgamation with 12th Royal Lancers)

**Honeywood's Regiment of Dragoons:** (1751) 11th Dragoons, (1840) 11th Prince Albert's Own Hussars, (1921) 11th Hussars (Prince Albert's Own), (1969) The Royal Hussars (Prince of Wales's Own) (on amalgamation with 10th Royal Hussars)

**Munden's Regiment of Dragoons:** (1751) 13th Dragoons, (1861) 13th Hussars, (1922) 13th/18th Royal Hussars (Queen Mary's Own) (on amalgamation with 18th Royal Hussars)

**Dormer's Regiment of Dragoons:** (1720) 14th Dragoons, (1861) 14th (King's) Hussars, (1922) 14th/20th Hussars (on amalgamation with 20th Hussars)

**Forfar's Regiment:** (1751) 3rd (or The Buffs) Foot, (1881) The Buffs (East Kent Regiment), (1961) The Queen's Own Buffs (on amalgamation with The Queen's Own Royal West Kent Regiment), (1966) 2nd Battalion The Queen's Regiment

**Morrison's Regiment:** (1751) 8th (The King's Regiment), (1881) The King's (Liverpool Regiment), (1958) The King's Regiment (Manchester and Liverpool) (on amalgamation with The Manchester Regiment)

**Montagu's Regiment:** (1751) 11th Foot, (1881) The Devonshire Regiment, (1958) The Devonshire and Dorset Regiment (on amalgamation with The Dorset Regiment)

**Clayton's Regiment:** (1751) 14th Foot, (1881) The Prince of Wales's Own (West Yorkshire Regiment), (1958) The Prince of Wales's Own Regiment of Yorkshire (on amalgamation with The East Yorkshire Regiment)

**Wightman's Regiment:** (1751) 17th Foot, (1881) The Leicestershire Regiment, (1964) 4th (Leicestershire) Battalion The Royal Anglian Regiment, (1970) Disbanded

**Orrery's Regiment:** (1751) 21st (Royal North British) Fusiliers, (1881) The Royal Scots Fusiliers, (1959) The Royal Highland Fusiliers (Princess Margaret's Own Glasgow and Ayrshire Regiment) (on amalgamation with The Highland Light Infantry)

**Shannon's Regiment:** (1751) 25th (Edinburgh) Foot (see Leven's Regiment, 1689)

**Preston's Regiment:** (1751) 26th Foot (The Cameronians) (see Earl of Angus's Regiment, 1689)

**Egerton's Regiment:** (1751) 36th Foot, (1881) The Worcestershire Regiment, (1970) The Worcestershire and Sherwood Foresters Regiment (29th/45th Foot) (on amalgamation with The Sherwood Foresters)

## PRESTONPANS 1745

**Gardiner's Regiment of Dragoons:** (1751) 13th Dragoons (see Munden's Regiment of Dragoons)

**Hamilton's Regiment of Dragoons:** (1720) 14th Dragoons (see Dormer's Regiment of Dragoons)

**Guise's Regiment:** (1751) 6th Foot, (1881) The Royal Warwickshire Regiment, (1963) The Royal Warwickshire Fusiliers, (1968) The Royal Regiment of Fusiliers (on amalgamation with the Northumberland, Royal and Lancashire Fusiliers)

**Lee's Regiment:** (1748) 44th Foot, (1881) The Essex Regiment, (1958) 3rd East Anglian Regiment (16th/44th Foot) (on amalgamation with the Bedfordshire and Hertfordshire Regiment), (1968) 3rd Battalion, The Royal Anglian Regiment

**Murray's Regiment:** (1748) 46th Foot, (1881) The Duke of Cornwall's Light Infantry, (1959) The Somerset and Cornwall Light Infantry (on amalgamation with The Somerset Light Infantry), (1968) 1st Battalion, The Light Infantry

**Lascelles's Regiment:** (1751) 47th Foot, (1881) The Loyal North Lancashire Regiment, (1921) The Loyal Regiment (North Lancashire), (1970) The Queen's Lancashire Regiment (on amalgamation with the Lancashire Regiment)

## CLIFTON 1745

**Bland's Regiment of Dragoons:** (1751) 3rd (King's Own) Dragoons (see Carpenter's Regiment of Dragoons, 1715)

**Cobham's Regiment of Dragoons:** (1751) 10th Dragoons, (1806) 10th, or Prince of Wales's Own Hussars, (1921) 10th Royal Hussars (Prince of Wales's Own), (1969) The Royal Hussars (on amalgamation with 11th Hussars)

**Kerr's Regiment of Dragoons:** (1751) 11th Dragoons (see Honeywood's Regiment of Dragoons, 1715)

## FALKIRK 1746

**Cobham's Regiment of Dragoons:** (1751) 10th Dragoons (see Cobham's Regiment of Dragoons, Clifton, 1745)

**Ligonier's Regiment of Dragoons:** (1751) 13th Dragoons (see Munden's Regiment of Dragoons, 1715)

**Hamilton's Regiment of Dragoons:** (see Dormer's Regiment of Dragoons, 1715)

**The Royal Regiment:** (1751) 1st, or Royal Regiment of Foot (see Dumbarton's Regiment, 1685)

**Howard's Regiment:** (1751) 3rd (or the Buffs) Foot (see Forfar's Regiment, 1715)

**Barrell's Regiment:** (1751) 4th, or The King's Own Regiment, (1881) The King's Own Royal Regiment (Lancaster), (1959) The King's Own Royal Border Regiment (on amalgamation with The Border Regiment)

**Wolfe's Regiment:** (1751) 8th (The King's Regiment) (see Morrison's Regiment, 1715)

**Pulteney's Regiment:** (1751) 13th Foot (see Hasting's Regiment, 1689)

**Price's Regiment:** (1751) 14th Foot (see Clayton's Regiment, 1715)

**Blakeney's Regiment:** (1751) 27th (Inniskilling) Foot, (1881) The Royal Inniskilling Fusiliers, (1968) The Royal Irish Rangers (on amalgamation with The Royal Ulster Rifles and The Royal Irish Fusiliers)

**Cholmondeley's Regiment:** (1751) 34th Foot, (1881) The Border Regiment, (1959) The King's Own Royal Border Regiment (on amalgamation with The King's Own Regiment (Lancaster))

**Fleming's Regiment:** (1751) 36th Foot (see Egerton's Regiment, 1715)

**Munro's Regiment:** (1751) 37th Foot, (1881) The Hampshire Regiment, (1946) The Royal Hampshire Regiment

**Ligonier's Regiment:** (1751) 48th Foot, (1881) The Northamptonshire Regiment, (1960) The 2nd East Anglian Regiment (Duchess of Gloucester's Own Royal

Lincolnshire and Northamptonshire) (on amalgamation with The Royal Lincolnshire Regiment), (1968) 2nd Battalion, The Royal Anglian Regiment

## CULLODEN 1746

**Cobham's Regiment of Dragoons:** (1751) 10th Dragoons (see Cobham's Regiment of Dragoons, Clifton, 1745)

**Kerr's Regiment of Dragoons:** (1751) 11th Dragoons (see Honeywood's Regiment of Dragoons, 1715)

**The Royal Regiment:** (1751) 1st, or Royal Regiment of Foot (see Dumbarton's Regiment, 1685)

**Howard's Regiment:** (1751) 3rd (or the Buffs) Foot (see Forfar's Regiment, 1715)

**Barrell's Regiment:** (1751) 4th, or The King's Own Regiment (see Barrell's Regiment, Falkirk, 1746)

**Wolfe's Regiment:** (1751) 8th (The King's Regiment) (see Morrison's Regiment, 1715)

**Pulteney's Regiment:** (1751) 13th Foot (see Hasting's Regiment, 1689)

**Price's Regiment:** (1751) 14th Foot (see Clayton's Regiment, 1715)

**Bligh's Regiment:** (1751) 20th Foot, (1881) The Lancashire Fusiliers, (1968) 4th Battalion, The Royal Regiment of Fusiliers, (1969) Disbanded

**Campbell's Regiment:** (1751) 21st (Royal North British) Fusiliers (see Orrery's Regiment, 1715)

**Sempill's Regiment:** (1751) 25th (Edinburgh) Foot (see Leven's Regiment, 1689)

**Blakeney's Regiment:** (1751) 27th (Inniskilling) Foot (see Blakeney's Regiment, Falkirk, 1746)

**Cholmondeley's Regiment:** (1751) 34th Foot (see Cholmondeley's Regiment, Falkirk, 1746)

**Fleming's Regiment:** (1751) 36th Foot (see Egerton's Regiment, 1715)

**Munro's Regiment:** (1751) 37th Foot (see Munro's Regiment, Falkirk, 1746)

**Ligonier's Regiment:** (1751) 48th Foot (see Ligonier's Regiment, Falkirk, 1746)

# GAZETTEER

**ENGLAND**

AVON
Dyrham

BERKSHIRE
Ashdown (Aldworth)
First and Second Battle of Newbury

CORNWALL
Lostwithiel
Stratton

DURHAM
Neville's Cross

EAST SUSSEX
Hastings (Battle)
Lewes

ESSEX
Maldon
Assandun (Ashingdon)

GLOUCESTERSHIRE
Tewkesbury

HAMPSHIRE
Cheriton

HEREFORD AND WORCESTER
Evesham
Mortimer's Cross
Worcester

HERTFORDSHIRE
First and Second Battle of St Albans
Barnet

KENT
Medway

LANCASHIRE
Preston

LEICESTERSHIRE
Bosworth Field (Market Bosworth)

NORTHAMPTONSHIRE
Northampton
Naseby

NORTHUMBERLAND
Hadrian's Wall
Halidon Hill
Homildon Hill
Hedgeley Moor
Hexham
Flodden (Branxton)

NOTTINGHAMSHIRE
Stoke (East Stoke)

OXFORDSHIRE
Edgcote
Chalgrove Field
Cropredy Bridge

SALOP
Shrewsbury

SOMERSET
Lansdown
Langport
Sedgemoor

STAFFORDSHIRE
Blore Heath

WARWICKSHIRE
Boudicca (Mancetter?)
Edgehill

WILTSHIRE
Mt Badon
Ellandun (Wroughton)
Ethandun (Edington)
Roundway Down

NORTH YORKSHIRE
Stamford Bridge
Battle of the Standard (Northallerton)
Otterburn
Towton
Marston Moor

WEST YORKSHIRE
Wakefield

## SCOTLAND

CENTRAL
Stirling Bridge
Falkirk
Bannockburn
Sheriffmuir
Clifton
Falkirk

GRAMPIAN
Mons Graupius (near Aberdeen?)

HIGHLAND
Glenshiel
Culloden

LOTHIAN
Pinkie Cleuch
Dunbar
Prestonpans

STRATHCLYDE
Drumclog
Bothwell Bridge

TAYSIDE
Nechtanesmere (Dunnichen)
Killiecrankie
Dunkeld

## WALES

POWYS
Cefn Carnedd

# GLOSSARY

**Battle:** One of the groupings into which medieval armies were often divided. An army would normally, but not always, be formed in three 'battles' for ease of movement and control, and to facilitate tactical deployment. The first 'battle' would function as a vanguard, the second as the main 'battle', and the third as a rearguard.

**Bill/Billmen:** A staff weapon derived from the agricultural implement commonly known as a billhook. The head of the bill had a curved cutting hook in front topped by a spike, with lugs protruding from the base of the head to form a parrying guard. The recorded use of the bill stretches from the thirteenth to the seventeenth century and it was particularly popular with British infantry. Those wielding this weapon were known as billmen.

**Brigade:** An administrative and tactical grouping of squadrons of horse, regiments of foot, dragoons, or artillery. The number of units in a brigade was not a precise establishment but may generally be said to have comprised three regiments or six battalions in the case of foot, and eight, ten, or twelve squadrons in the case of horse. Brigades were usually temporary groupings that were dispersed at the conclusion of a campaign.

**Commission of Array:** From the beginning of the fourteenth century to the middle of the sixteenth, troops were arrayed and mustered in response to commissions from the Crown. These were issued to two or more persons of position and authority in each country to enable them to raise troops in the king's name. Soldiers thus raised could be employed on military expeditions outside England as well as for local defence.

**Dragoon:** A soldier normally trained to fight on foot but who used a horse for mobility when not in action. The term is derived from the short musket, or 'dragon', originally issued to such troops c.1600.

**Enfilade:** To rake the enemy with fire from the flank.

**Forlorn Hope:** A party of troops charged with a particularly hazardous duty, often in advance of the main body of the army, during the execution of which they are likely to be seriously outnumbered and to suffer disproportionately heavy casualties. Troops leading a charge or storming operation are often said to be a forlorn hope, as are those placed in an exposed position as skirmishers to delay the advance of the enemy. In the 17th and 18th centuries a role which dragoons found themselves increasingly called upon to play as they were often the first to fall in with the enemy.

**Glaive:** A term applied in early periods to the lance and later to swords and large daggers, but which is more generally used to describe staff weapons possessing a long blade, particularly those with a blade resembling a cleaver or scythe.

**Grape shot:** Although strictly descriptive of shot containing nine large bullets wired together, the term 'grape' was loosely and inaccurately applied by contemporaries to case shot. This comprised a tin case, wooden box or linen bag filled with loose bullets which left the container as it emerged from the bore of the cannon on firing. The bullets thereafter spread out in flight across the frontage of the gun and were an extremely effective killing agent at short ranges.

**Mêlée:** A close-quarter fight in which formal battle lines dissolve in a mass of intermingled combatants.

**Militia:** The body of the nation's active male citizens (normally aged between fifteen and sixty) who may be called upon to muster with weapons in defence of the realm. Although an obligation from time immemorial, the term is specifically used from the late sixteenth century to denote the non-professional forces maintained at the expense of the counties rather than of the Exchequer. The obligation to fulfil the county quota of men and arms fell upon the Lord Lieutenant and through him upon the owners of property, although those required to serve could supply substitutes.

**New Model Army:** An army raised by Parliament, through an ordinance passed by the Commons on 27 January 1645, as a permanent, national force which was capable of deployment and sustained campaigning anywhere in the United Kingdom. The Army's commander, Sir Thomas Fairfax, was authorized to nominate his own officers subject to Parliamentary scrutiny, and the New Model's field officers were generally men of outstanding ability. Although the New Model's particular identity was submerged in the numerous contractions and expansions of the standing Cromwellian army, several of its veteran regiments continued to serve into the 1650s. The standardized command and organization of the Army brought an increasing tendency towards uniformity of dress, discipline, armament and tactical doctrine among its regiments.

**Oppidum:** Literally a town, but normally used by Roman authors to describe a fortified centre of native settlement in Britain or Gaul. The term was applied to hill-forts, particularly by Pliny, and also to enclosures, such as Camulodunum, protected by dykes.

**Ordnance:** In general military materials and stores, but specifically artillery pieces.

**Picquet:** A small detachment of horse or foot stationed in advance of the main body of an army to provide warning of an attack.

**Pike:** A term frequently employed to describe all types of spear carried by infantry, but which normally refers to the long pike ranging in length from 16 to 22 feet (5 to 6.75 metres). The wooden pike-staff was protected at its end by metal strips called langets and it was topped by a leaf-shaped steel head.

**Round shot:** A solid stone or cast iron spherical shot which represented by far the commonest type of ammunition fired by smooth-bore ordnance.

**Schiltron:** A formation of pikemen providing for all-round defence.

**Siege train:** A convoy of heavy artillery pieces, together with ammunition and stores, specifically allocated for employment in the reduction of fortifications.

**Squadron:** A unit of horse formed by grouping two to four troops of cavalry together, often, in the past, on an *ad hoc* basis for a particular action. The strength of a squadron can be roughly estimated at 150 all ranks. Also a tactical and administrative grouping of bomber, fighter, supply or reconnaissance aircraft.

**Standing Army:** A body of troops maintained as a professional military force through central Exchequer funding in peace as well as in war. A standing army developed in Britain in the seventeenth century and national politics were deeply affected by the possibility of an increase in the power of the state which Englishmen, in particular, associated with a professional military force. The existence of a Militia, and the Royal Navy, was held to render a standing army unnecessary and extravagant.

**Trained bands:** In 1573, in response to the threat of Spanish invasion and to the northern rebellion of 1569, Elizabeth I's government required the English counties to provide men for training in the use of the pike and the musket. Training was to take place at musters where, theoretically, the most able men of the Militia would be selected and formed as 'trained bands'. In practice the term 'trained bands' appears to have been applied particularly to men supplied by towns and the reputation of those formed by London, for example, was certainly higher than that of county bands.

**Troop:** A unit of horse with a strength of approximately 50 all ranks. A private soldier in such a unit was known as a trooper. See also *Squadron*.

**Vouge:** A staff weapon whose exact form cannot be defined but which exhibited similarities to both the *bill* and the *glaive*, and which in its Swiss development became an early form of halberd.

# FURTHER READING

Any author who seeks to cover a period of history spanning 2000 years must rely to a considerable degree upon the research of others. The following published works have proved of particular value and they can be recommended to those who wish to pursue the study of individual periods.

## THE ROMANS IN BRITAIN 55BC–AD409

Breeze, David J., *The Northern Frontiers of Roman Britain*, B.T.Batsford Ltd, London, 1982.

Butler, R.M. (editor), *Soldier and civilian in Roman Yorkshire*, Leicester University Press, 1971.

Frere, Sheppard, *Britannia, A History of Roman Britain*, Routledge & Kegan Paul, London 1978.

Mann, J.C., 'The Northern Frontier after AD369', *Glasgow Archaeological Journal* Vol 3, 1974 pp34–42.

Salway, Peter, *Roman Britain*, Oxford University Press, 1981.

Wacher, John, *Roman Britain*, Dent & Sons Ltd, London 1978.

Webster, Graham & Dudley, Donald R., *The Roman Conquest of Britain*, B.T.Batsford Ltd, London 1965.

Webster, Graham, *The Roman Imperial Army*, Adam & Charles Black, London, 1969.

Webster, Graham & Dudley, Donald R., *The Rebellion of Boudicca*, Routledge & Kegan Paul, London, 1962.

## EARLY ENGLAND 410–1060

Alcock, Leslie, *Arthur's Britain, History and Archaeology AD367–634*, Penguin Books Ltd, Harmondsworth, 1971.

Keynes, Simon & Lapidge, Michael (translators), *Alfred The Great, Asser's Life of King Alfred and other contemporary sources*, Penguin Books, Harmondsworth, 1983.

Laborde, E.D., 'The Site of the Battle of Maldon', *The English Historical Review* No CLVIII, April 1925.

Loyn, H.R., *Anglo-Saxon England and the Norman Conquest*, Longman Group Ltd, Harlow, 1970.

——*The Vikings in Britain*, B.T.Batsford Ltd, London, 1977.

Macrae-Gibson, O.D., 'How Historical is the Battle of Maldon', *Medium Ævum* Vol XXXIX No 2, 1970.

Whitelock, Dorothy (editor), *English Historical Documents c.500–1042*, Eyre Methuen, London, 1979.

Wilson, David, *The Anglo-Saxons*, Penguin Books, Harmondsworth, 1978.

## THE MIDDLE AGES 1066–1450

Beeler, John, *Warfare in England 1066–1189*, Cornell University Press, New York, 1966.

Douglas, David C., *William The Conqueror, The Norman Impact upon England*, Eyre Methuen, London, 1977.

Norman, Vesey, *The Medieval Soldier*, Arthur Barker Ltd, London, 1971.

Oman, Sir Charles, *A History of the Art of War in the Middle Ages* Vol I AD378–1278, Methuen & Co Ltd, London, 1978.

Sayles, G.O., *The Medieval Foundations of England*, Methuen & Co Ltd, London, 1966.

Stenton, D.M., *English Society in the Early Middle Ages 1066–1307*, Penguin Books, Harmondsworth, 1981.

## THE AGE OF THE WARS OF THE ROSES 1450–1550

Brooke, Richard, *Visits to Fields of Battle in England of the Fifteenth Century*, J.R.Smith, London, 1857 (reprinted in 1975 by Alan Sutton).

Goodman, Anthony, *The Wars of the Roses: Military Activity and English Society, 1452–97*, Routledge & Kegan Paul, London, 1981.

Reid, William, *The Lore of Arms*, Mitchell Beazley Ltd, London, 1976.

Storey, R.L., *The End of the House of Lancaster*, Barrie & Rockliff, London, 1966.

Williams, D.T., *The Battle of Bosworth*, Leicester University Press, 1973.

## THE ENGLISH CIVIL WARS 1642–51

Firth, C.H., *Cromwell's Army*, Methuen & Co Ltd, London, 1962.

Fletcher, Anthony, *The Outbreak of the English Civil War*, Edward Arnold, London, 1981.

Hutton, Ronald, *The Royalist War Effort 1642–1646*, Longman, London, 1982.

Newman, Peter, *The Battle of Marston Moor 1644*, Anthony Bird Publications Ltd, Chichester, 1981.

Young, Peter & Holmes, Richard, *The English Civil War: A Military History of the Three Civil Wars 1642–1651*, Eyre Methuen, London, 1974.

## WARFARE IN THE AGE OF REASON 1660–1746

Childs, John, *The Army, James II and the Glorious Revolution*, Manchester University Press, 1980.

Earle, Peter, *Monmouth's Rebels: The Road to Sedgemoor 1685*, Weidenfeld & Nicolson, London, 1977.

Jarvis, Rupert C., *Collected Papers on the Jacobite Risings* Vols I & II, Manchester University Press, 1971–72.

Lenman, Bruce, *The Jacobite Rising in Britain 1689–1746*, Eyre Methuen, London, 1980.

McLynn, F.J., *The Jacobite Army in England 1745: The Final Campaign*, John Donald Ltd, Edinburgh, 1983.

Tomasson, Katherine & Buist, Francis, *Battles of the '45*, B.T.Batsford Ltd, London, 1962.

## THE BATTLE OF BRITAIN 1940

Bekker, Cajus, *The Luftwaffe War Diaries*, Macdonald & Co Ltd, London, 1968.

Deighton, Len, *Battle of Britain*, Jonathan Cape Ltd, London, 1980.

Richards, Denis, *Royal Air Force 1939–45. Volume I: The Fight at Odds*, HMSO, London, 1953.

## SURVEY WORKS

Barnett, C., *Britain and Her Army 1509–1970: A military, political and social survey*, The Penguin Press, London, 1970.

Burne, Alfred H., *The Battlefields of England*, Methuen & Co Ltd, London, 1950.

——*More Battlefields of England*, Methuen & Co Ltd, London, 1952.

# INDEX

*Page numbers in italics denote illustrations*

# ACKNOWLEDGEMENTS

*The author and publishers are grateful to the following for supplying illustrations:*

### Colour
Aerofilms *7*; British Library *36, 58*; British Museum *14, 28, 29*; British Tourist Authority *20, 25, 41, 75, 78, 79, 116, 125, 142, 143, 157, 160*; By courtesy of the Duke of Buccleuch and Queensberry *190*; Cromwell Museum *161*; Anne-Marie Ehrlich *44, 165, 186*; E T Archive *135*; By courtesy of Her Majesty the Queen *182–3*; Michael Holford *55*; David James Gallery *3*; Oscar and Peter Johnson *198–9*; National Army Museum *132, 182, 206*; National Portrait Gallery *117, 134, 190, 194*; David Smurthwaite *117*; Geoff Walker and Philip Martin *43, 62, 120, 149, 191*.

### Black and White
Aerofilms *53, 99, 153, 162–3, 193*; Bodleian Library *24, 40, 48*; British Library *36, 42, 49, 52, 70, 90*; British Museum *12, 25*; British Tourist Authority *67, 74, 129*; By courtesy of the Duke of Buccleuch and Queensberry *173*; Central Bibliothek, Ghent *116*; Colchester and Essex Museum *22*; Malcolm Couch *26, 50, 86, 130, 178, 210*; By courtesy of the Earl of Dartmouth *154*; Constance and Brian Dear *10, 19, 33, 35, 39, 46, 61, 66, 69, 70, 73, 79, 80, 82, 85, 98, 101, 103, 105, 106, 109, 113, 115, 124, 129, 141, 146, 150, 152, 155, 159, 165, 167, 173, 175, 192, 196, 202, 204, 207*; E T Archive *56, 92, 93, 94, 95, 128, 129, 138, 139, 150, 168, 172, 174*; By courtesy of Her Majesty the Queen *80, 150, 208*; Imperial War Museum *212, 214, 215, 216*; Mansell Collection *13, 16*; National Army Museum *133, 137, 144, 147, 151, 153, 164, 176, 181, 187, 189, 192, 201*; National Museum of Antiquities of Scotland *24, 184*; National Portrait Gallery *96, 138, 141, 147, 180, 201*; Royal Commission for Historical Monuments *126*; Scottish National Portrait Gallery *136, 192, 200, 204*; Scottish Record Office *74*; Brian Shuel *38, 47, 65, 71, 72, 82, 84, 100, 105, 177*.